This coloring book belongs to:
_____

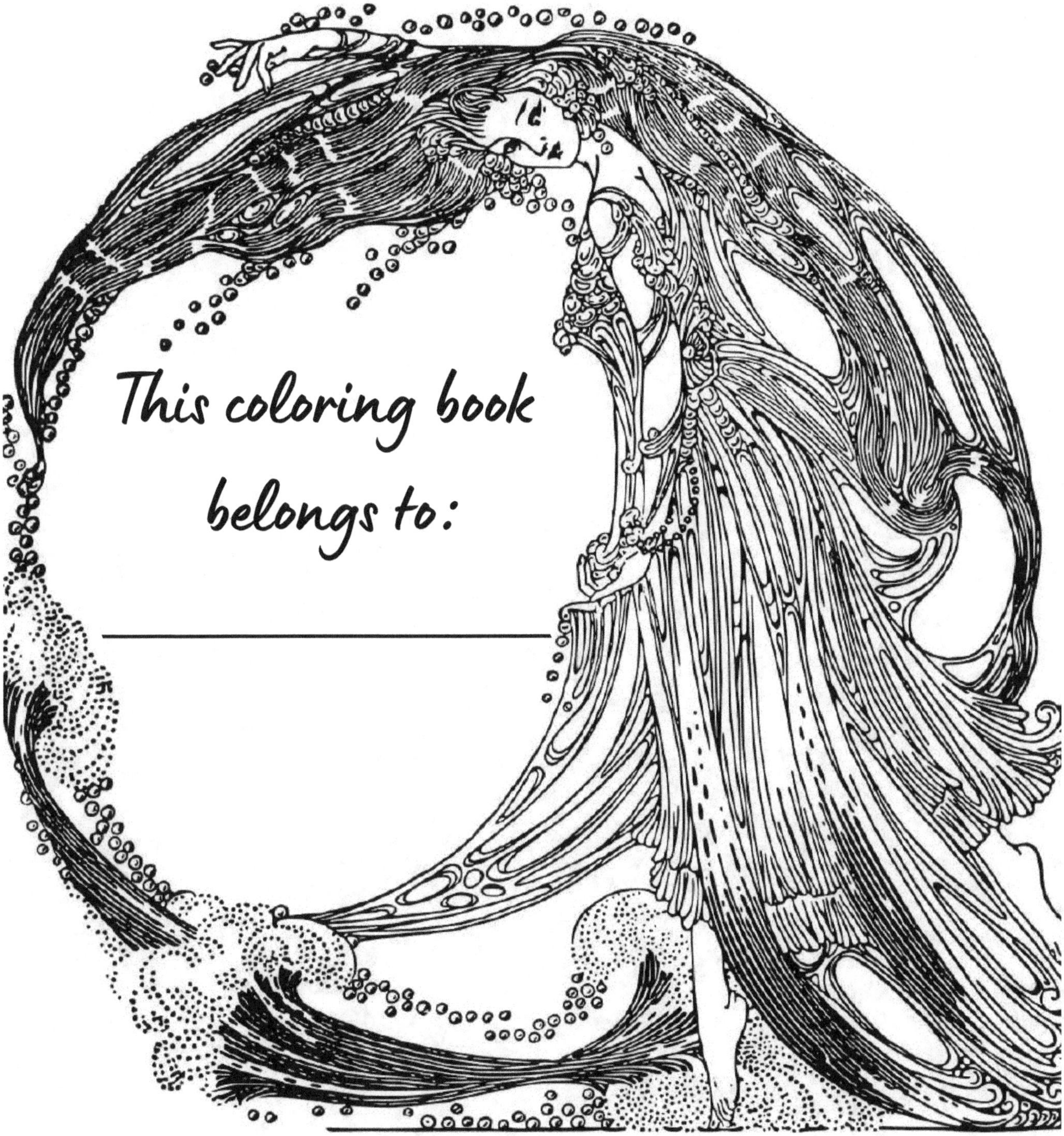

Book No. 1

Landscapes and Animals

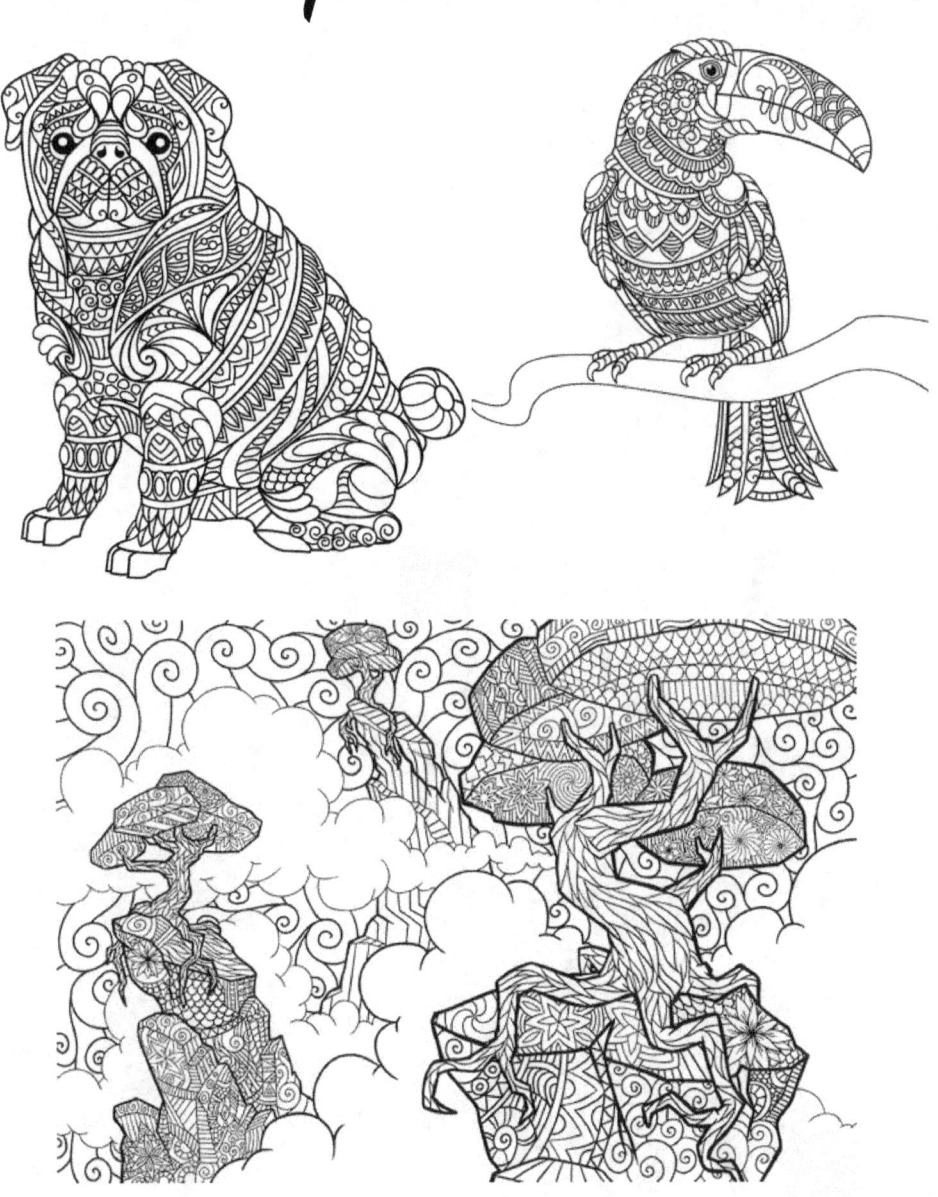

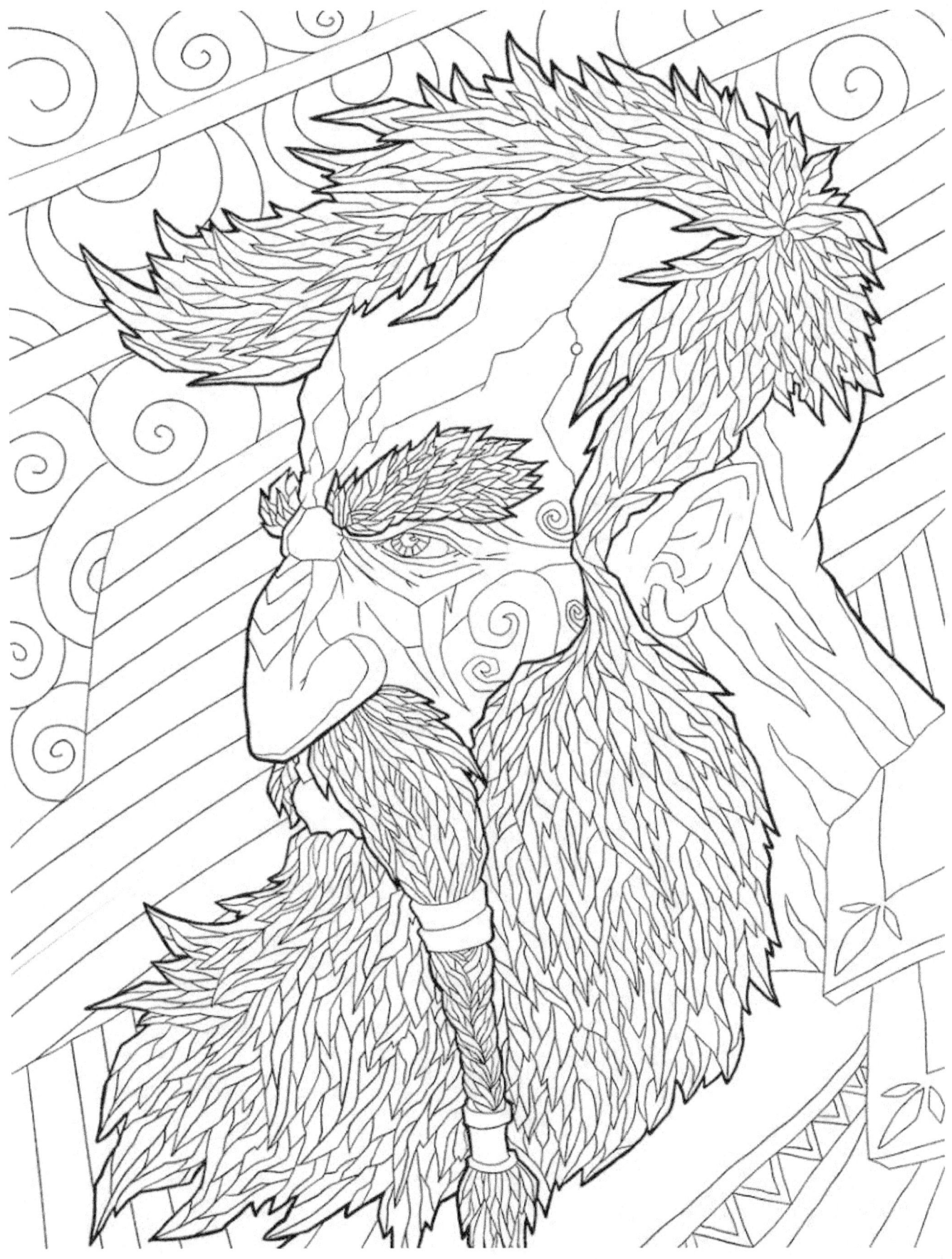

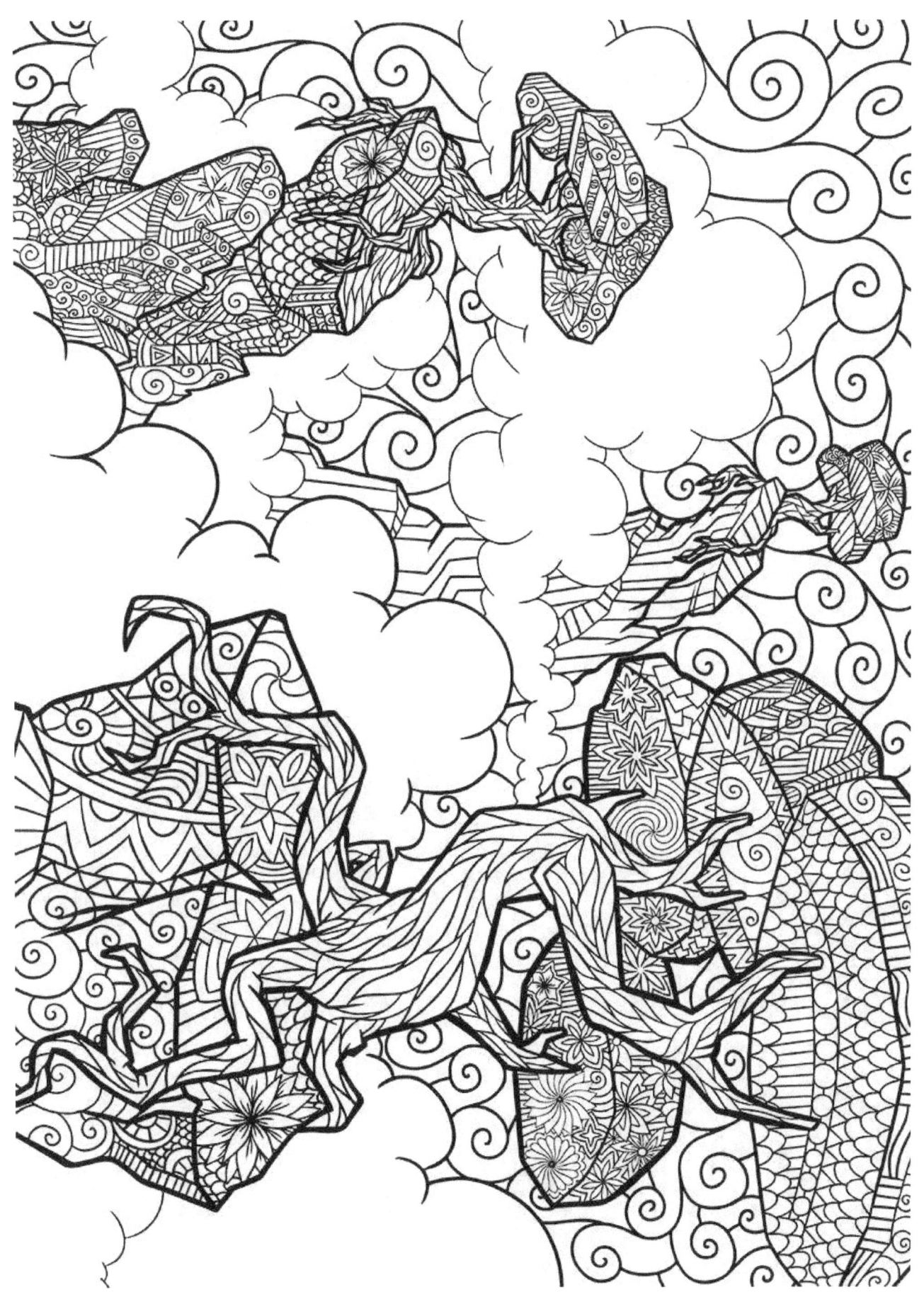

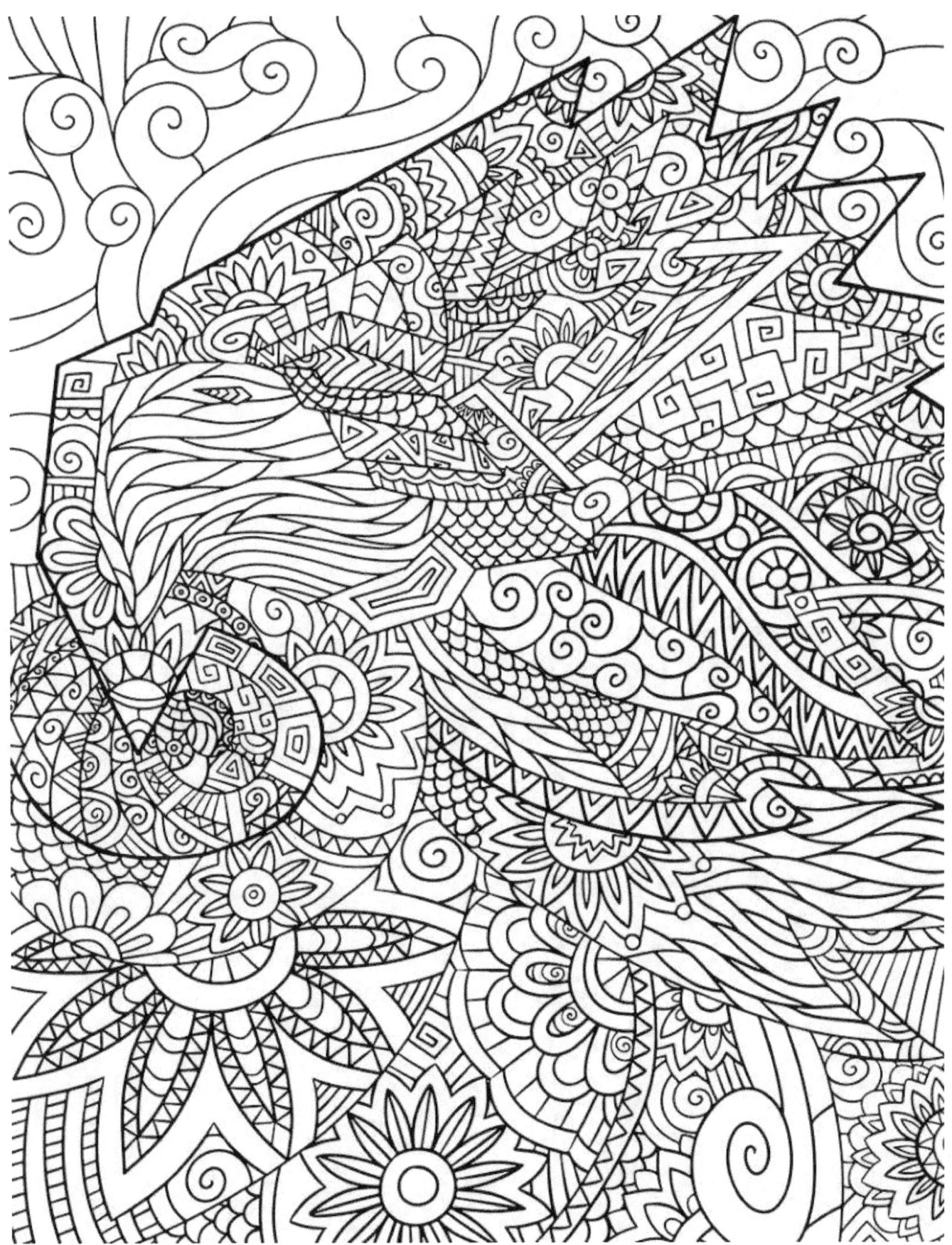

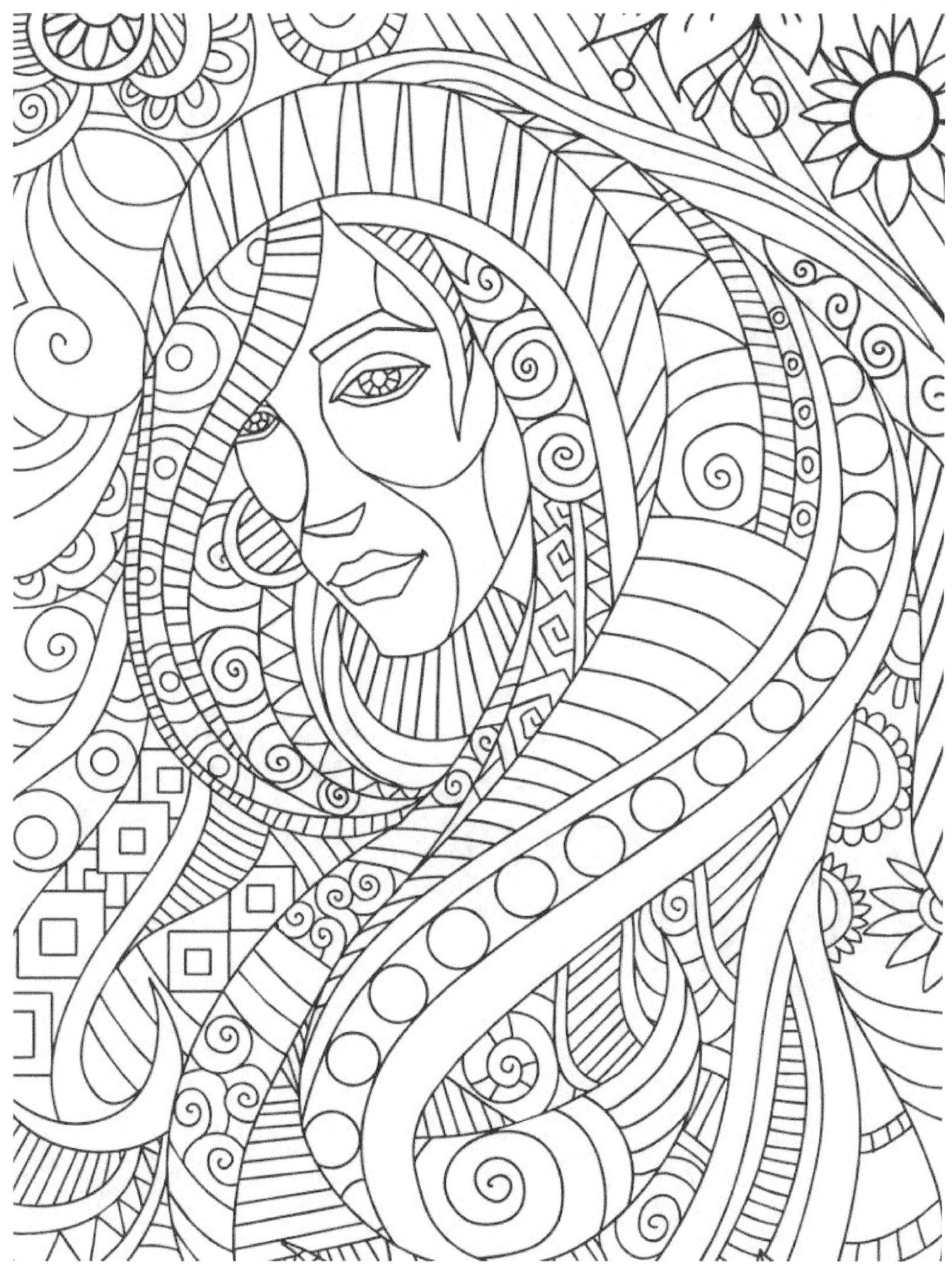

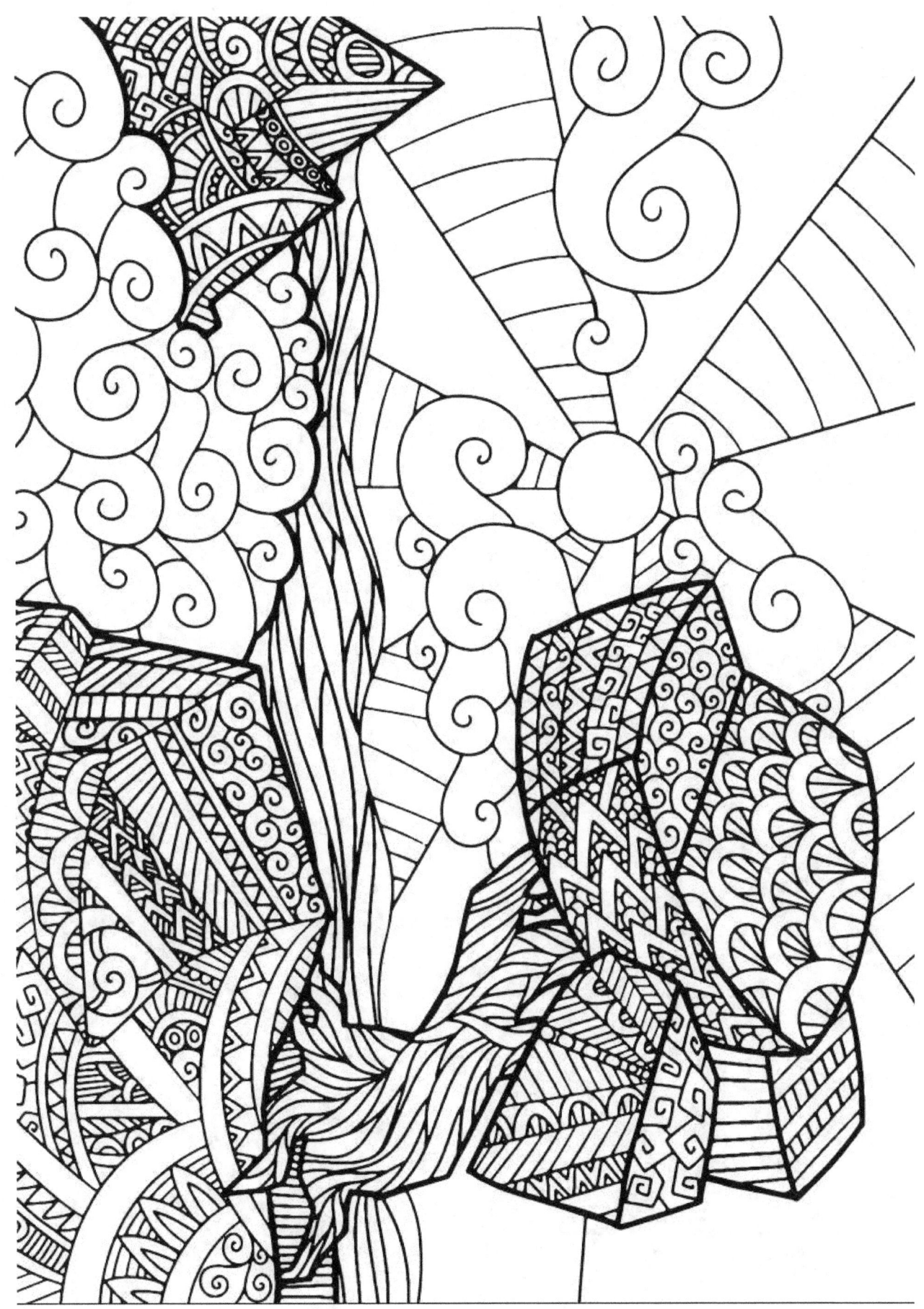

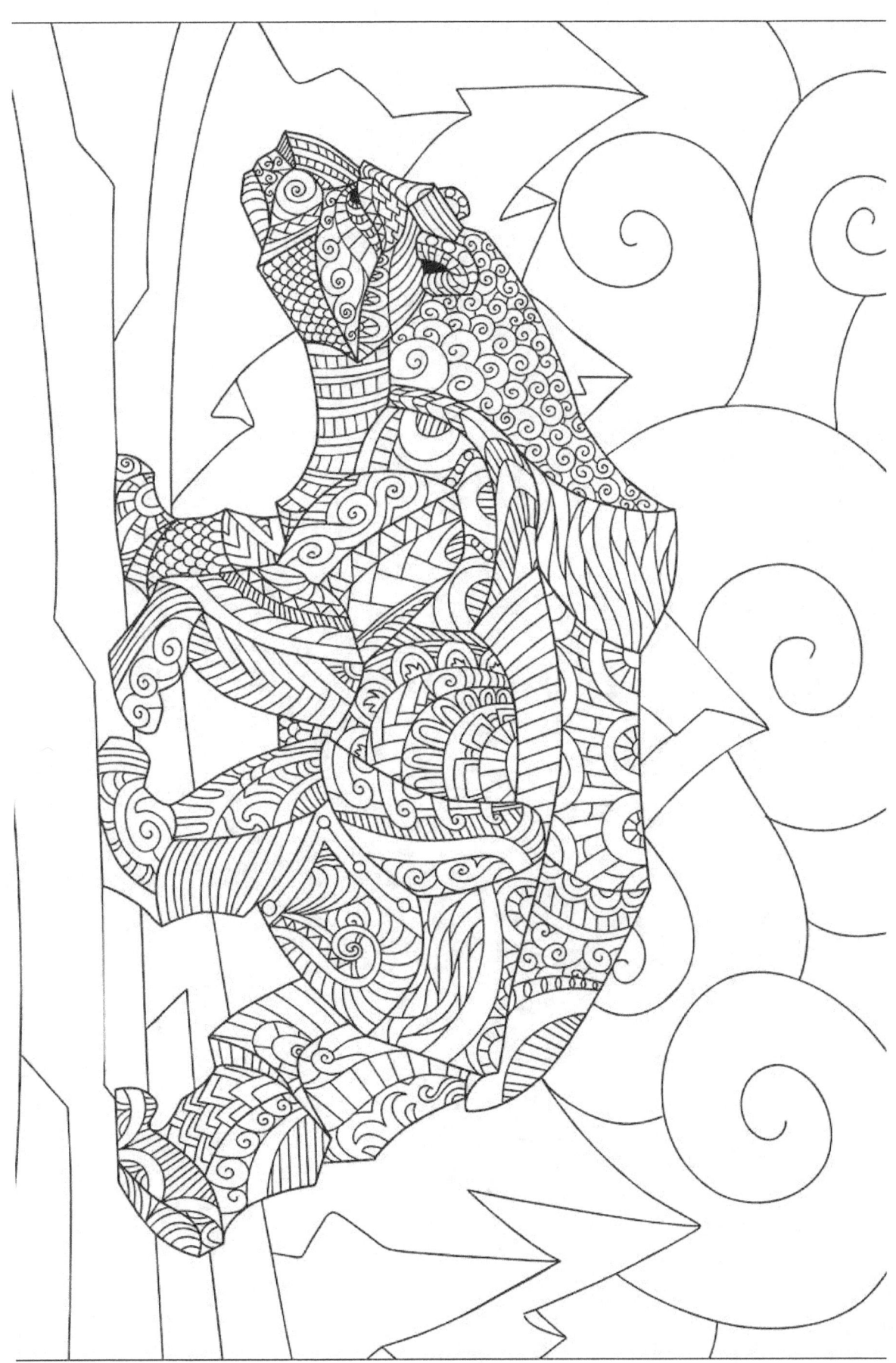

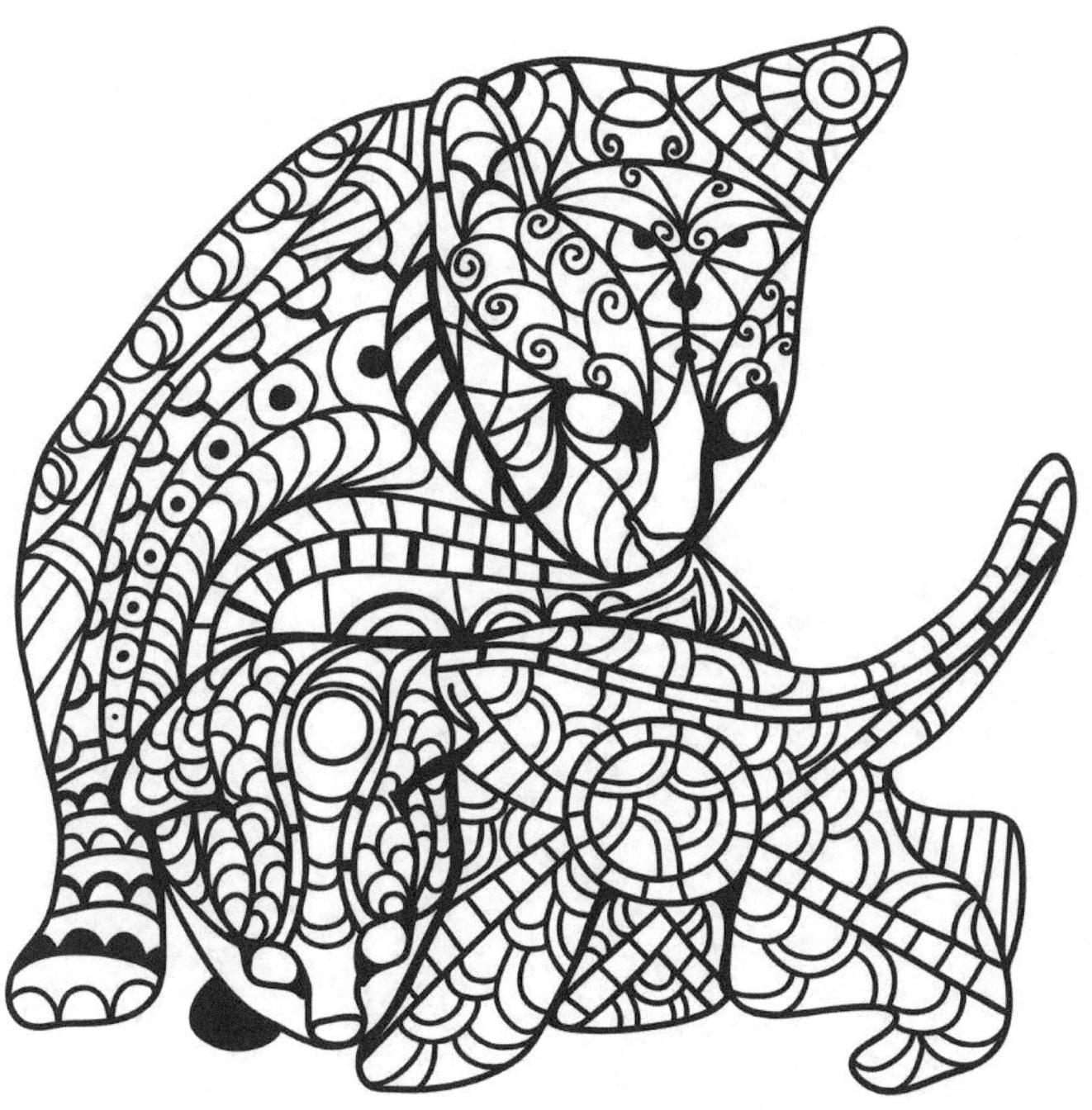

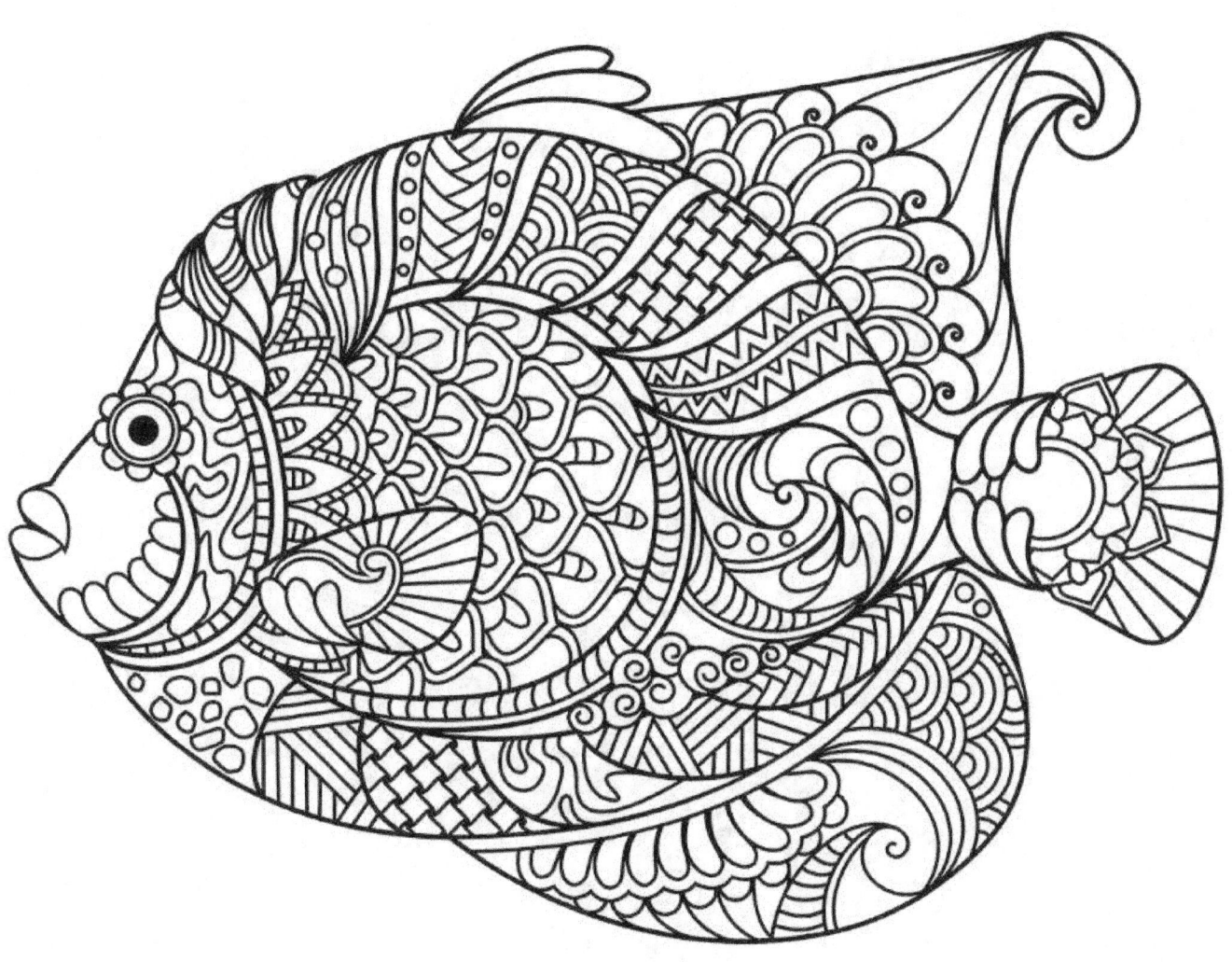

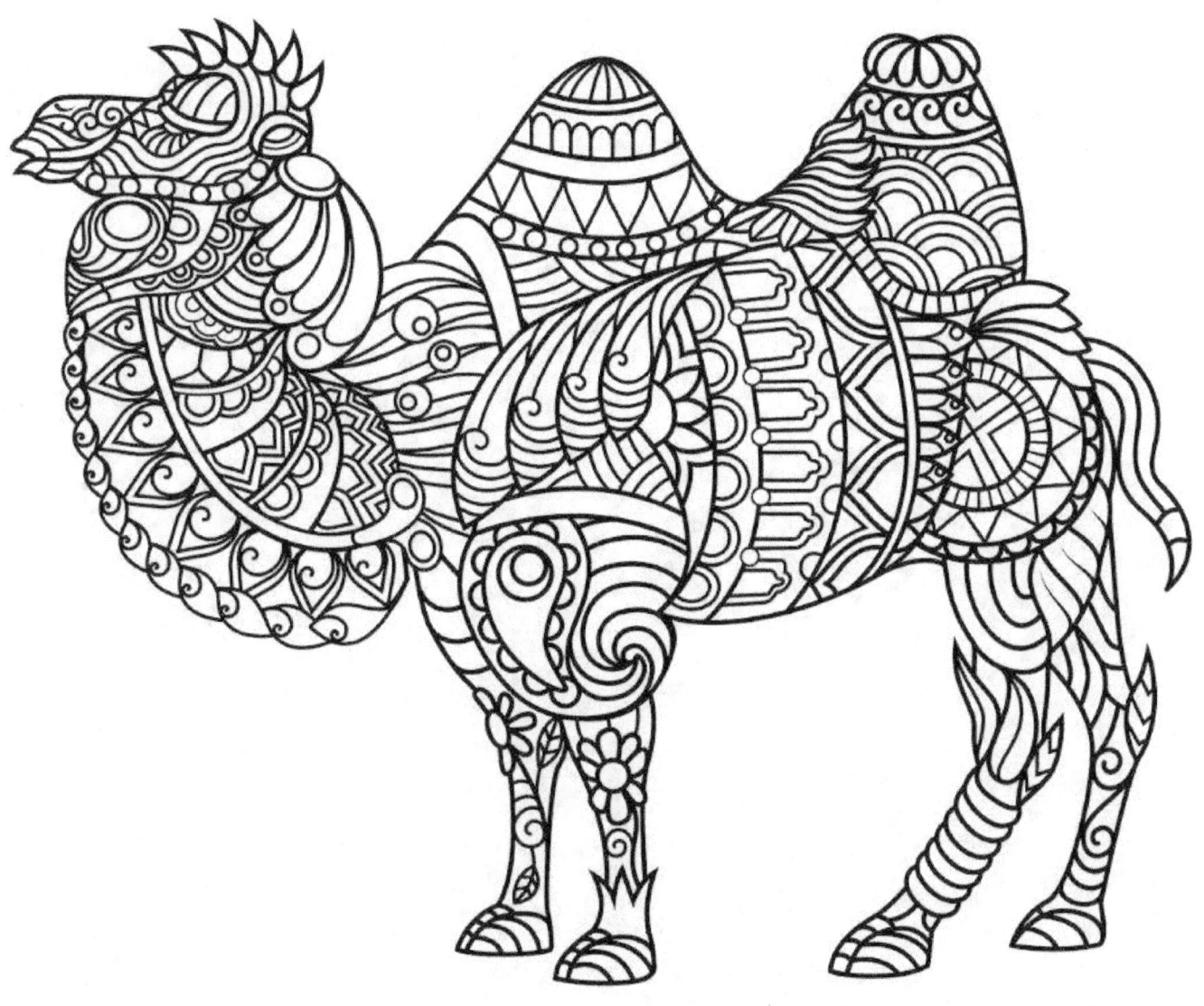

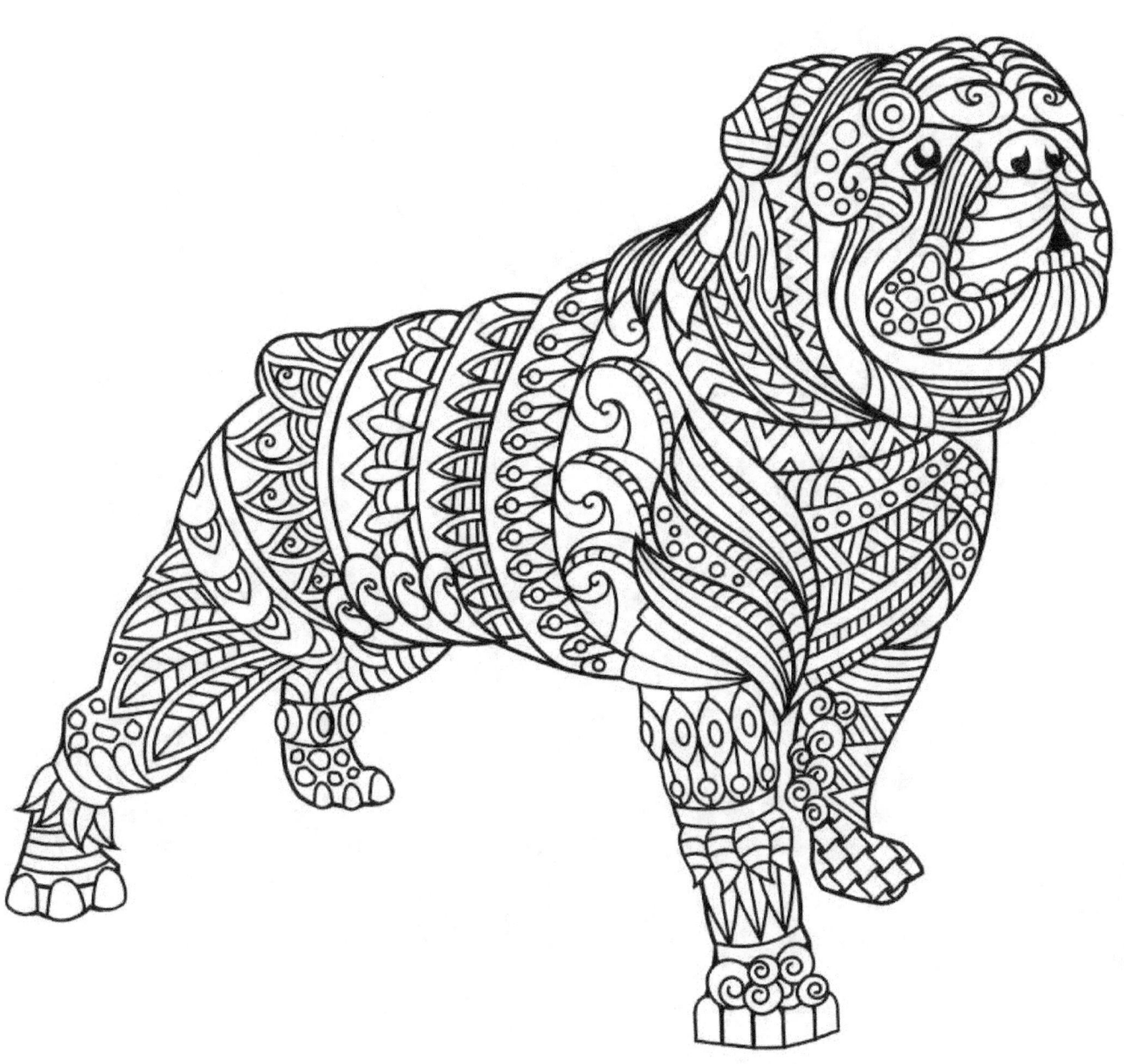

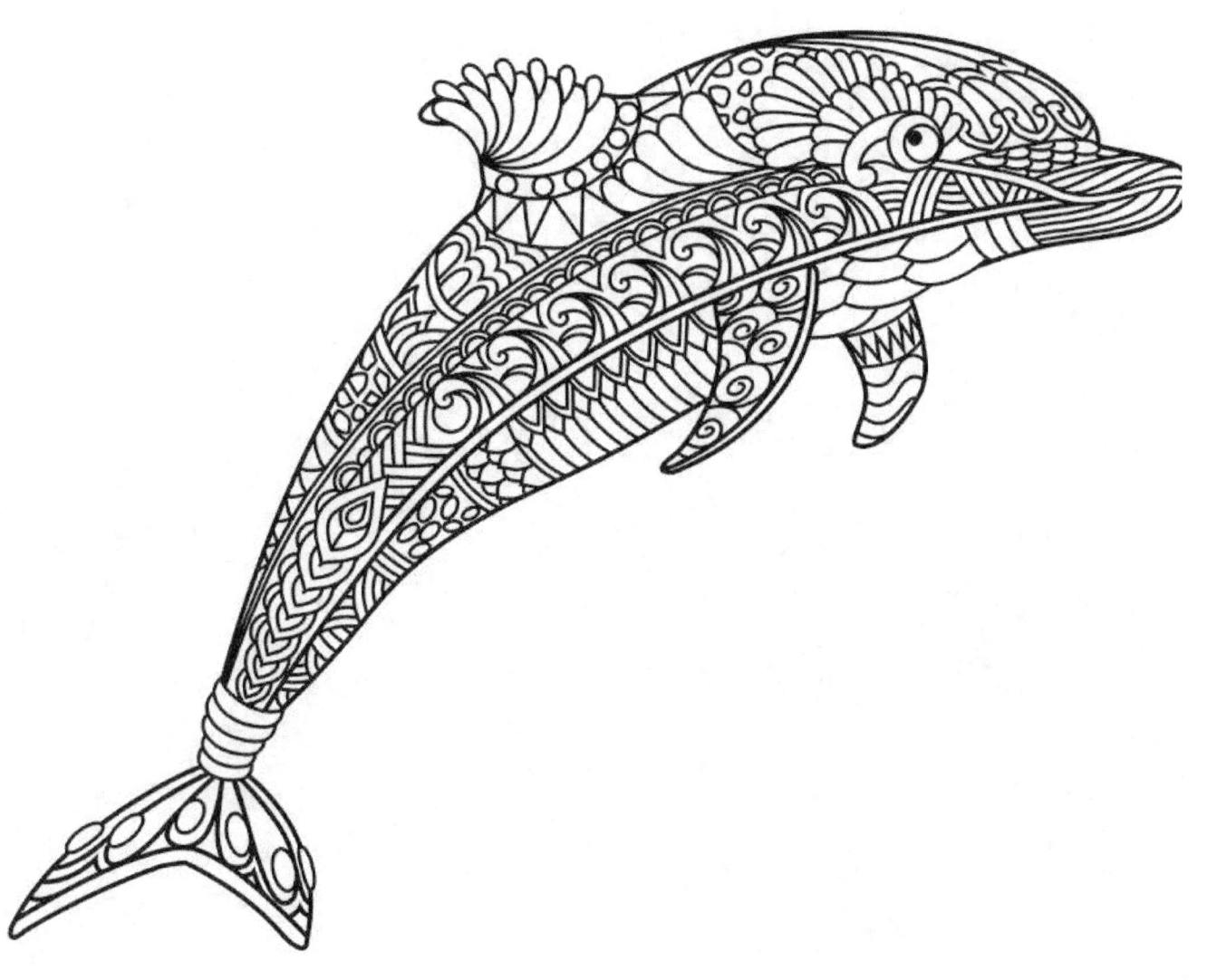

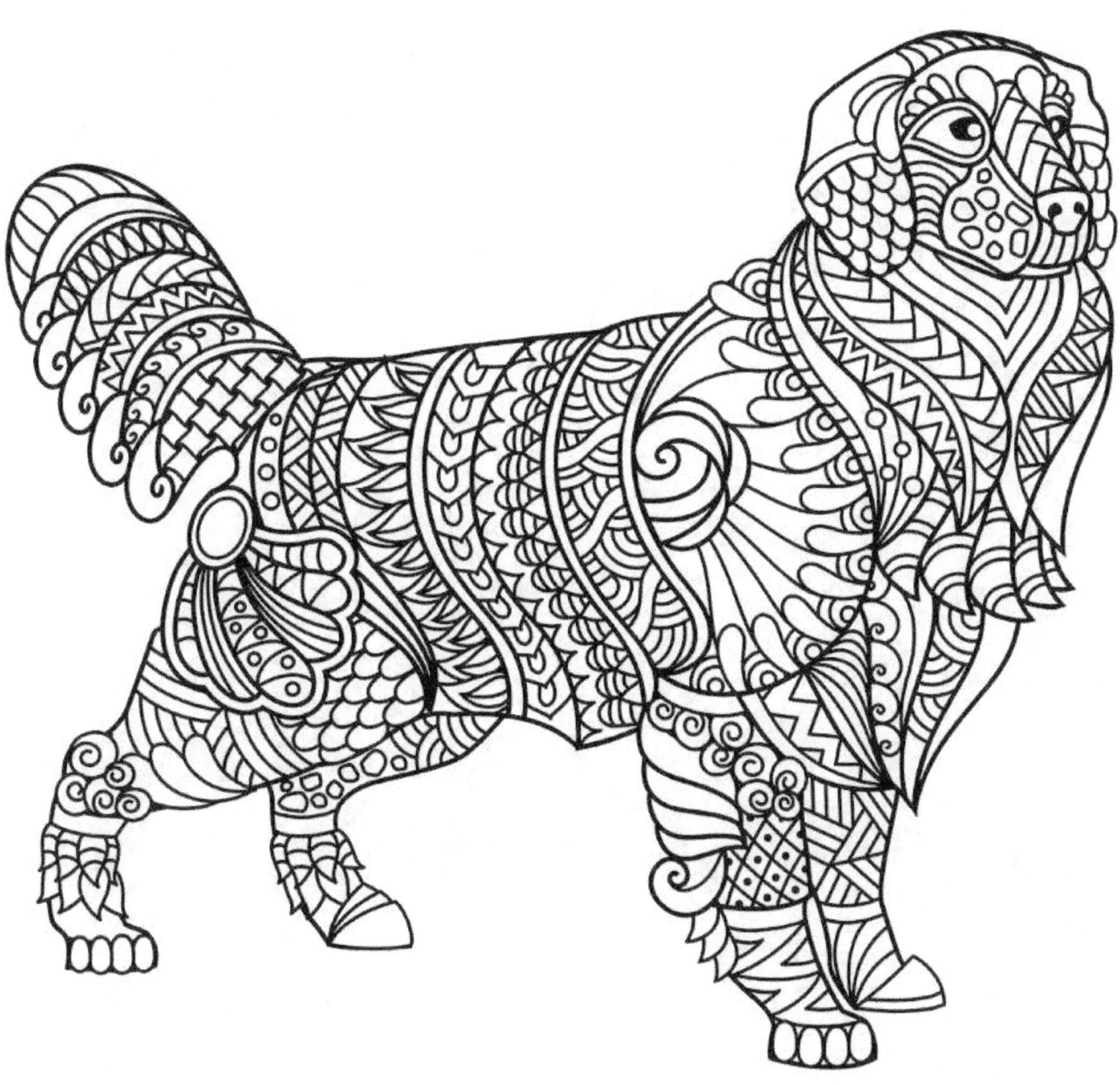

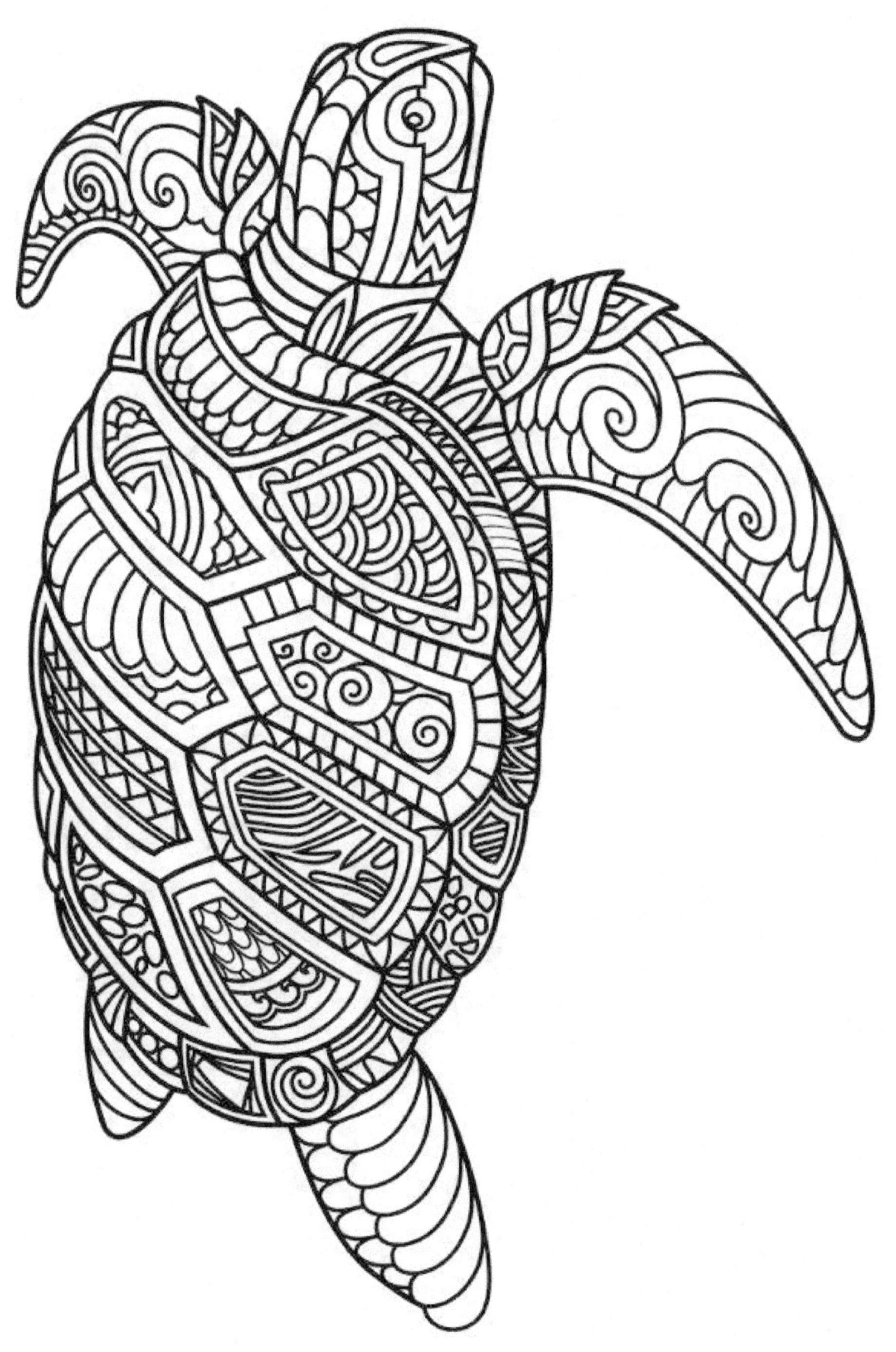

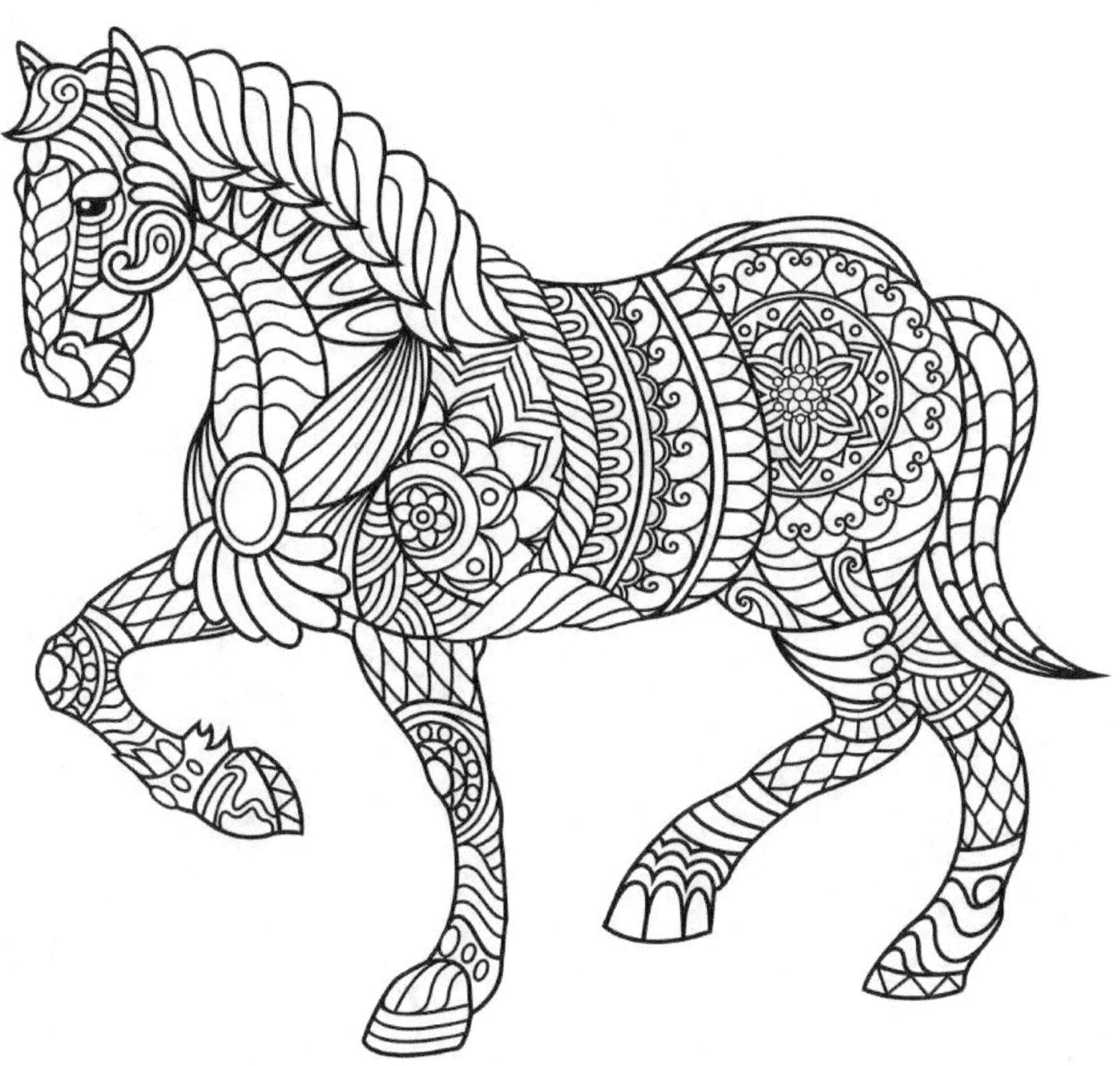

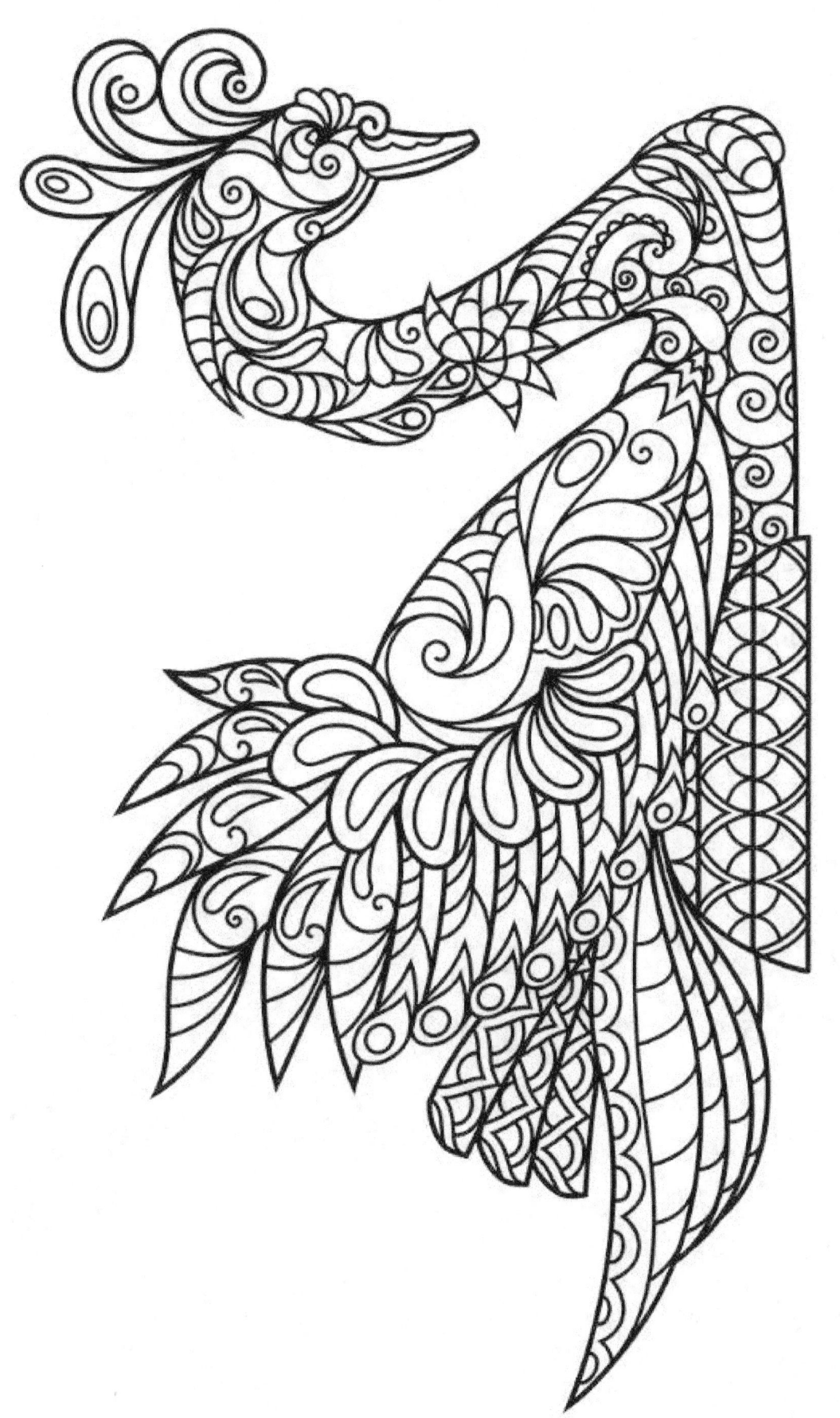

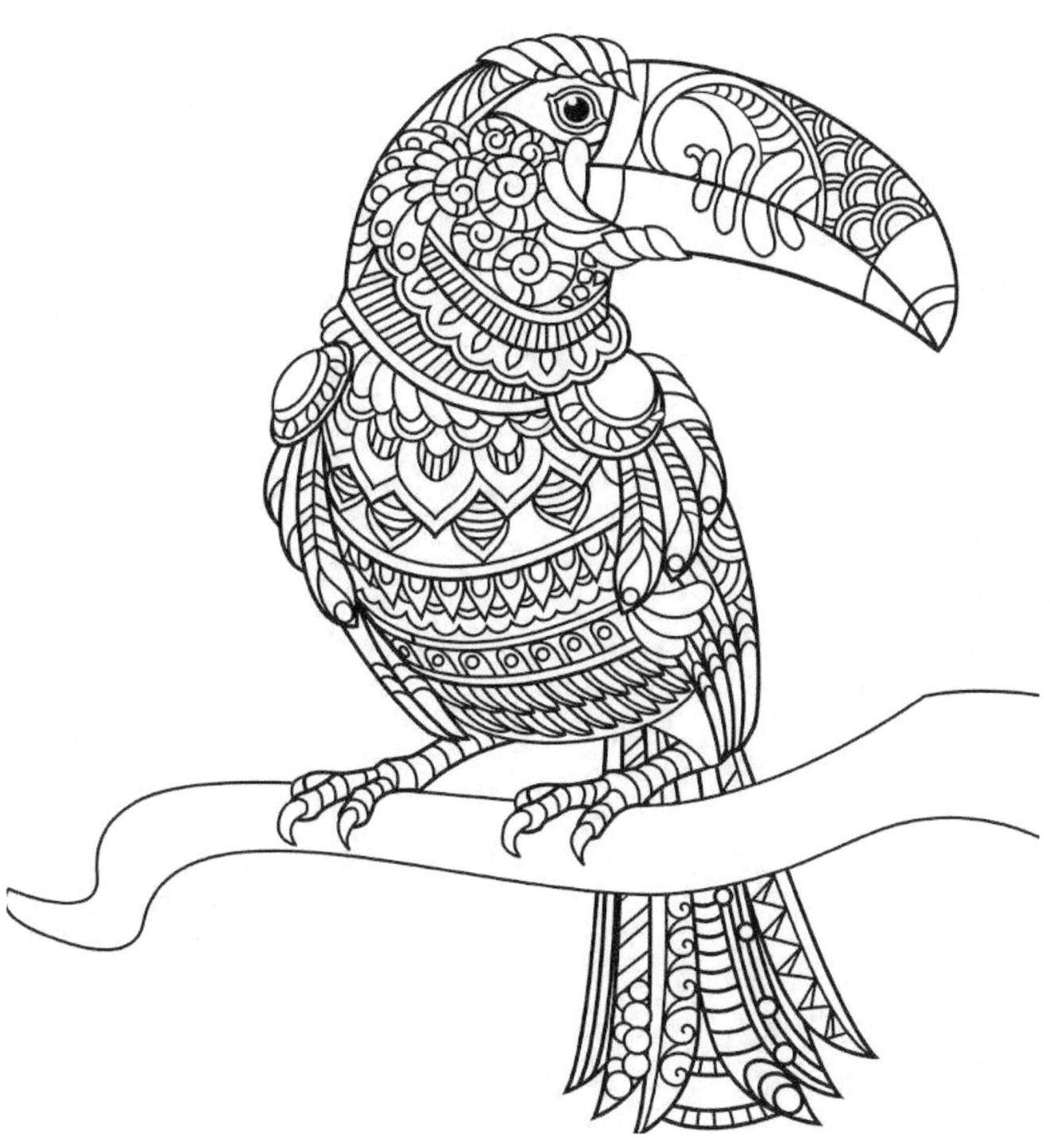

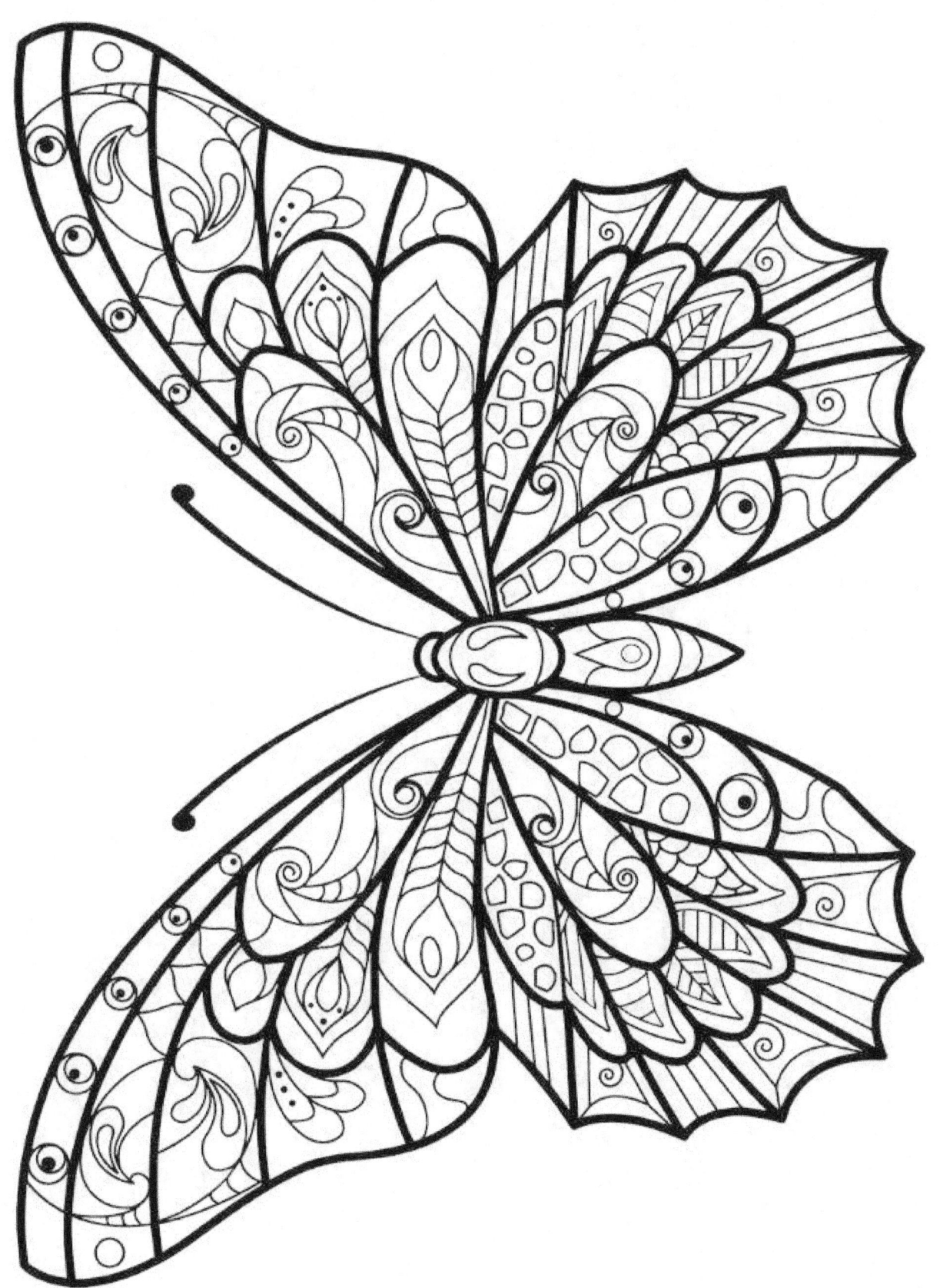

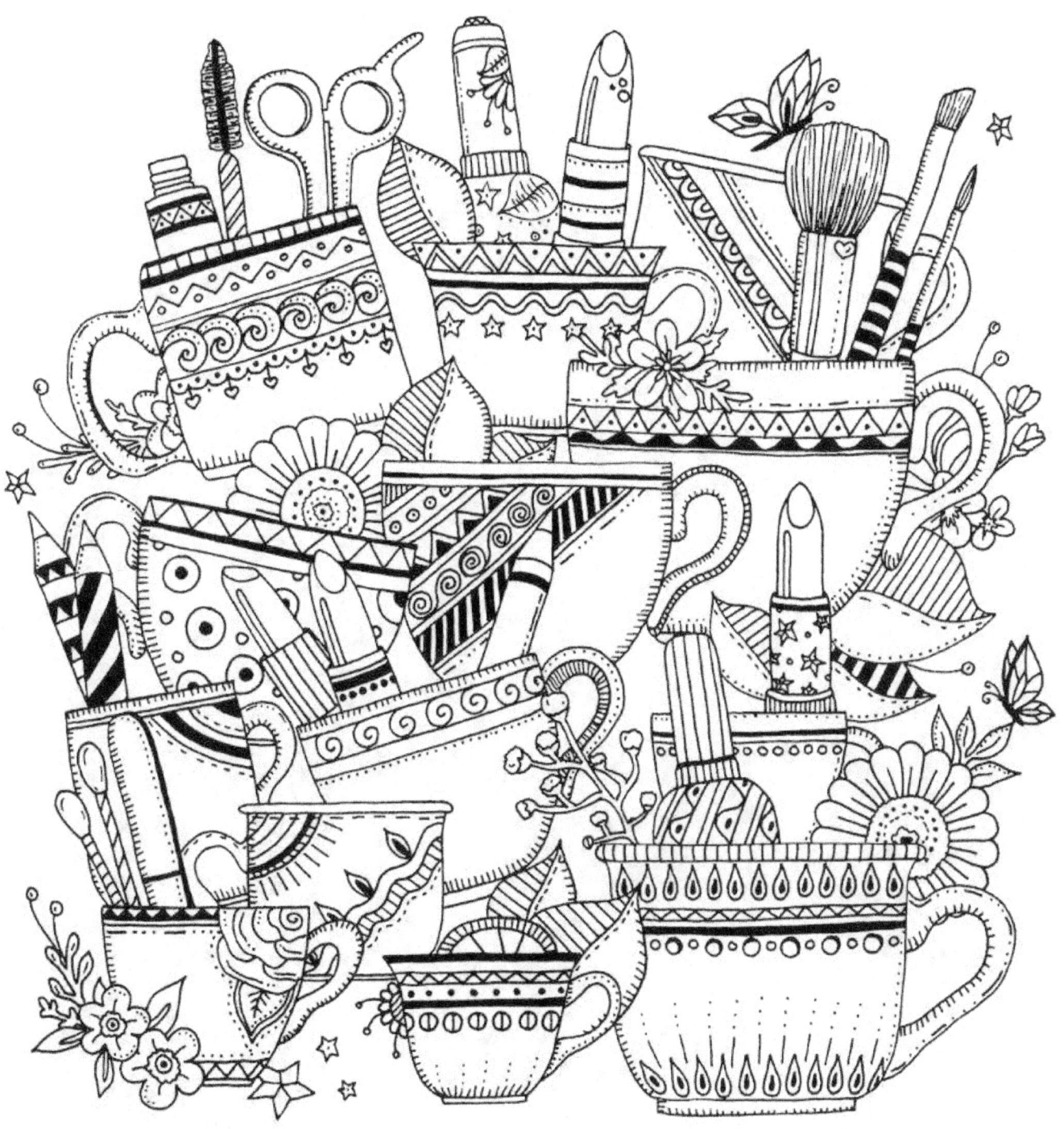

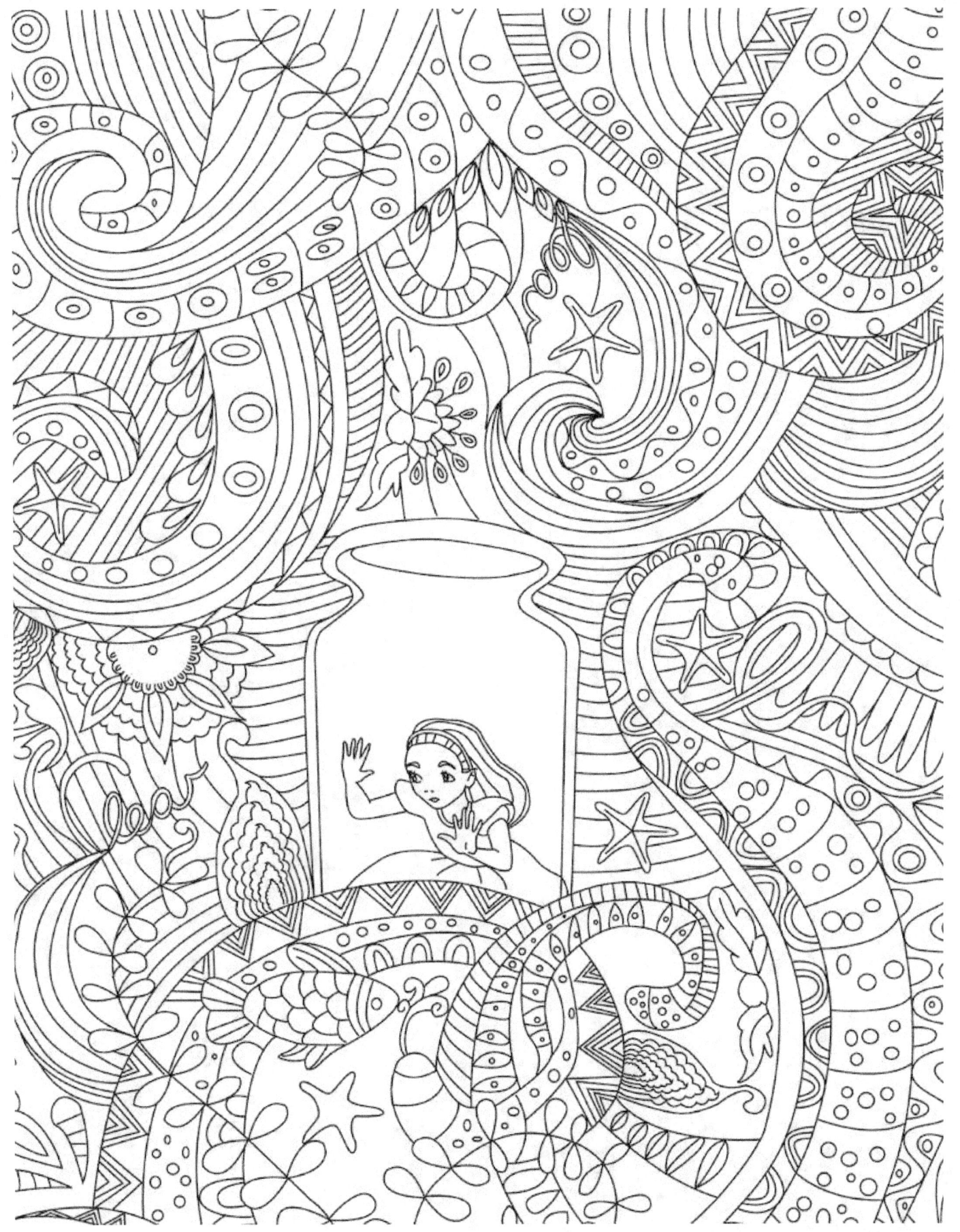

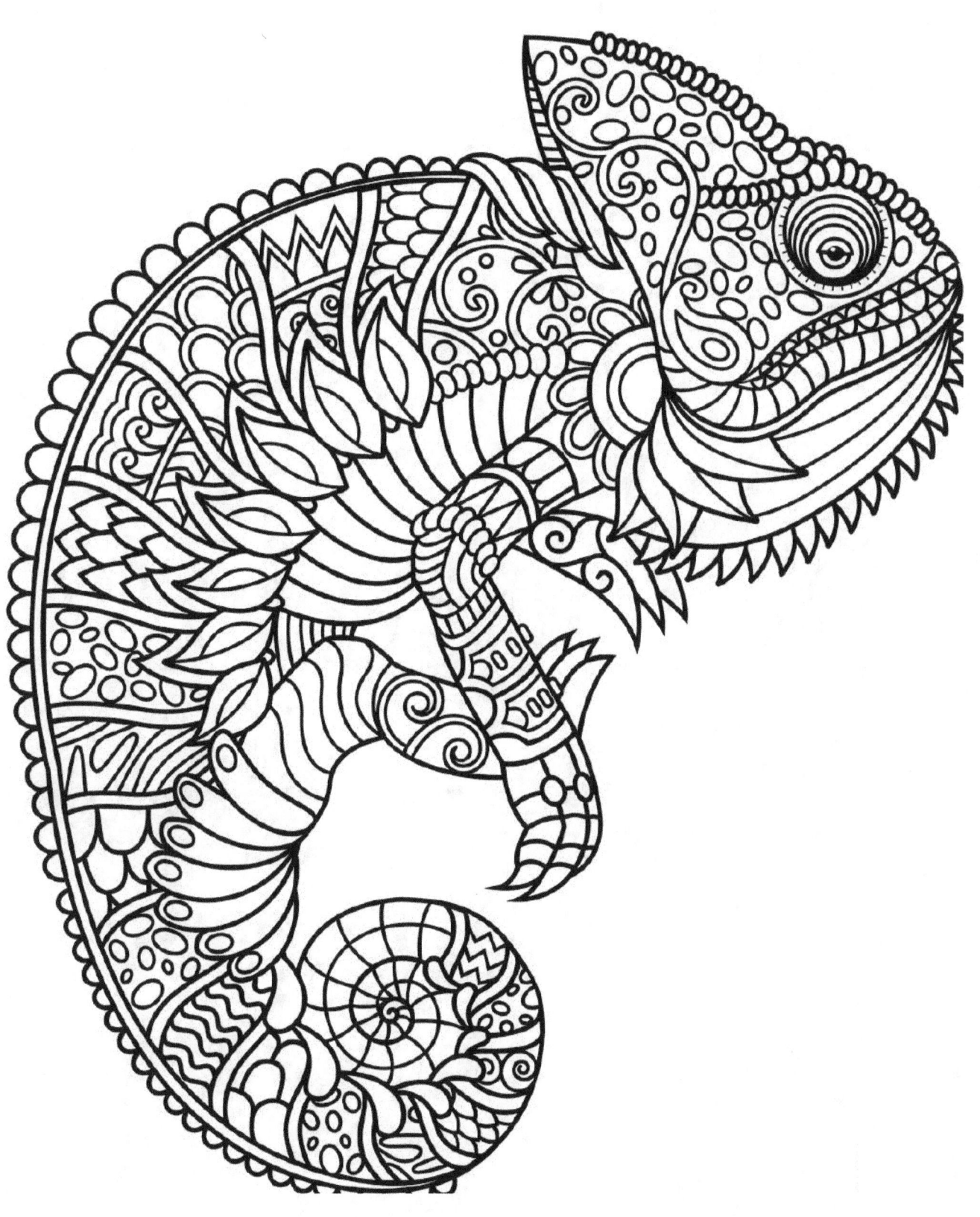

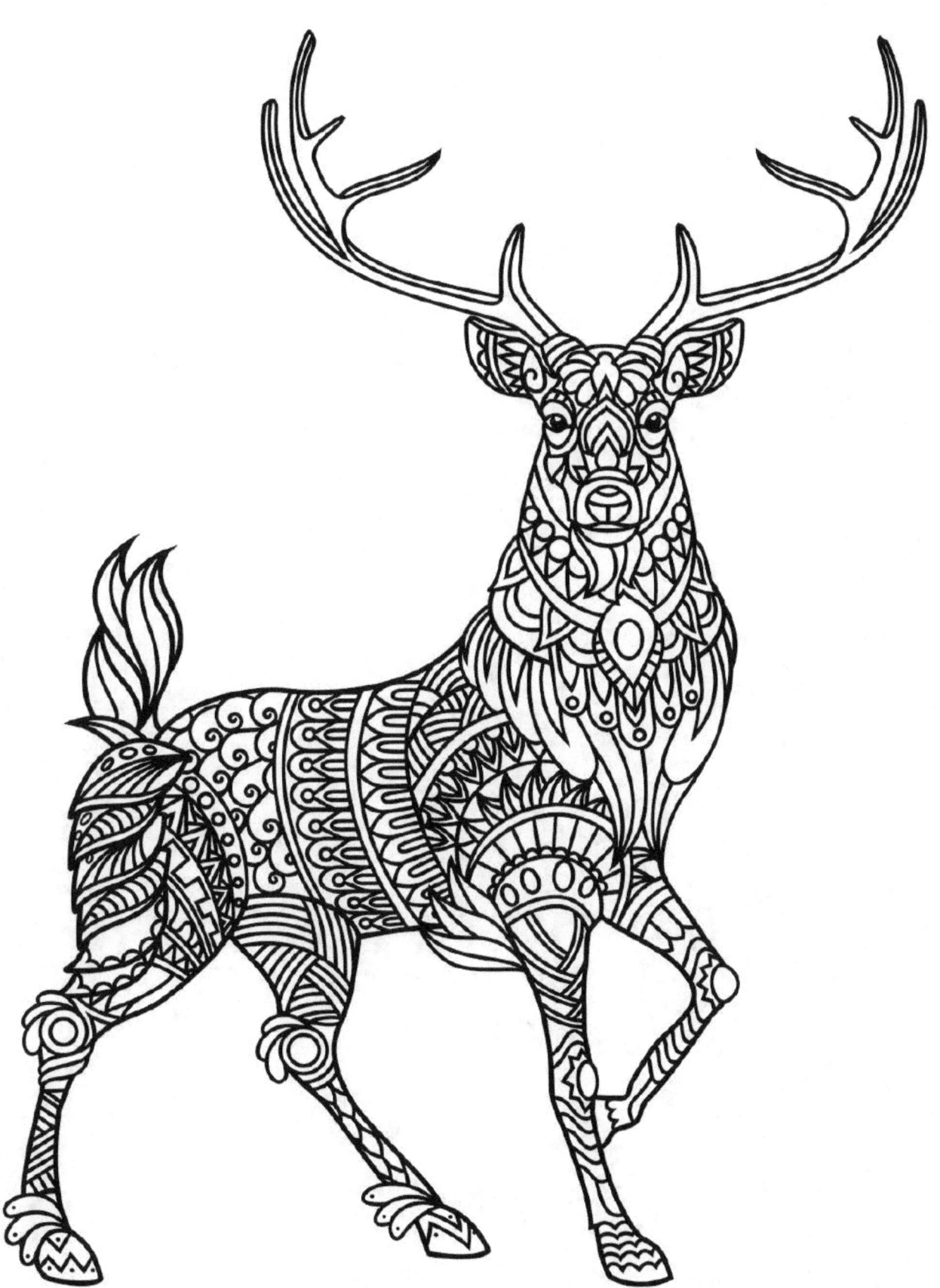

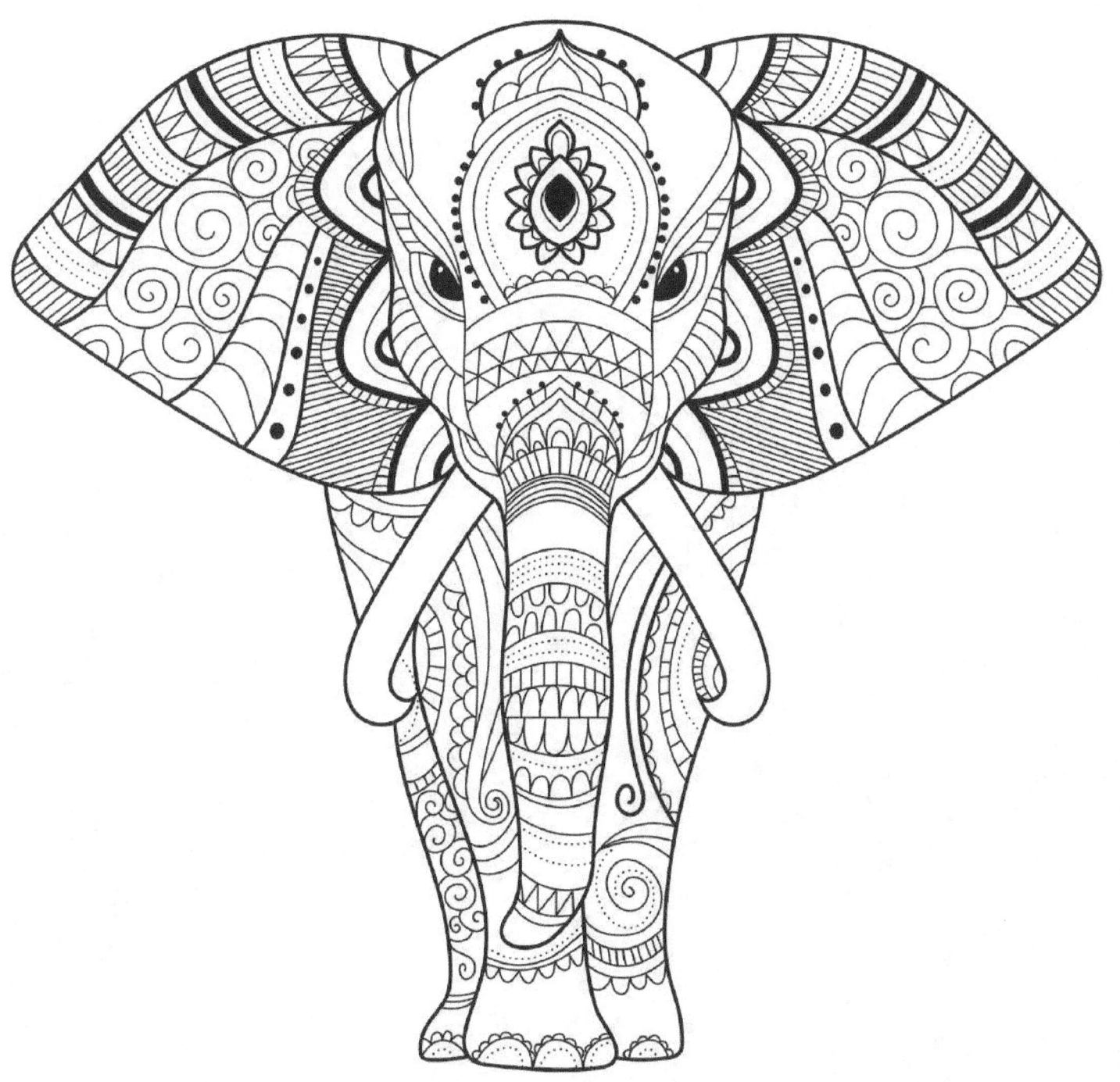

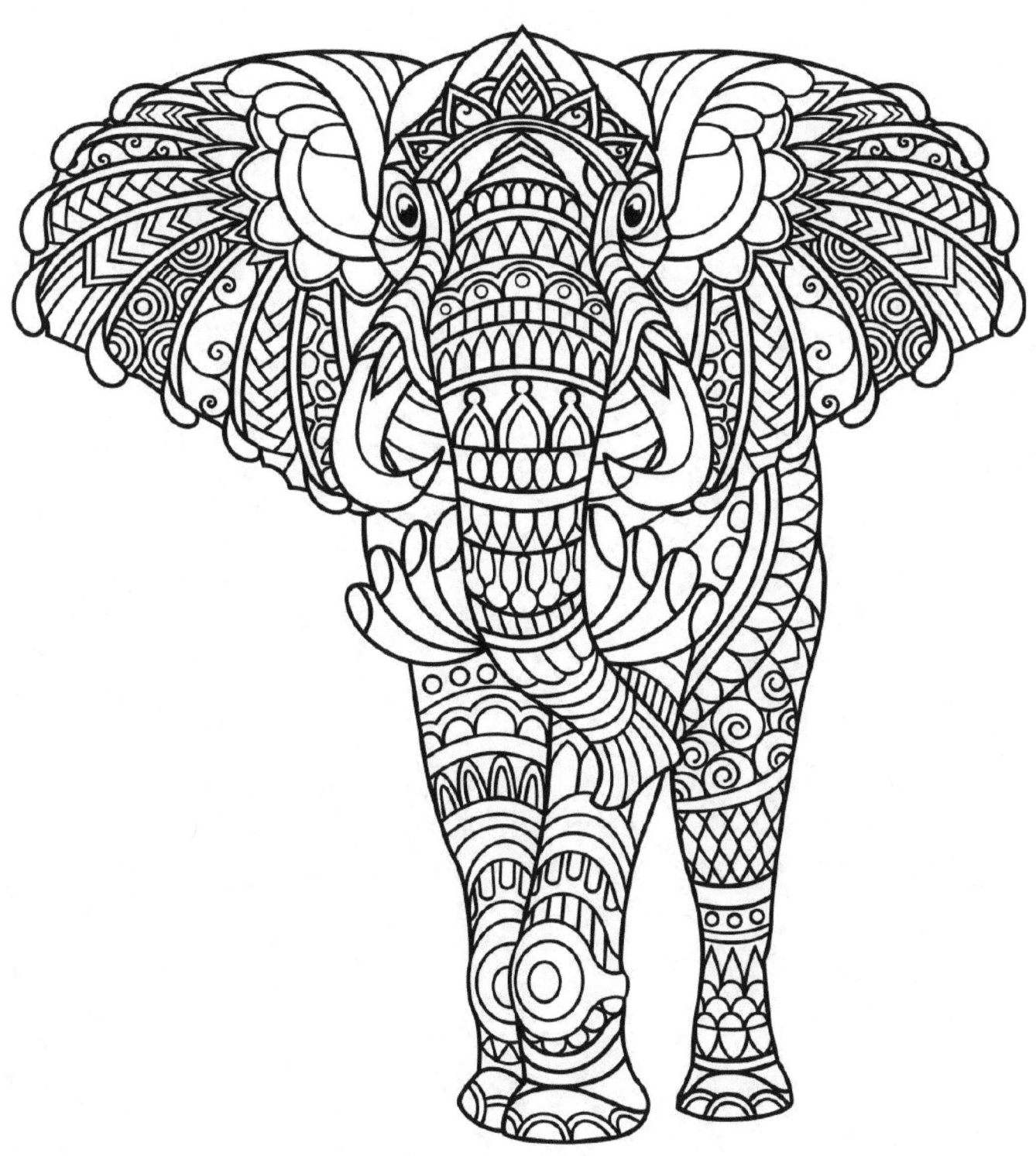

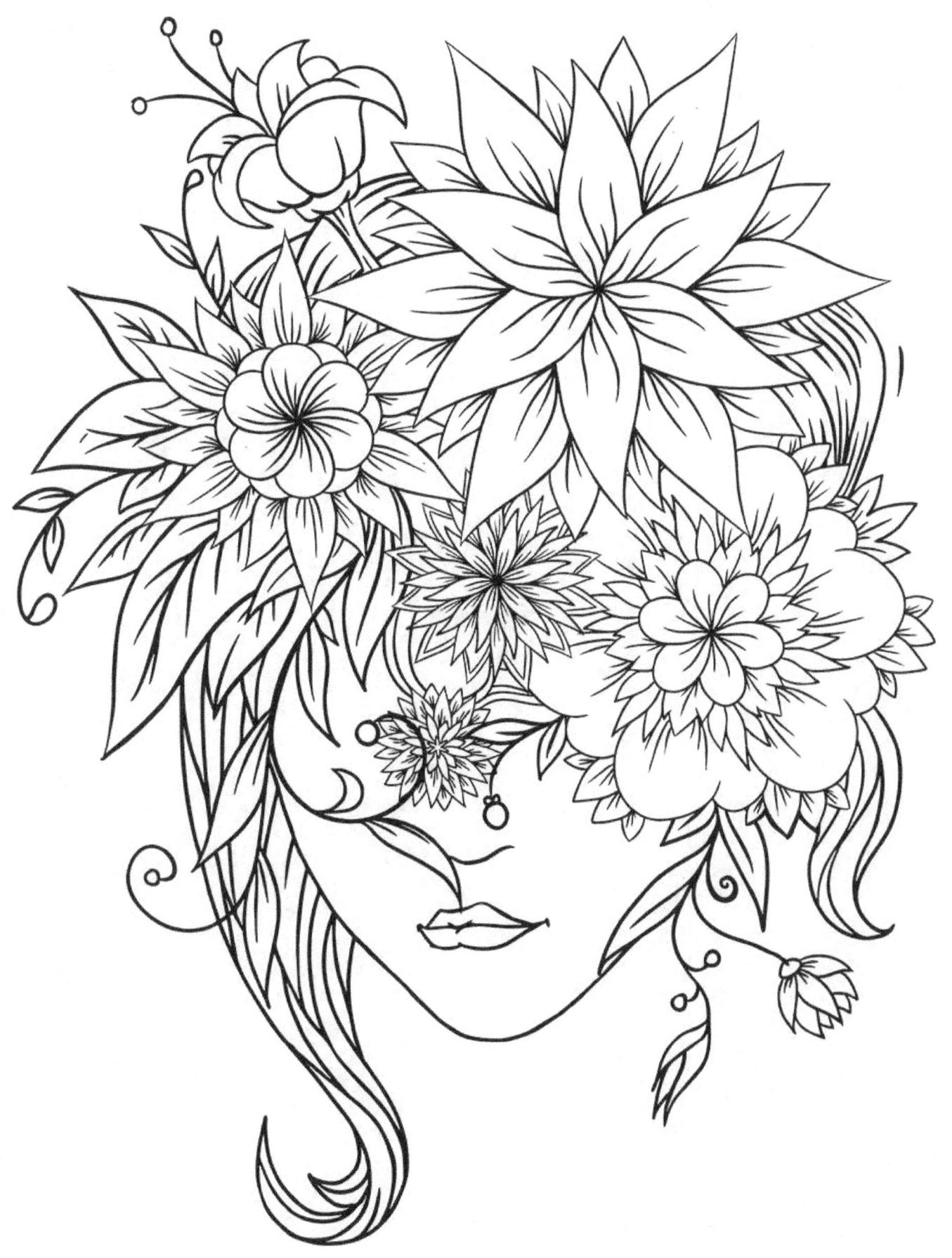

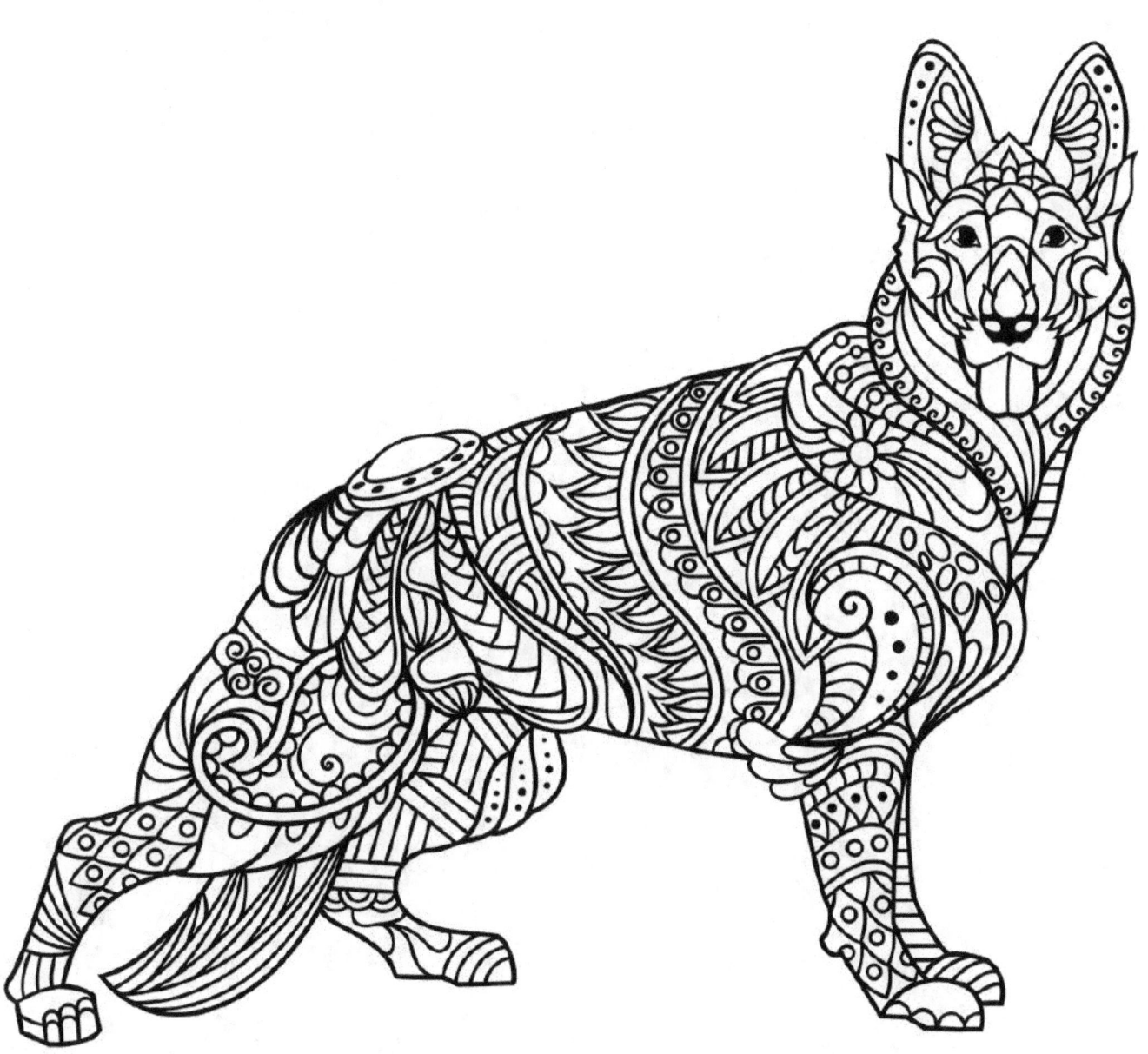

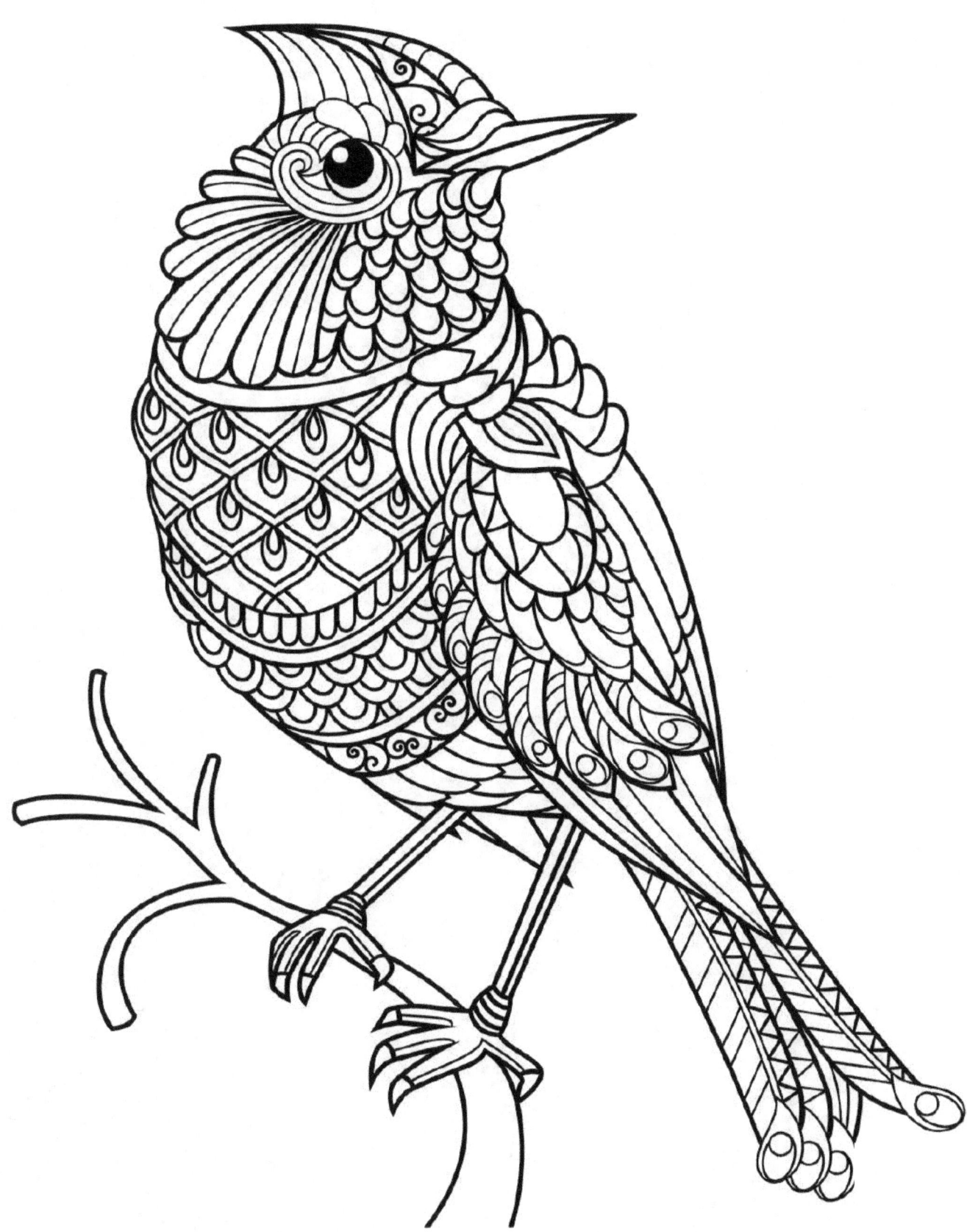

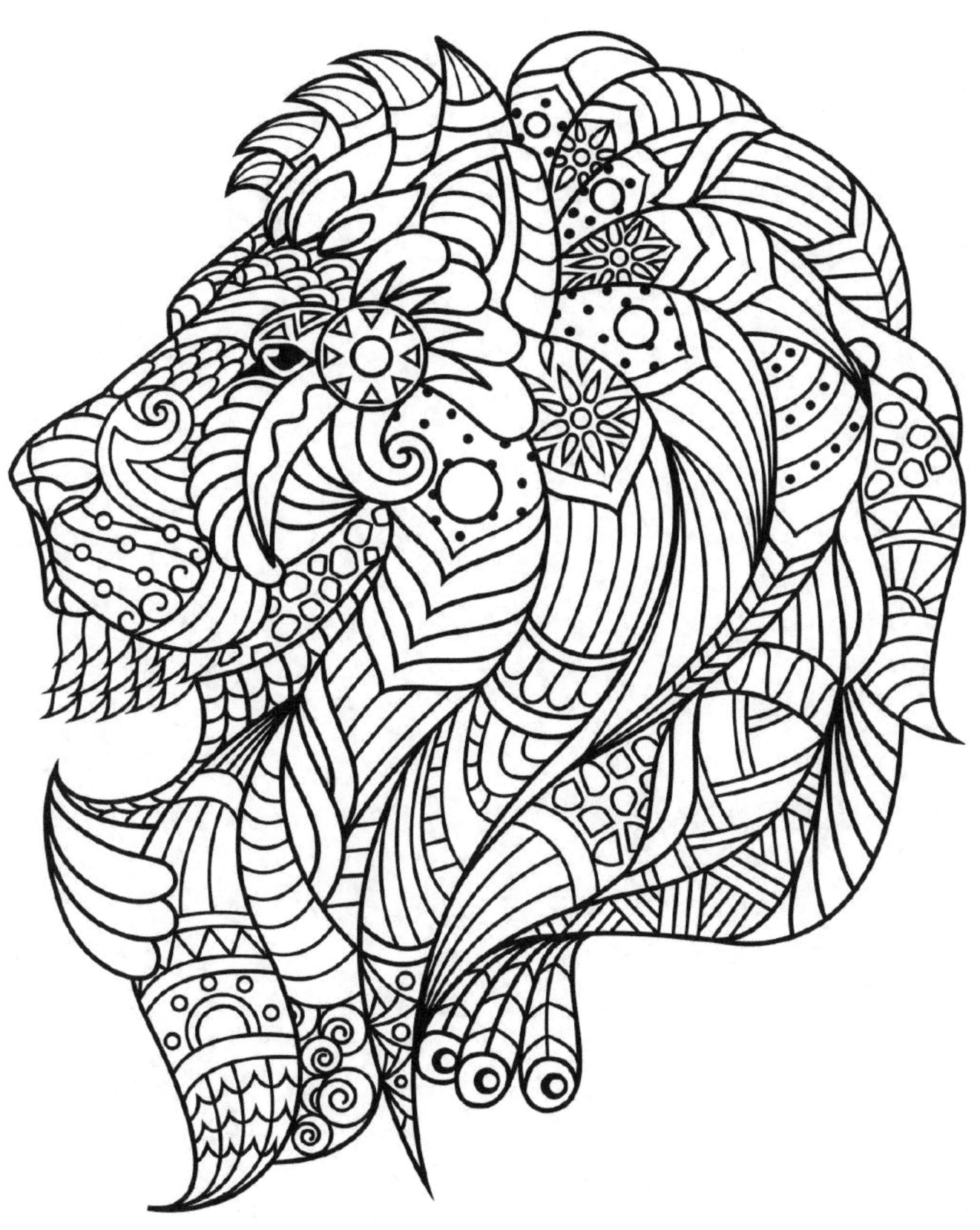

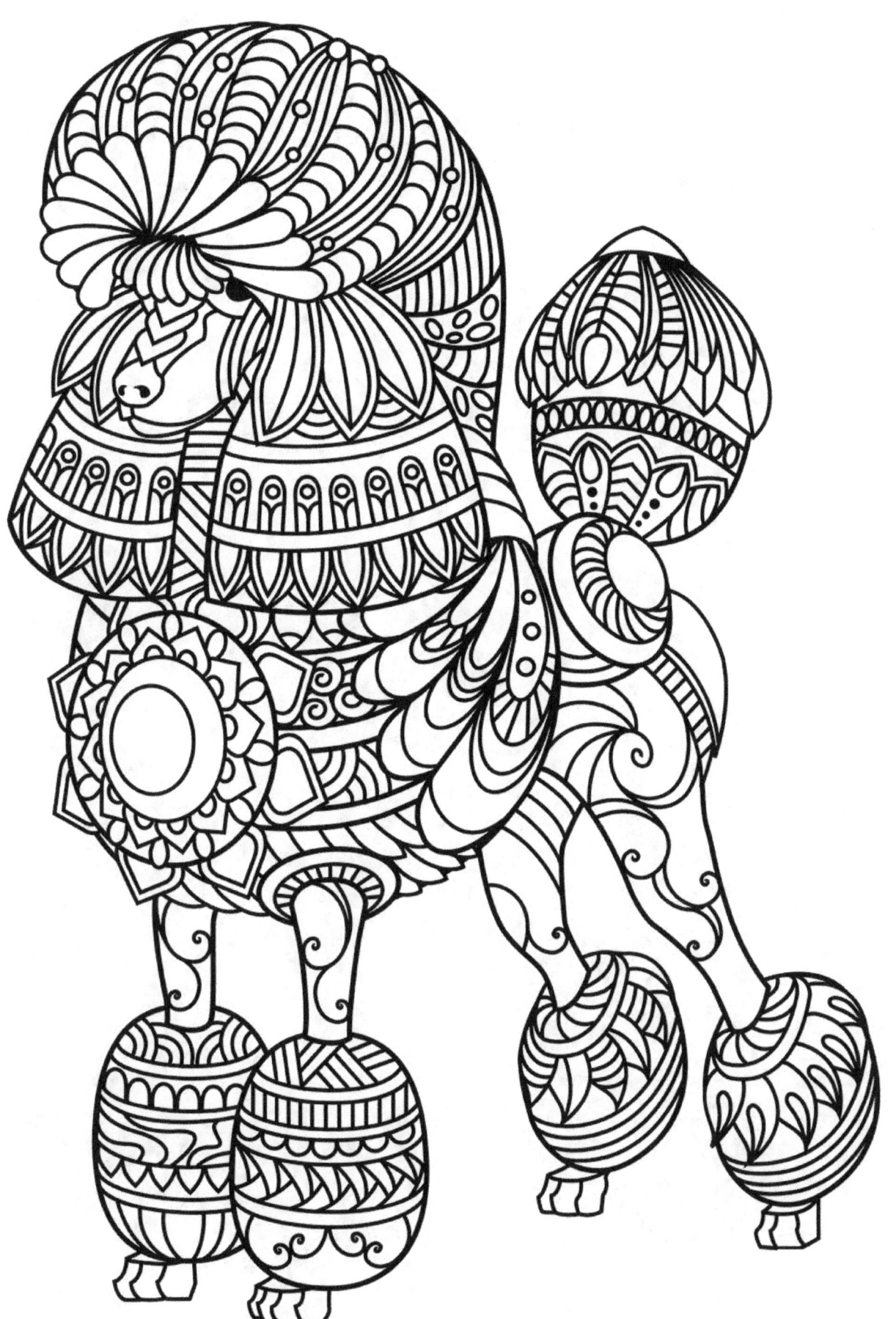

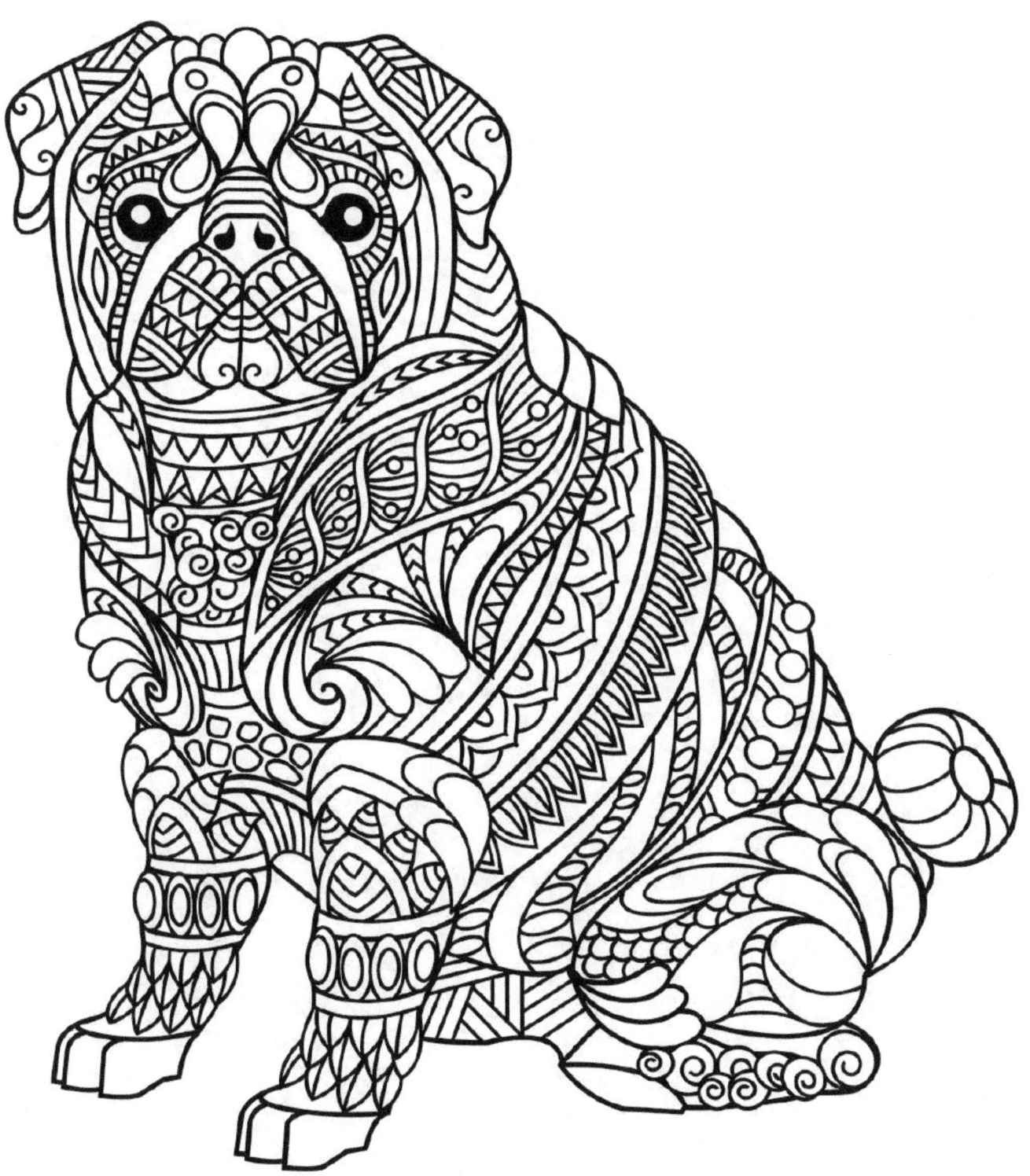

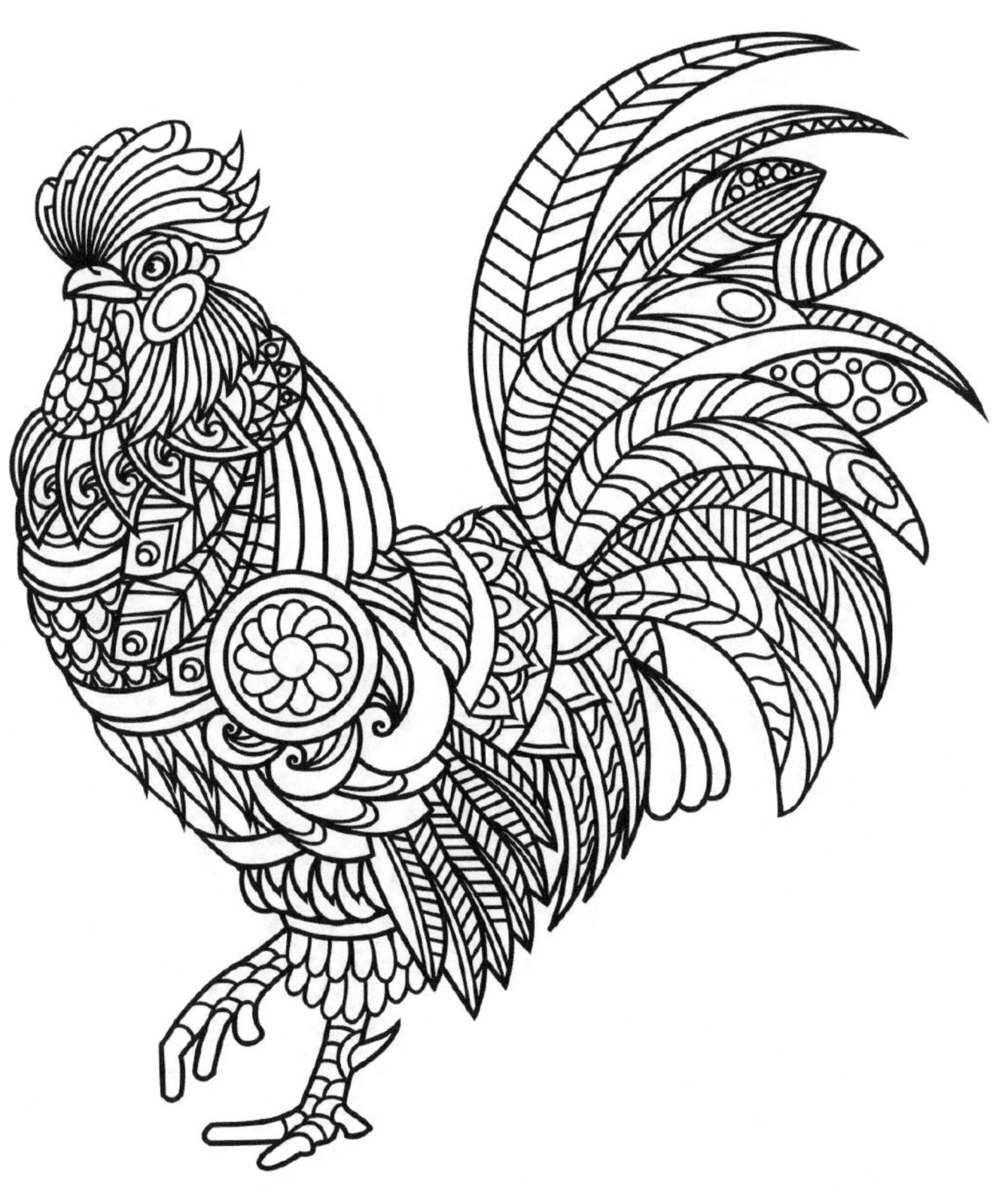

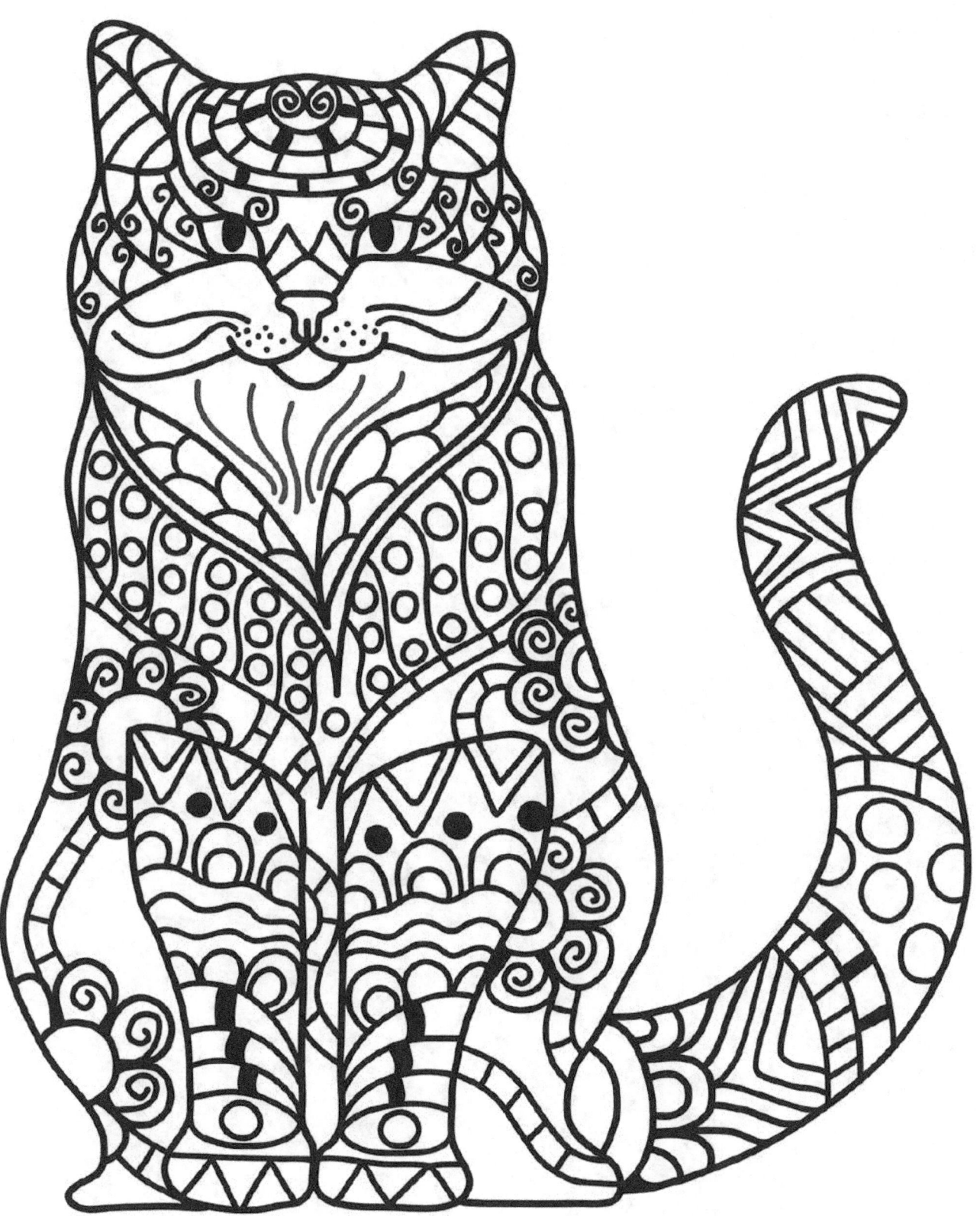

Book No. 2

Domestic Animals

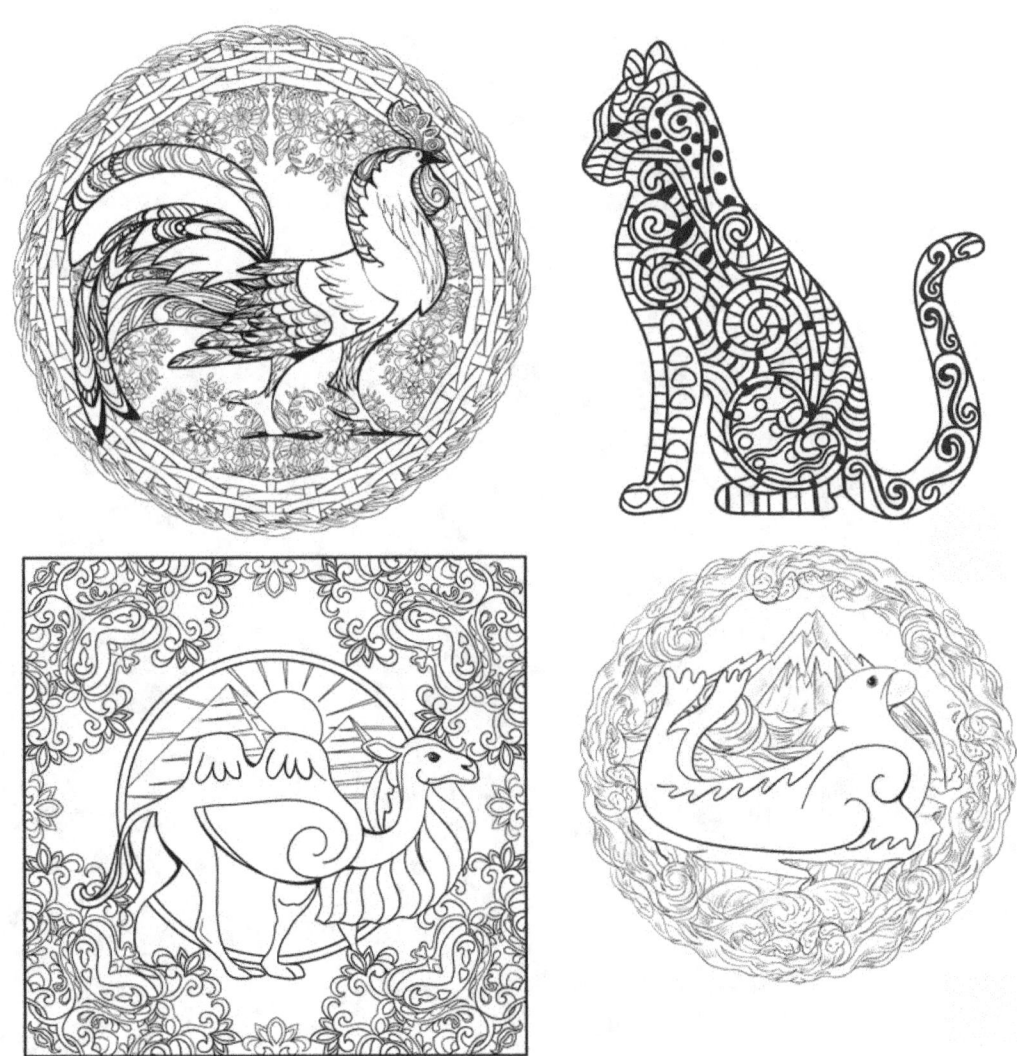

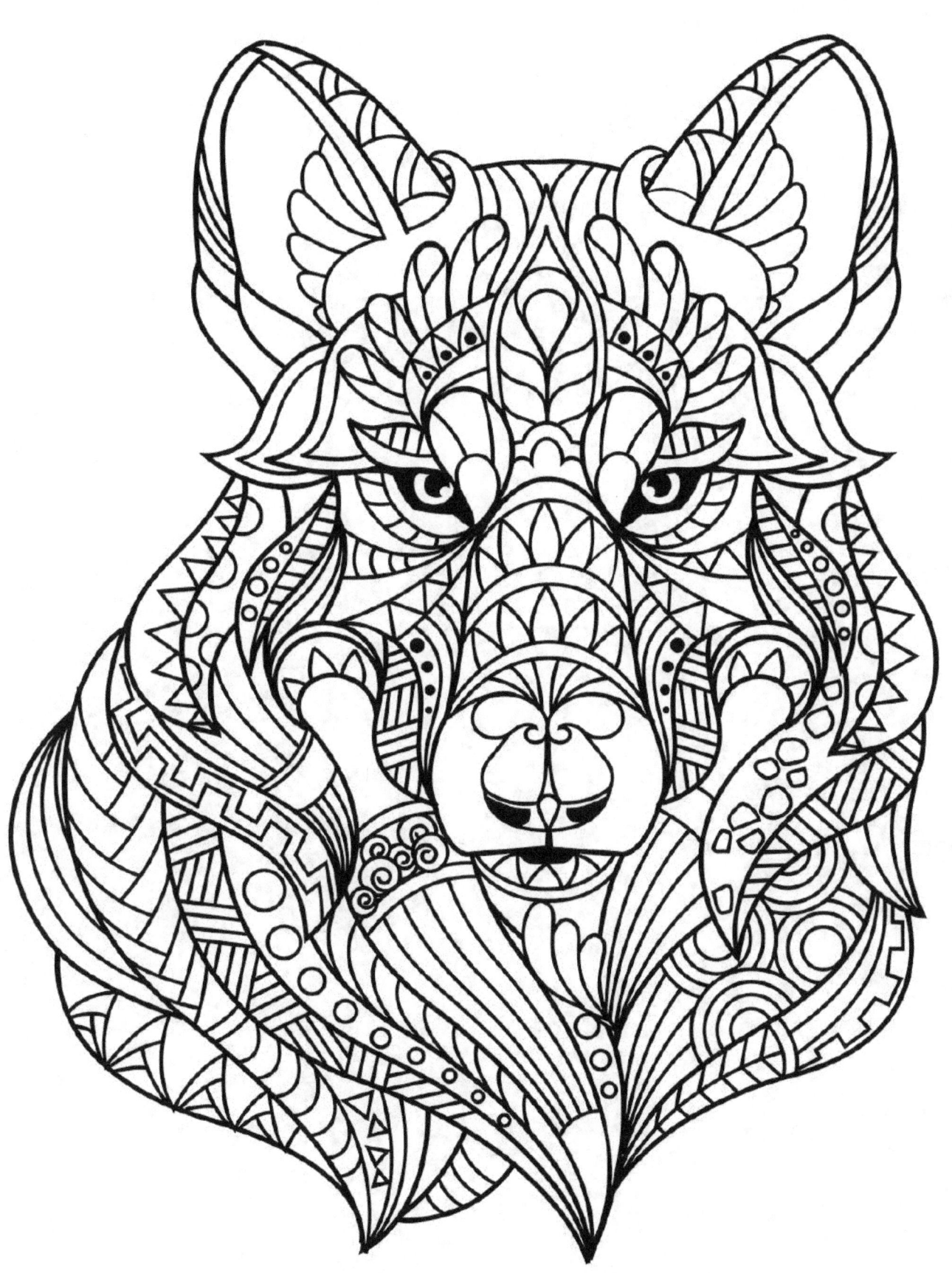

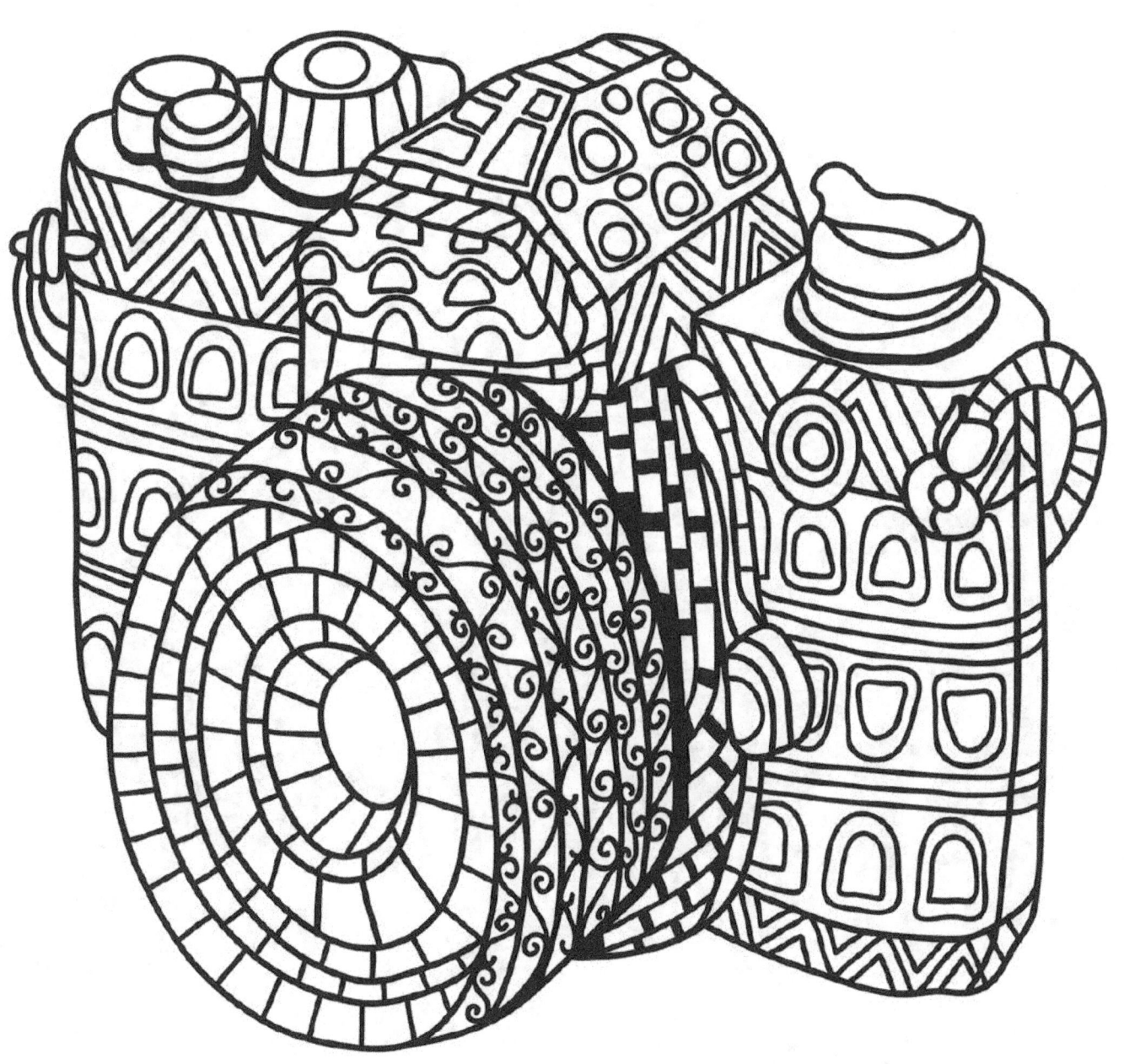

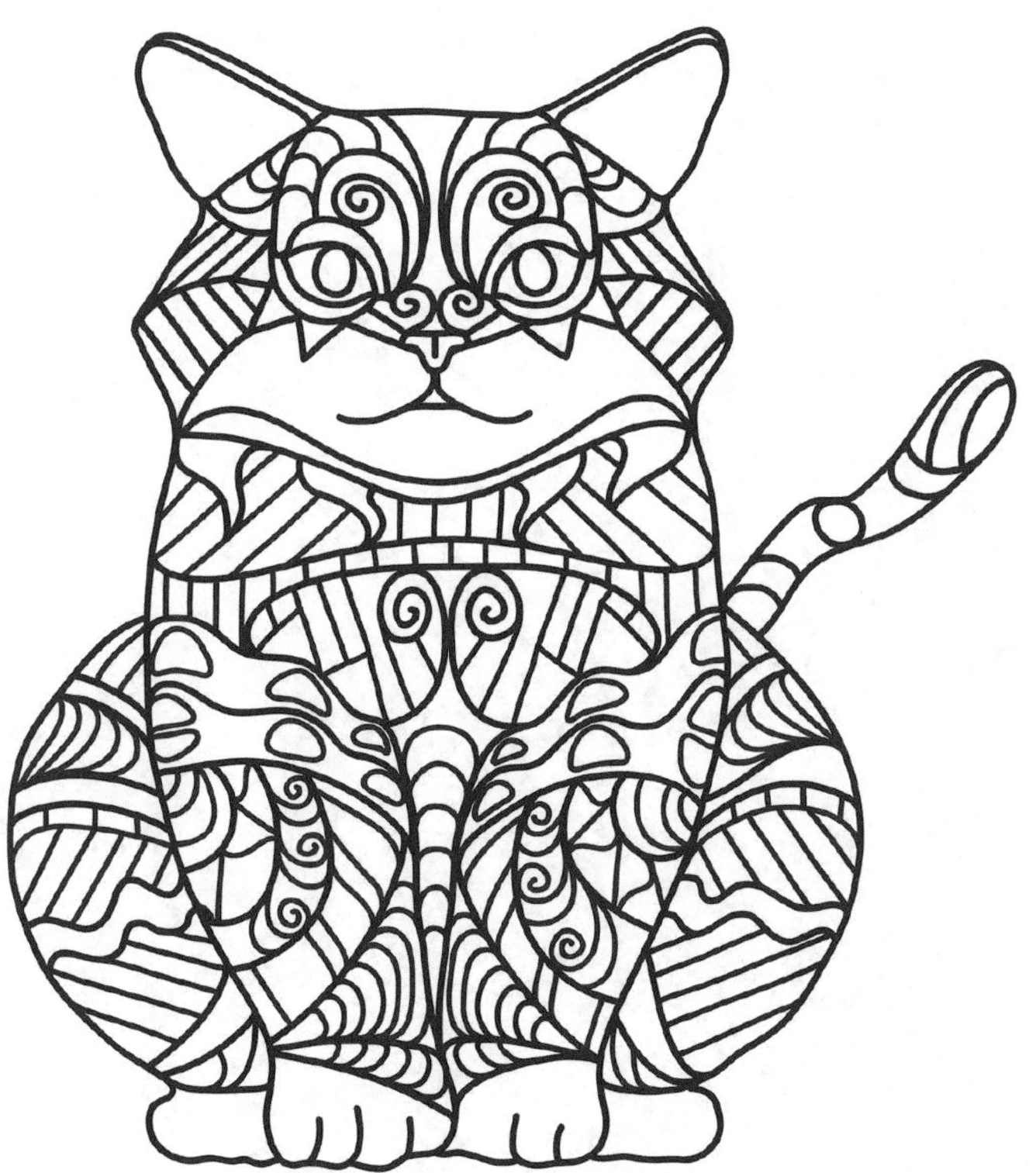

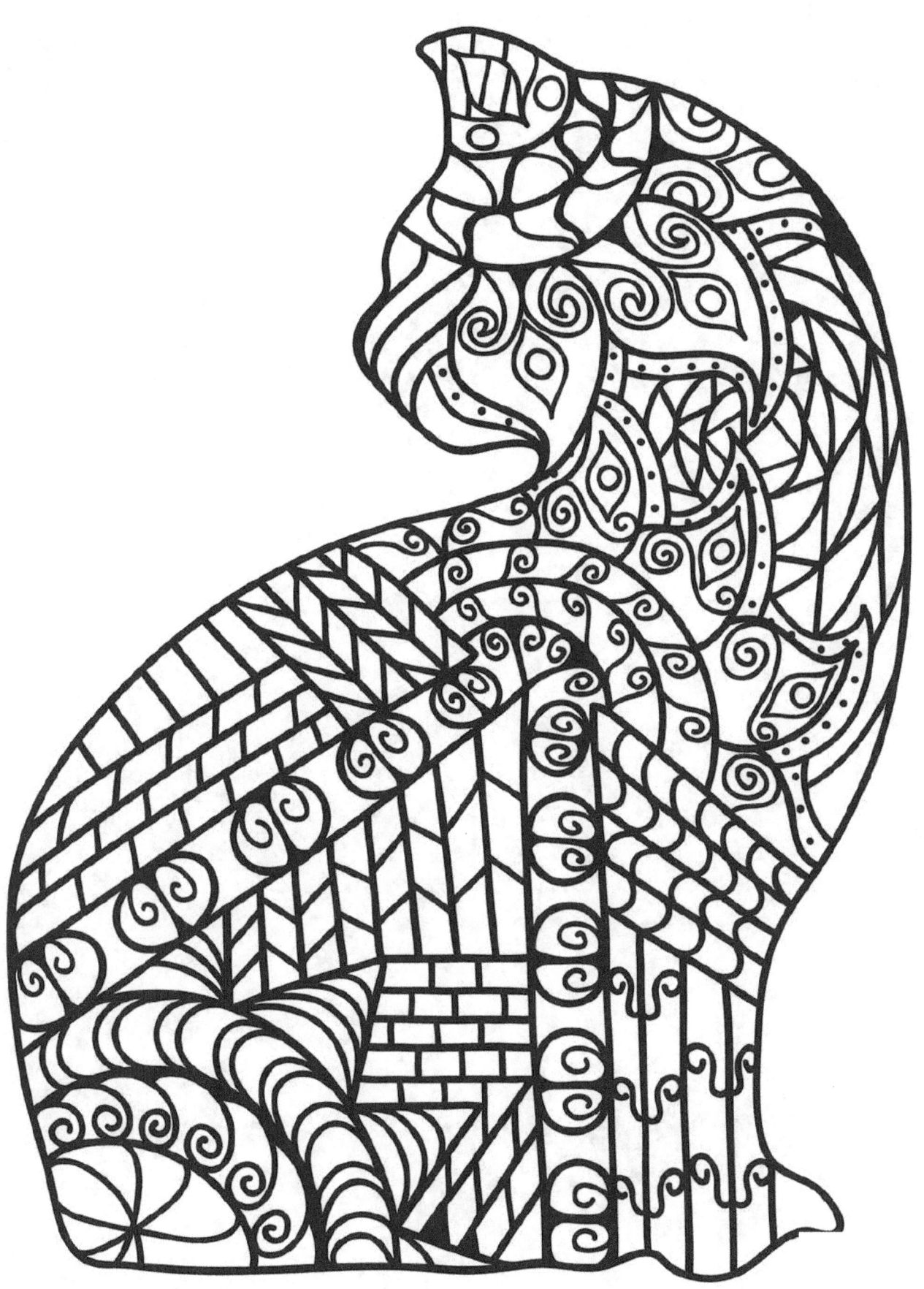

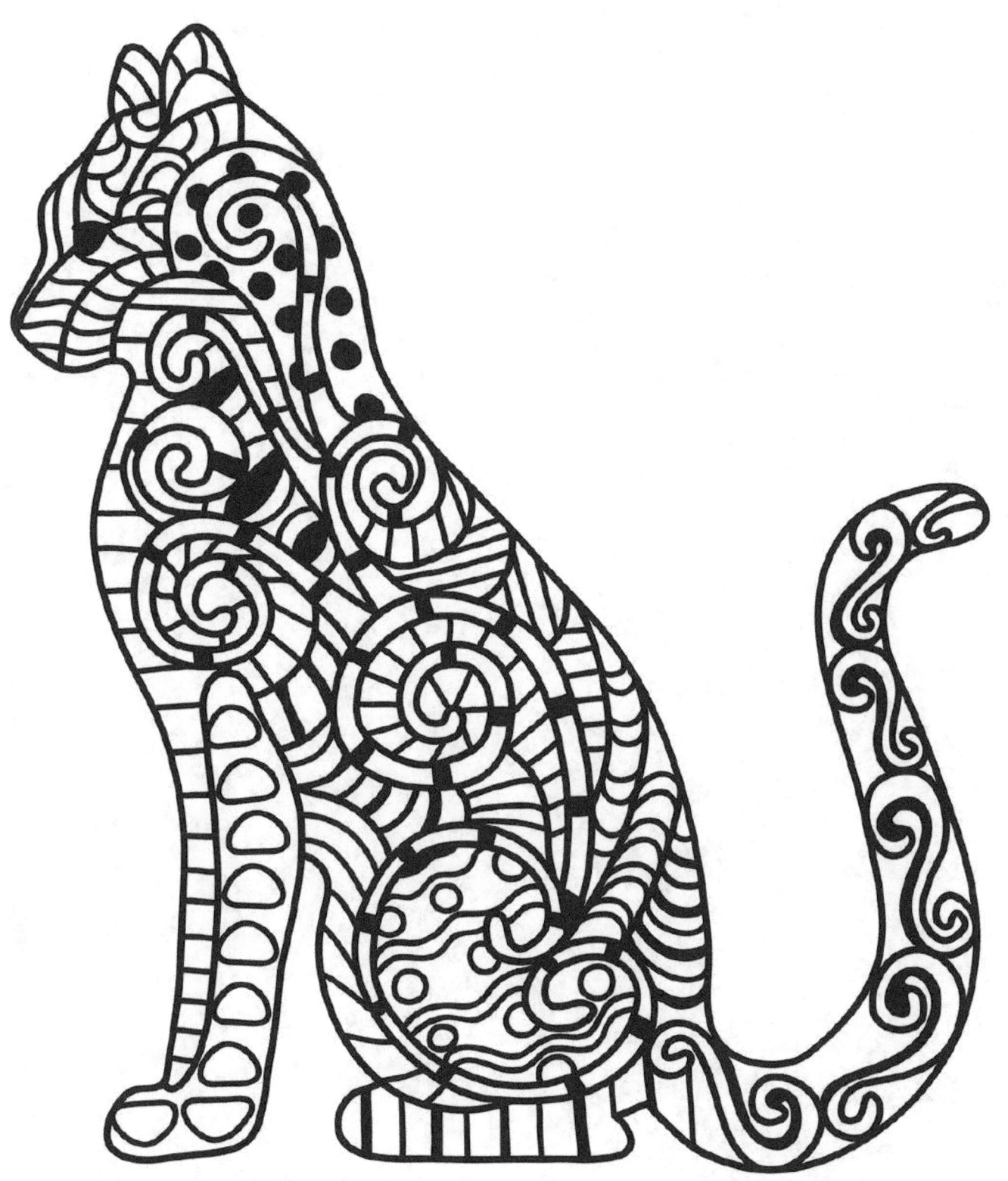

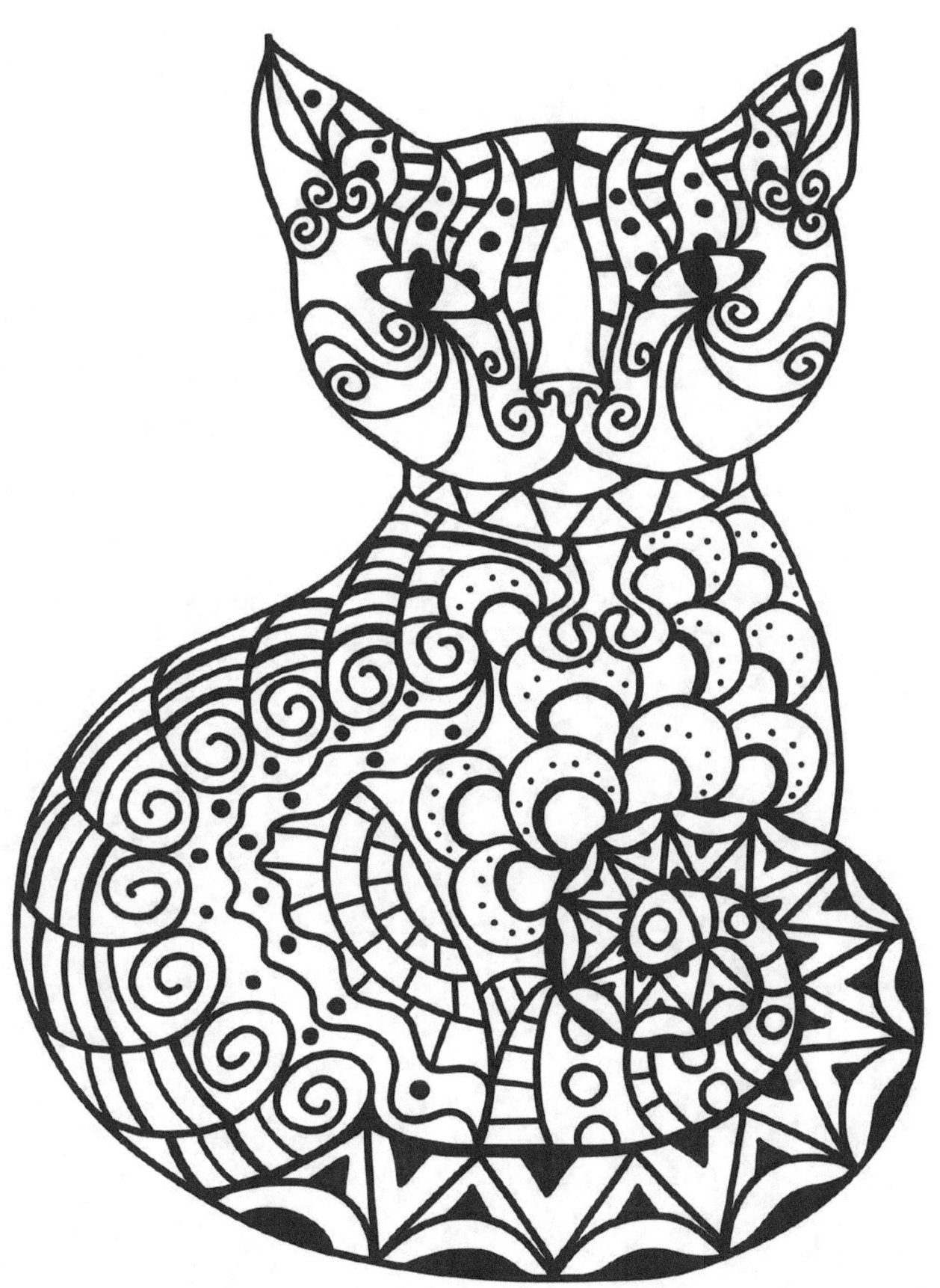

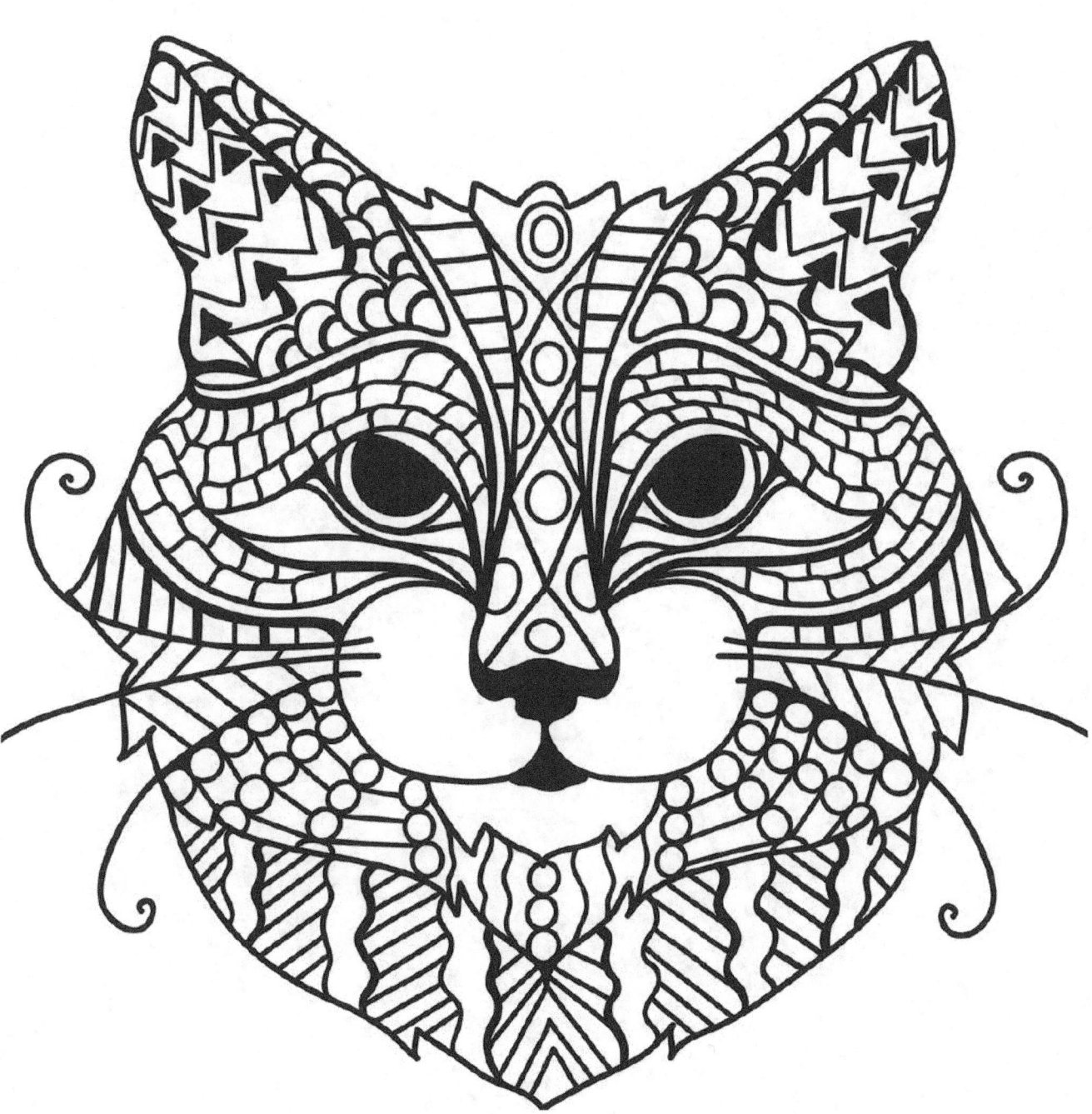

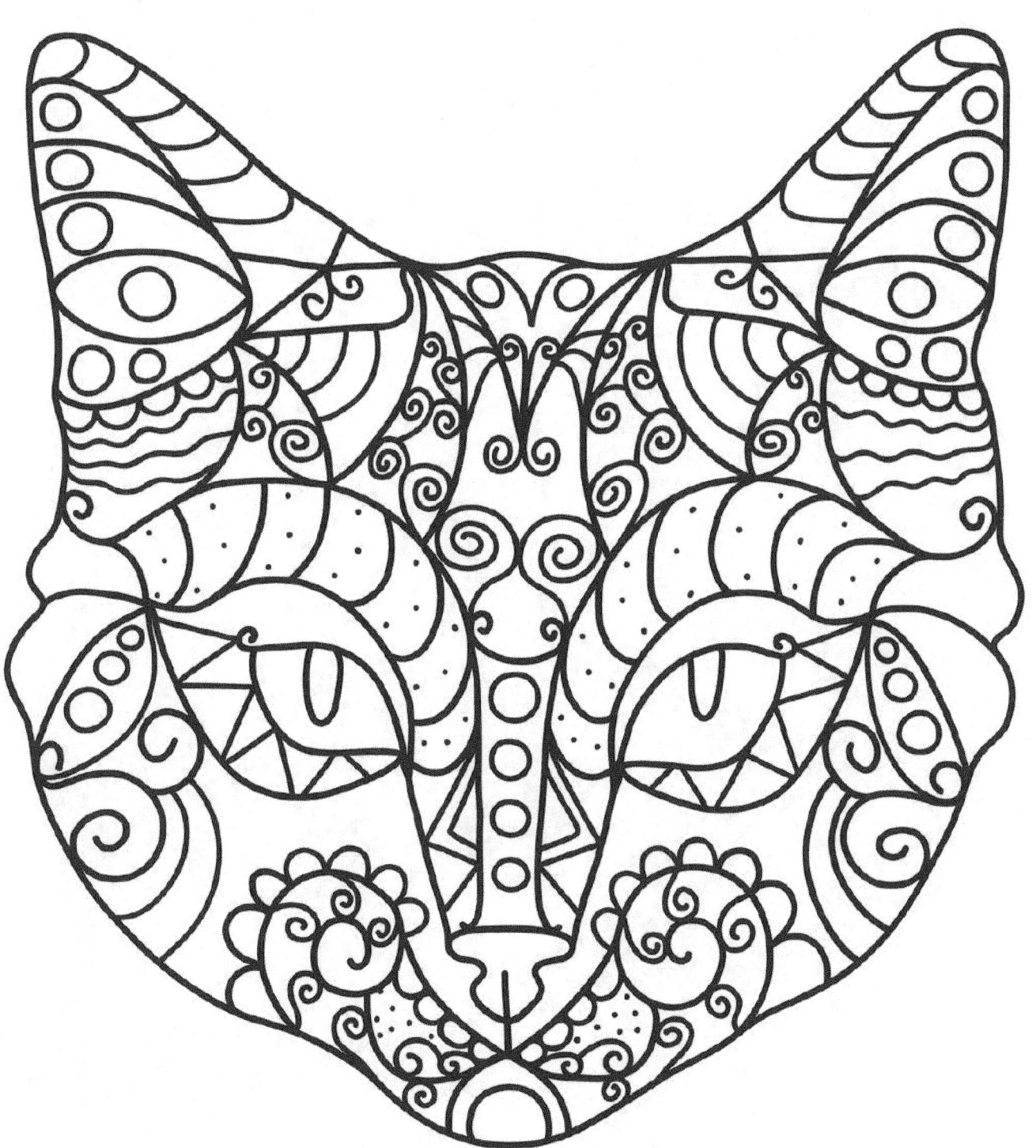

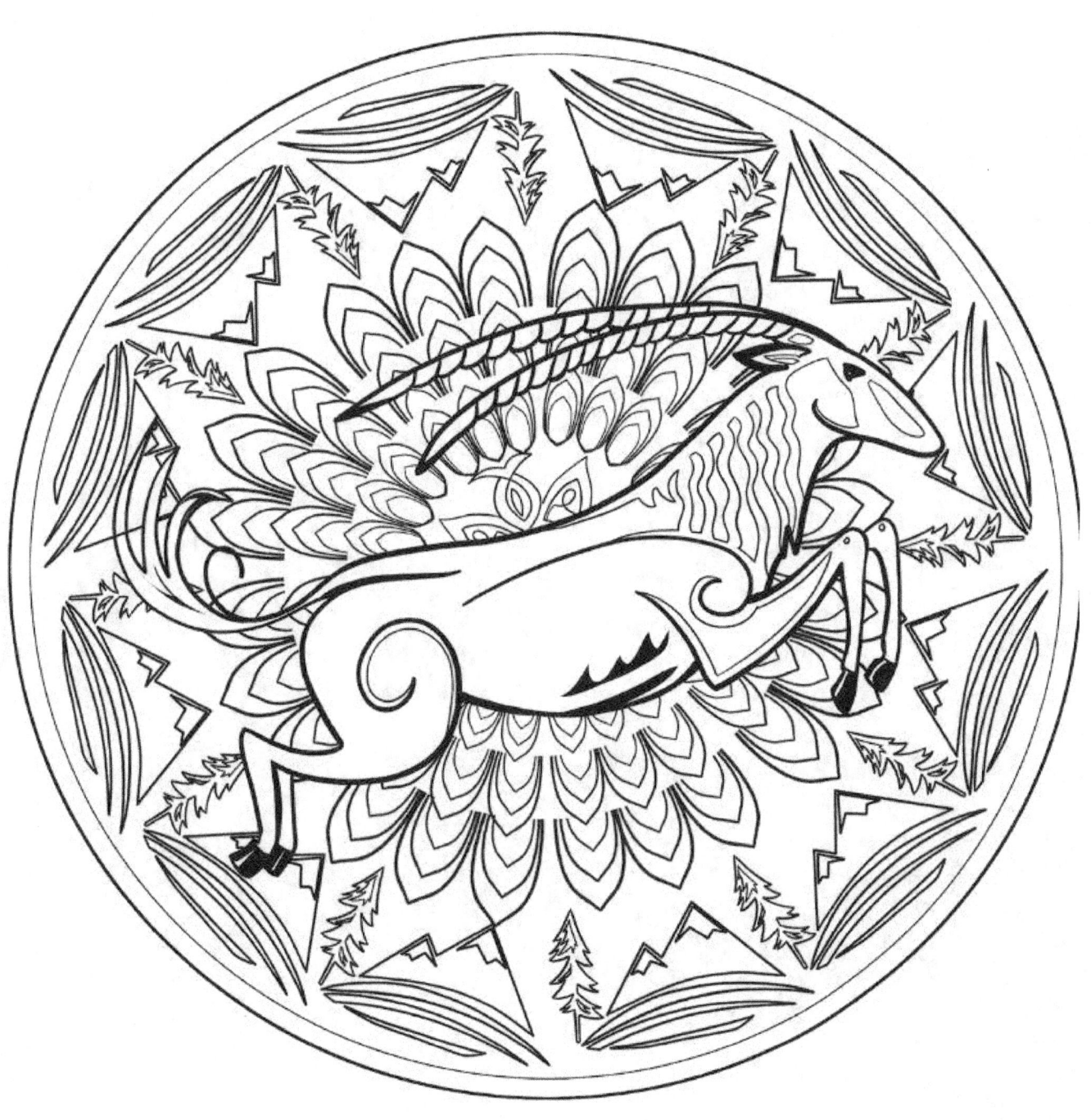

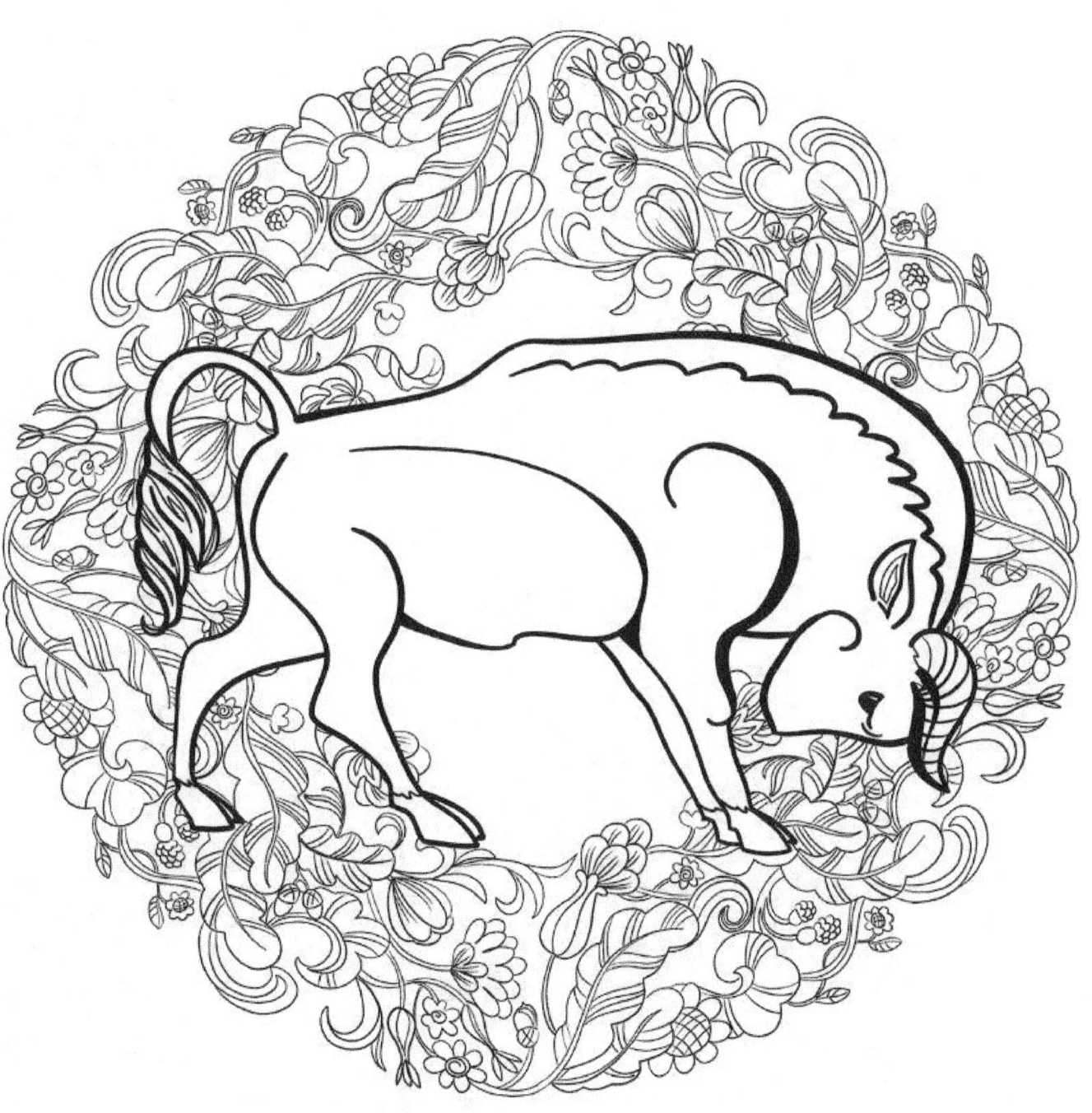

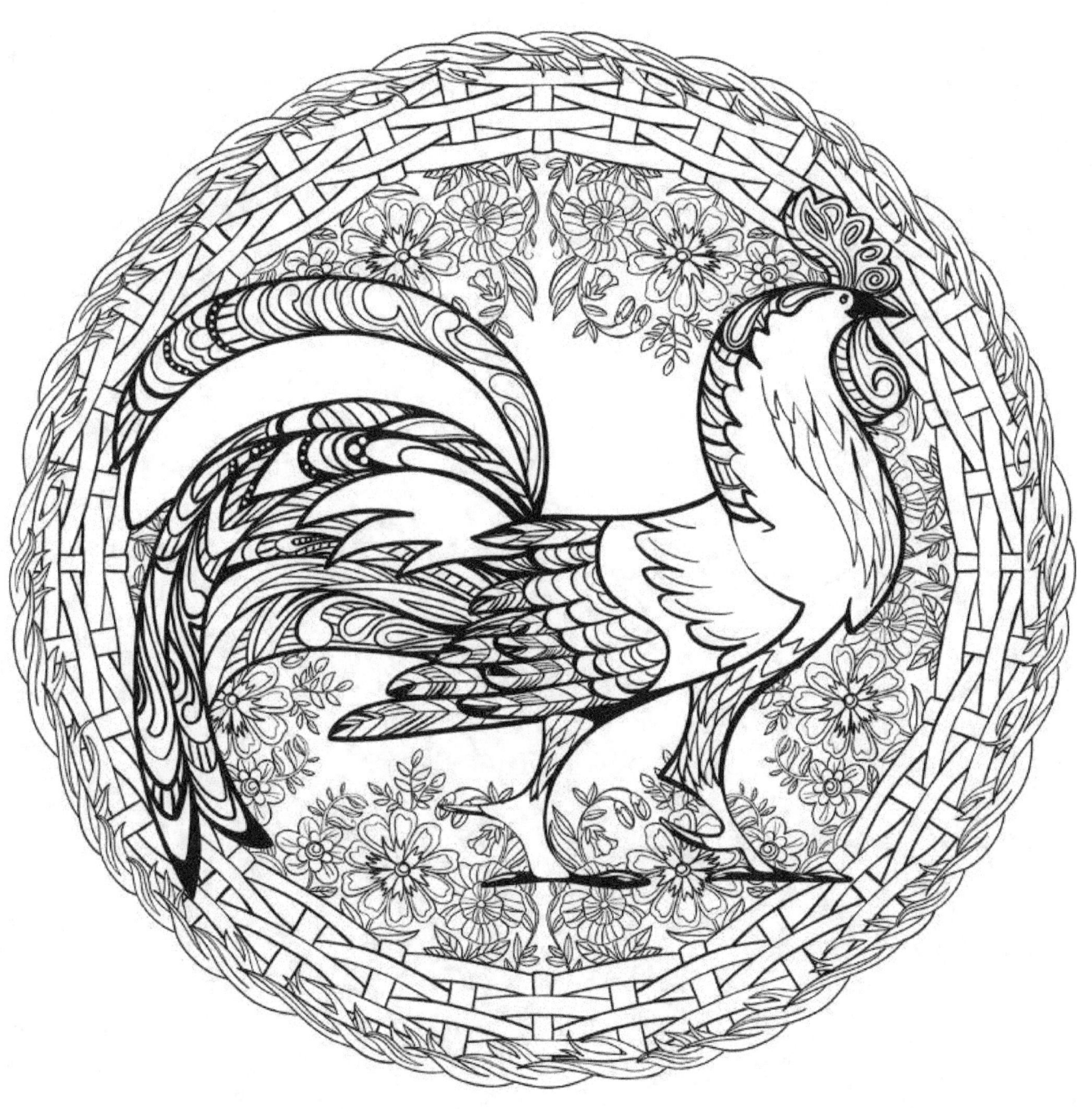

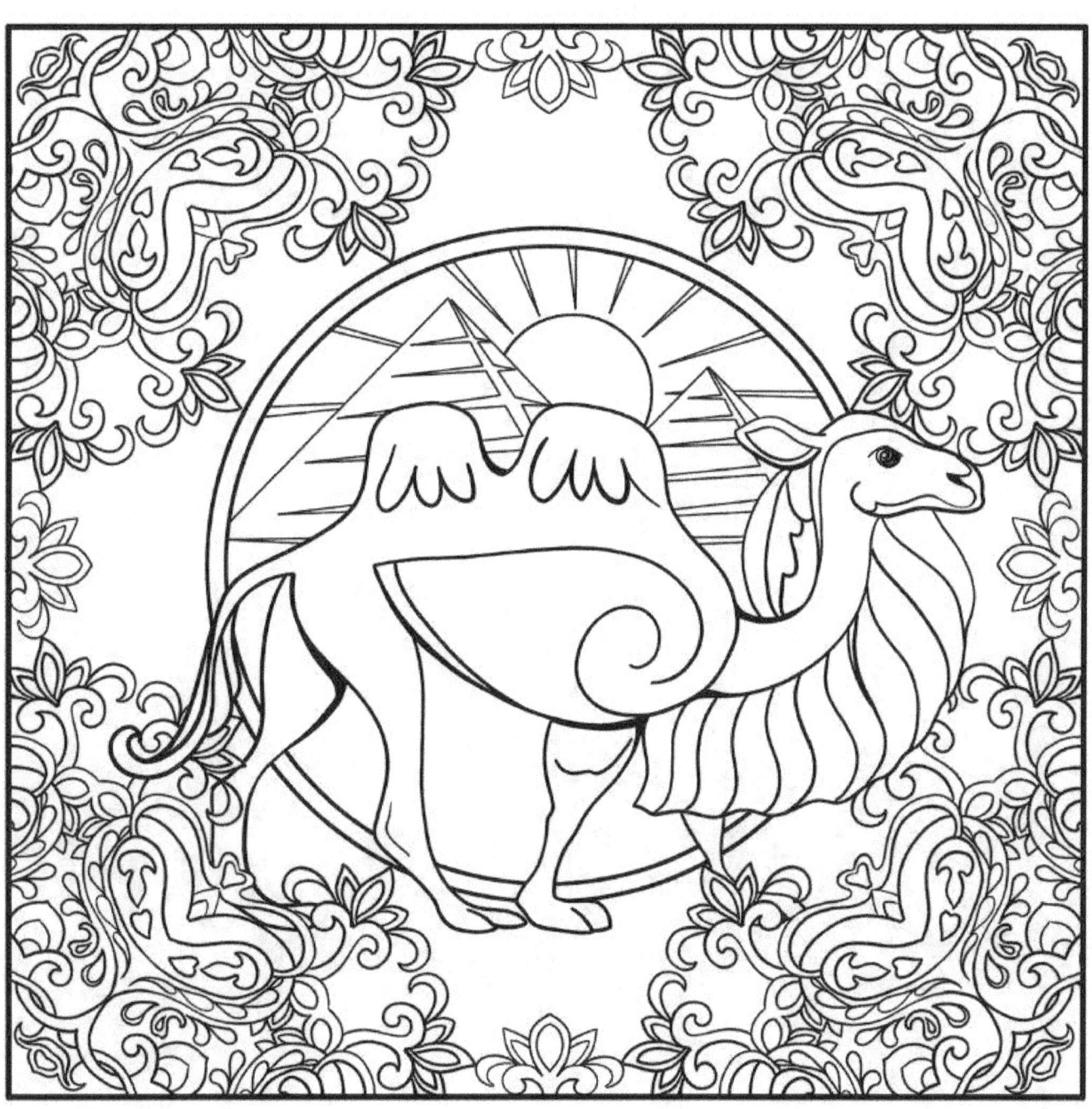

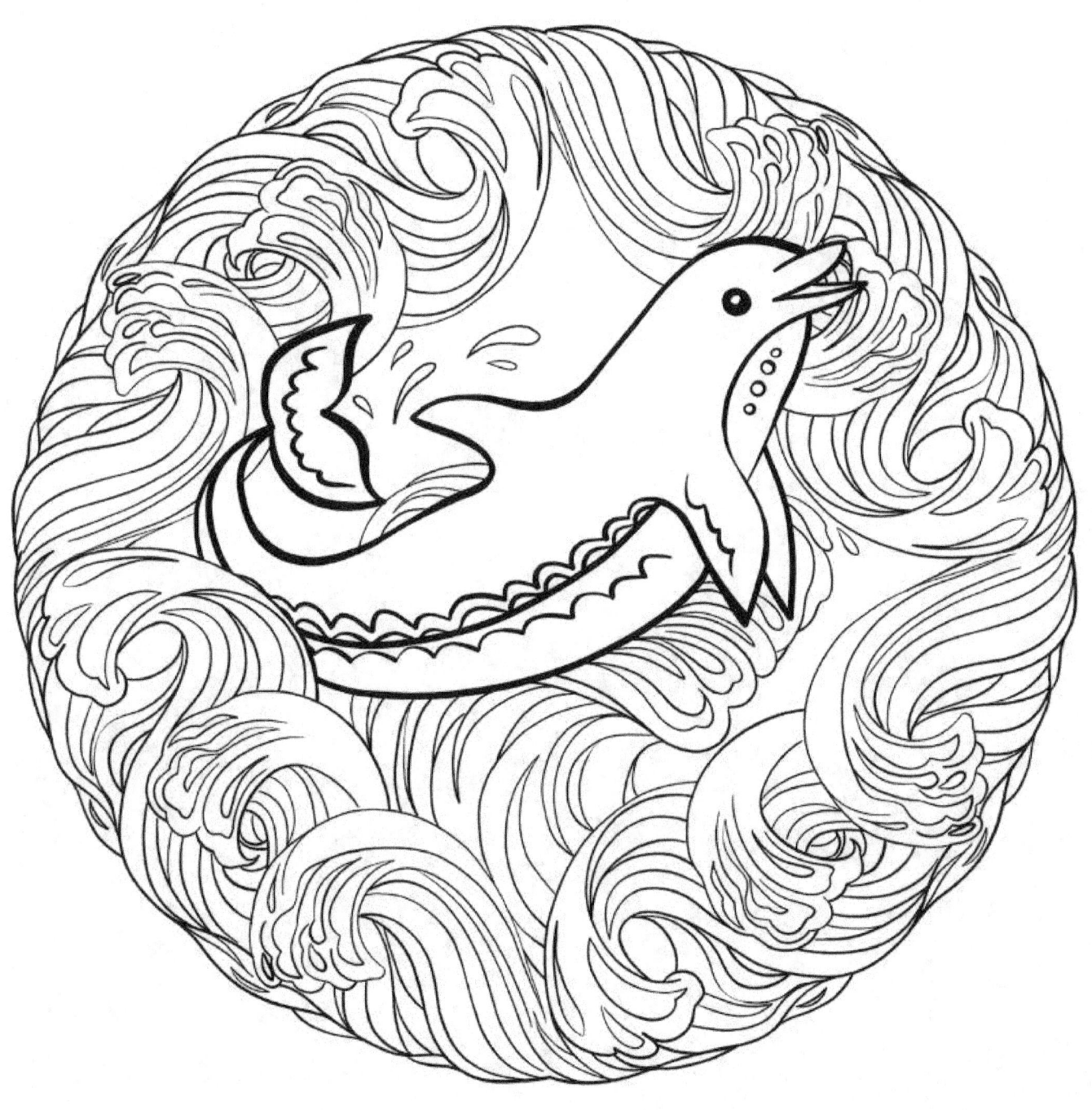

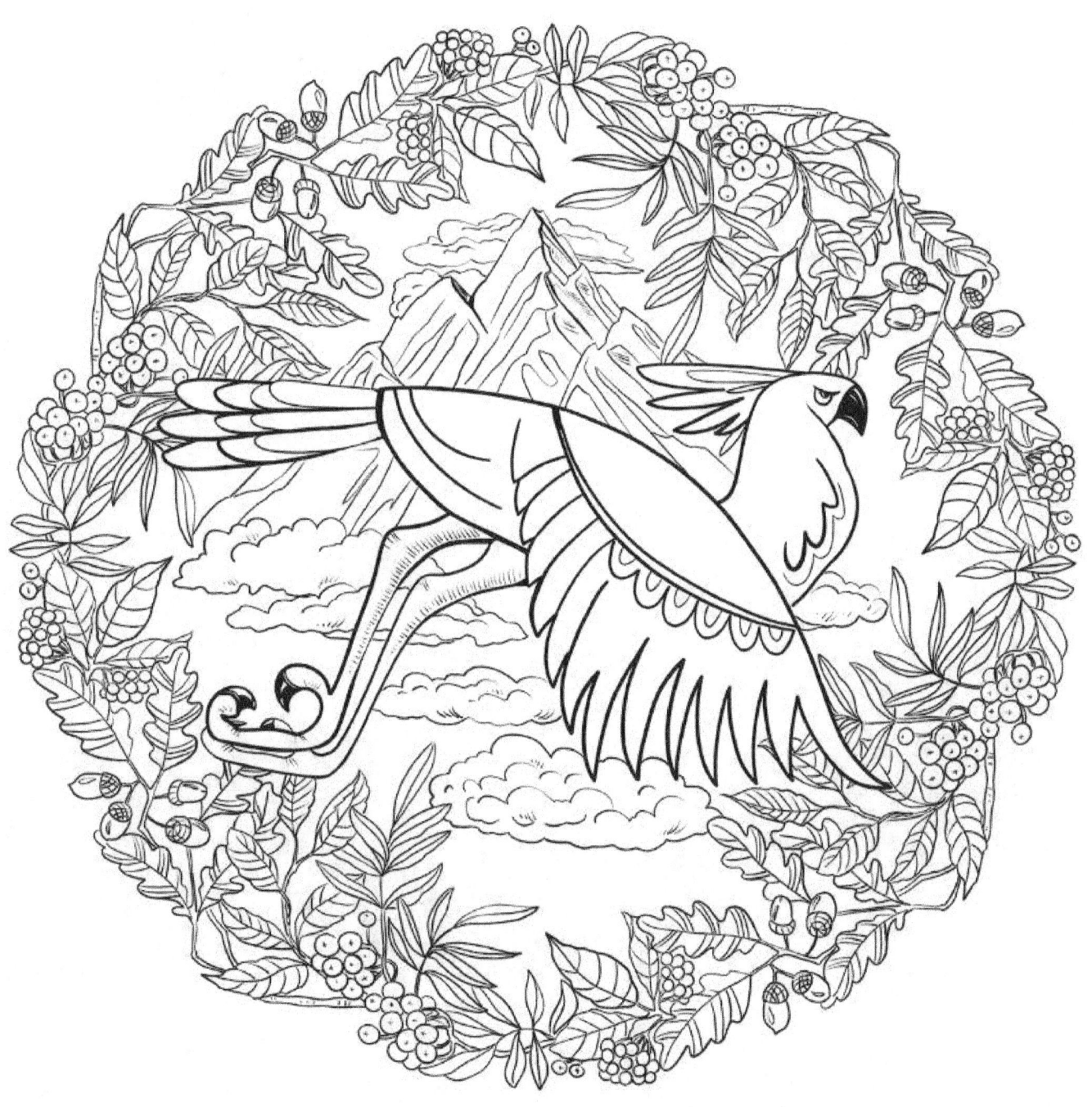

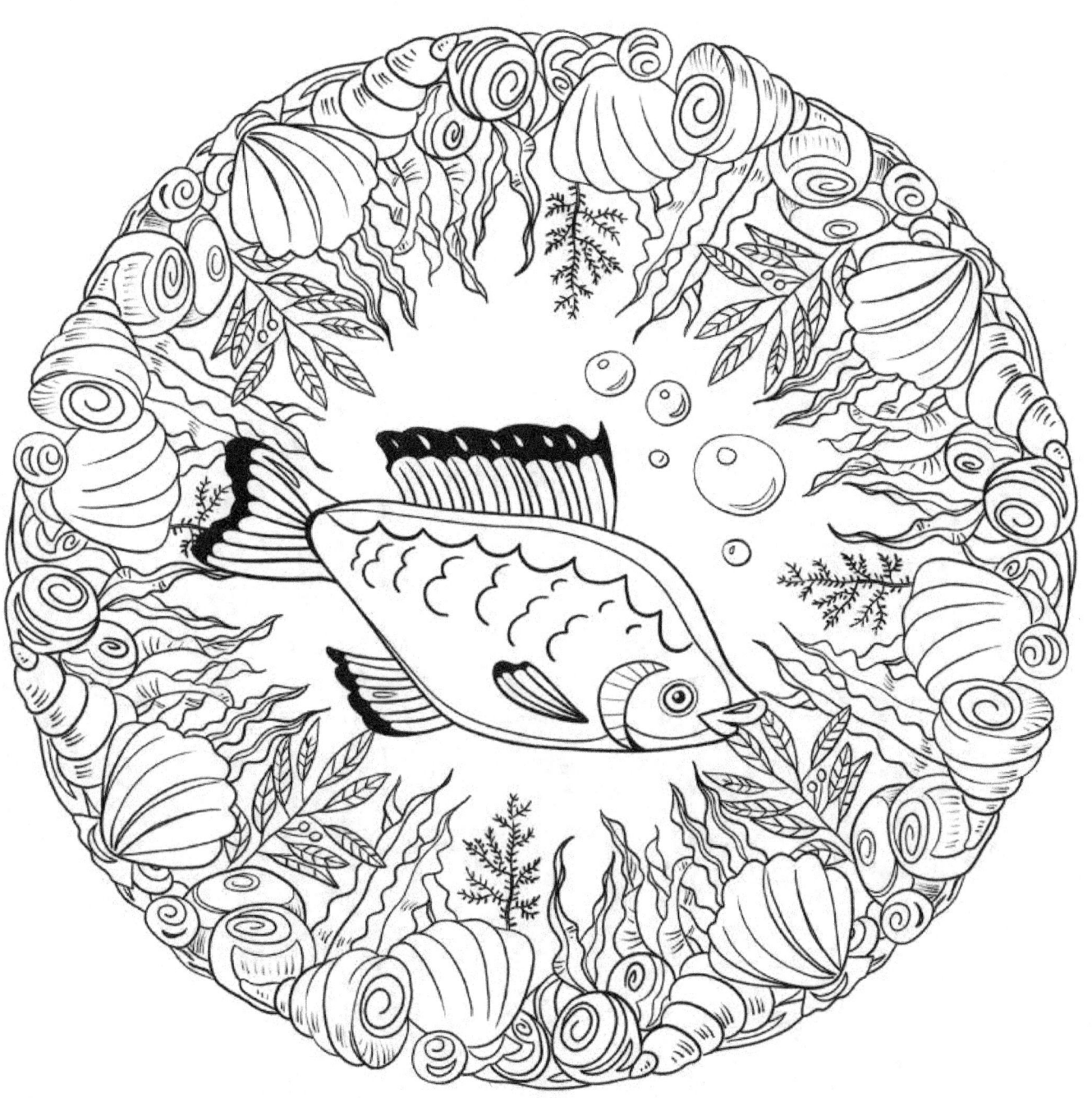

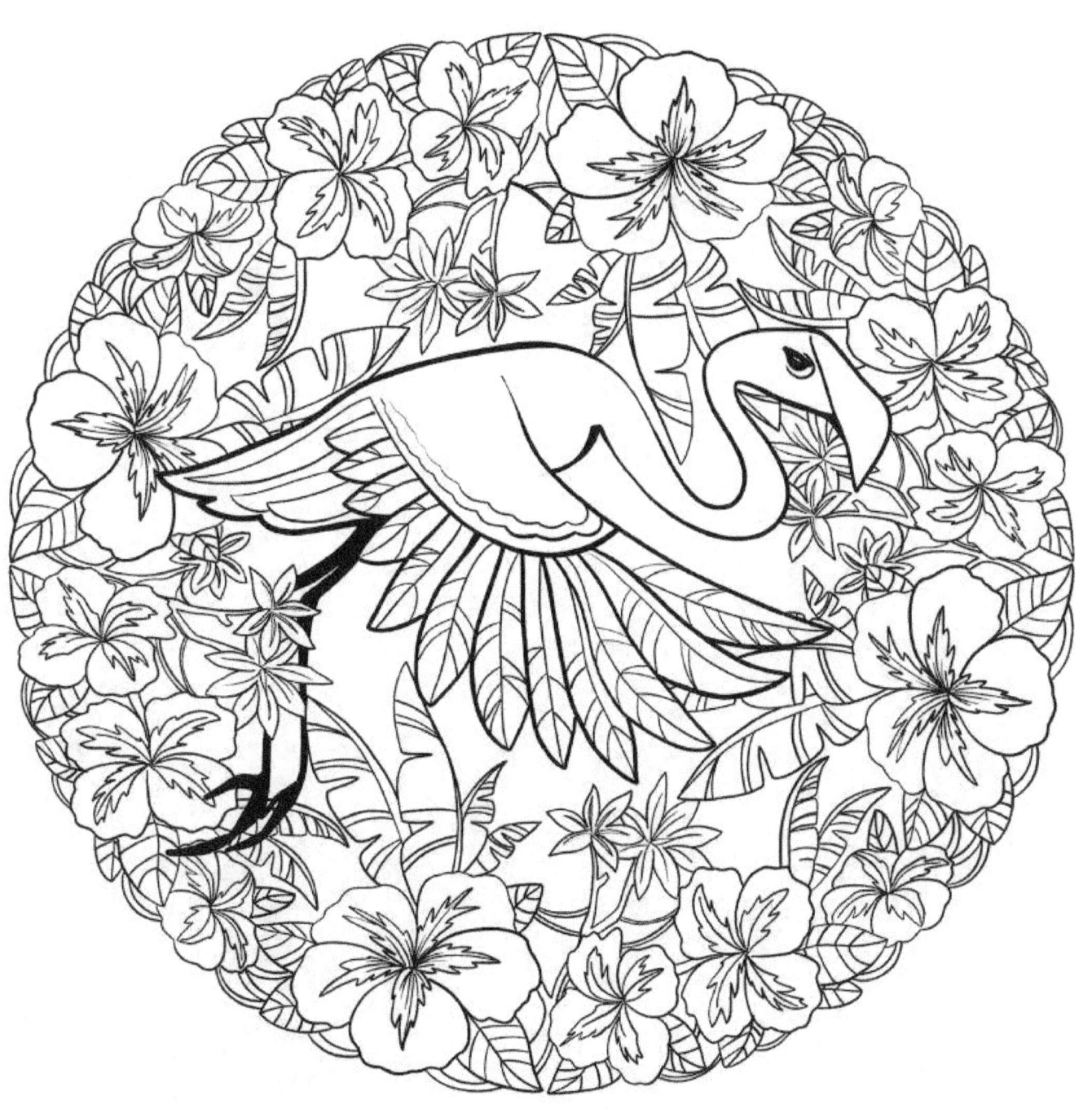

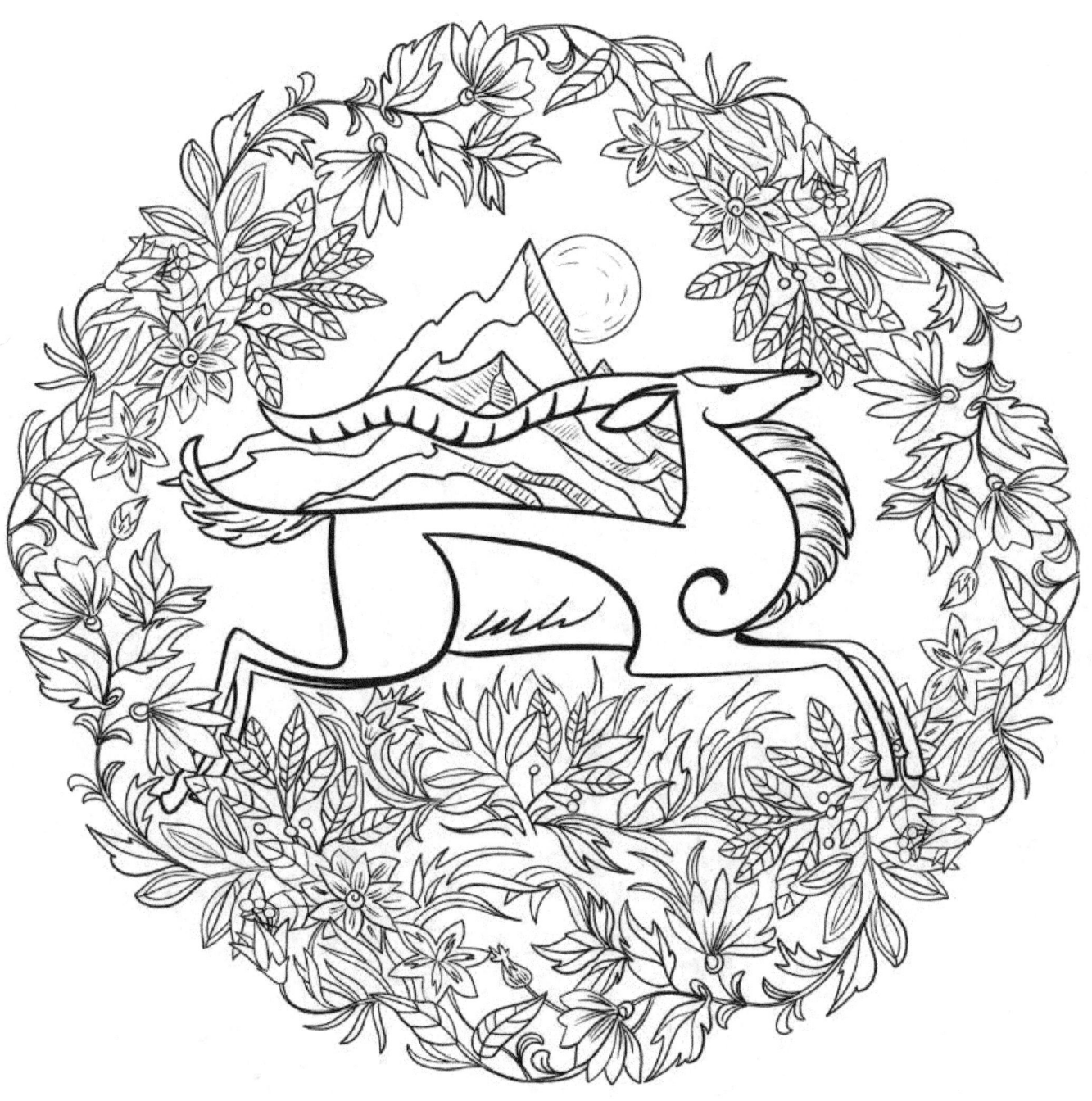

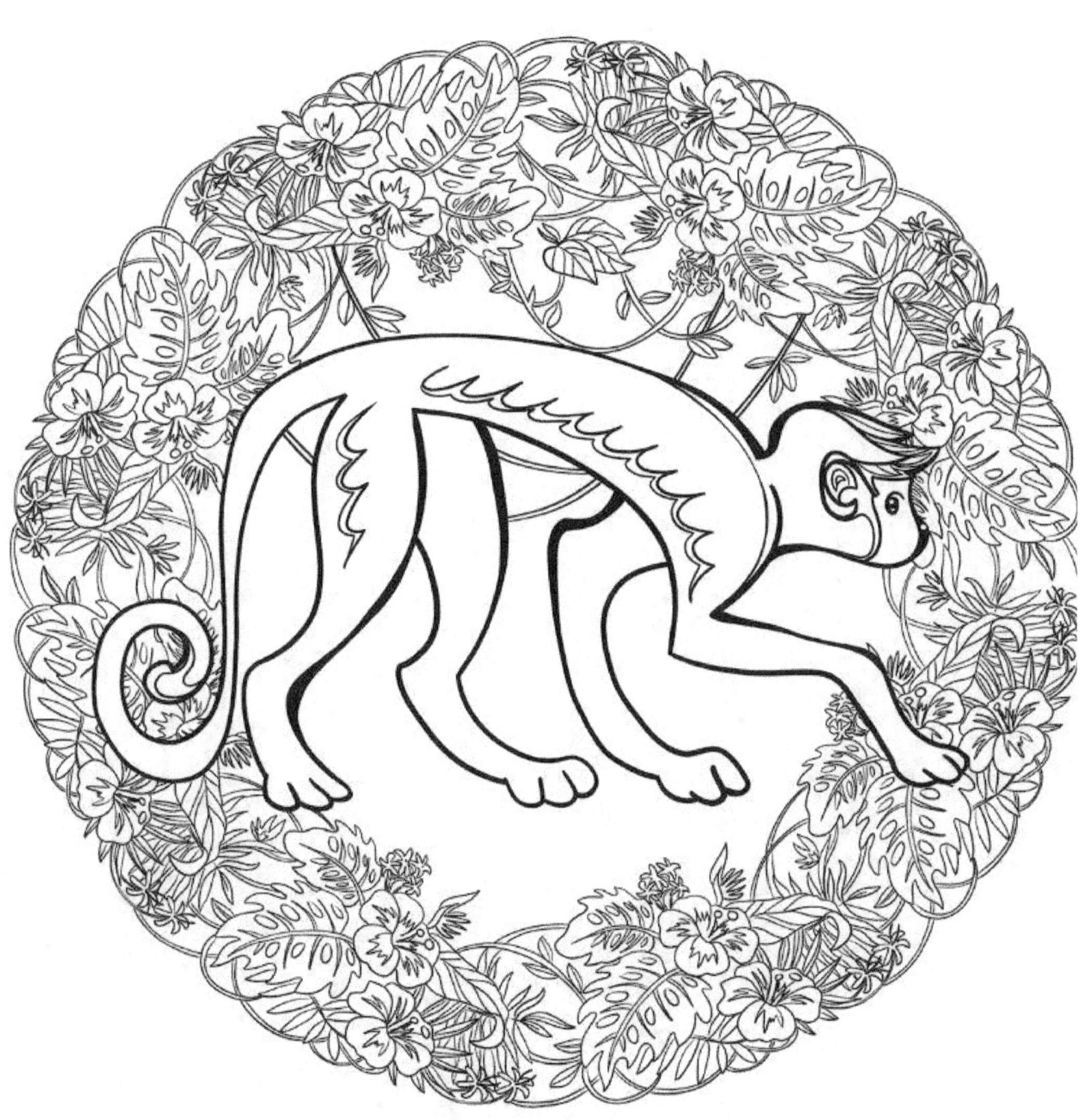

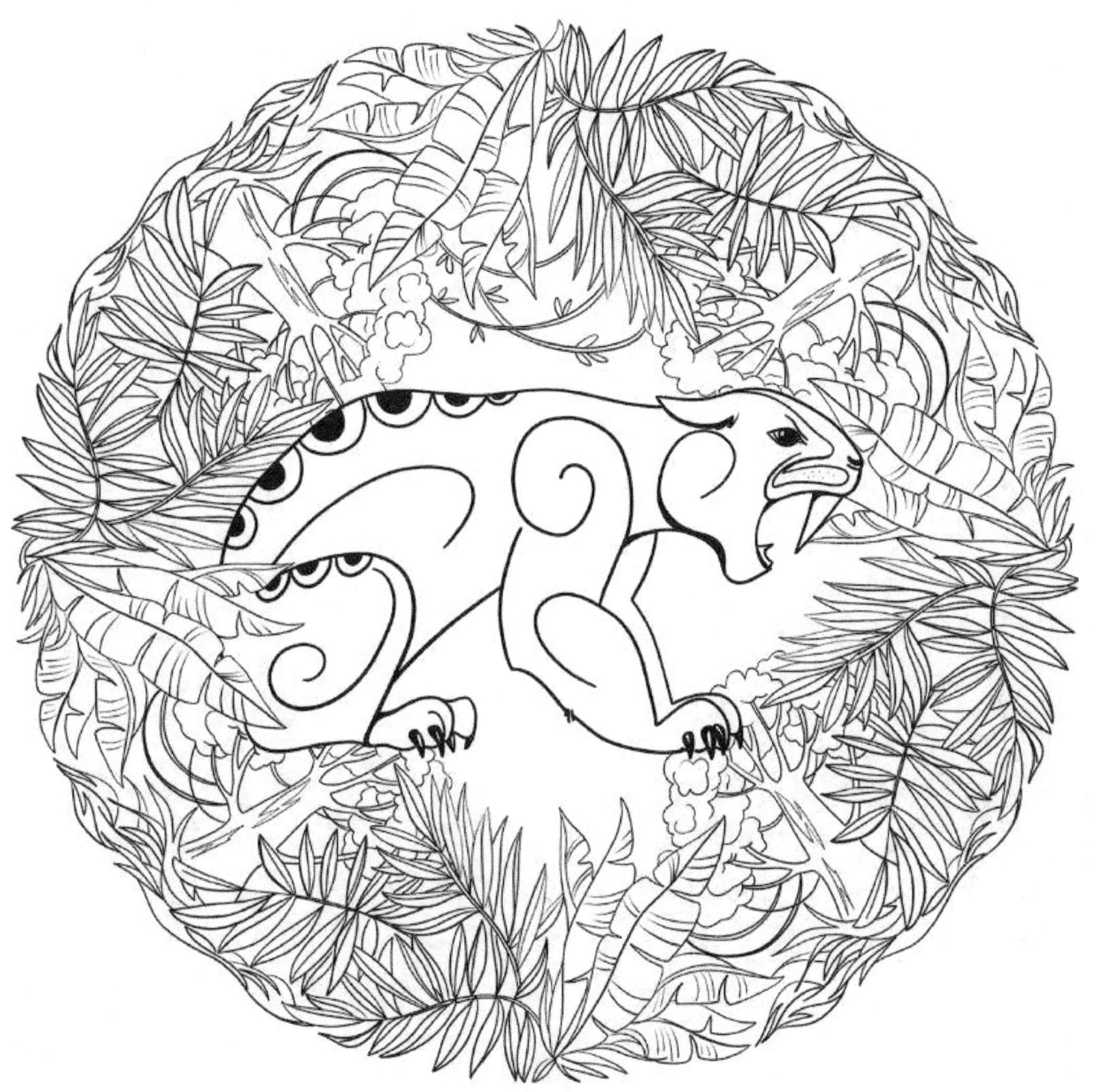

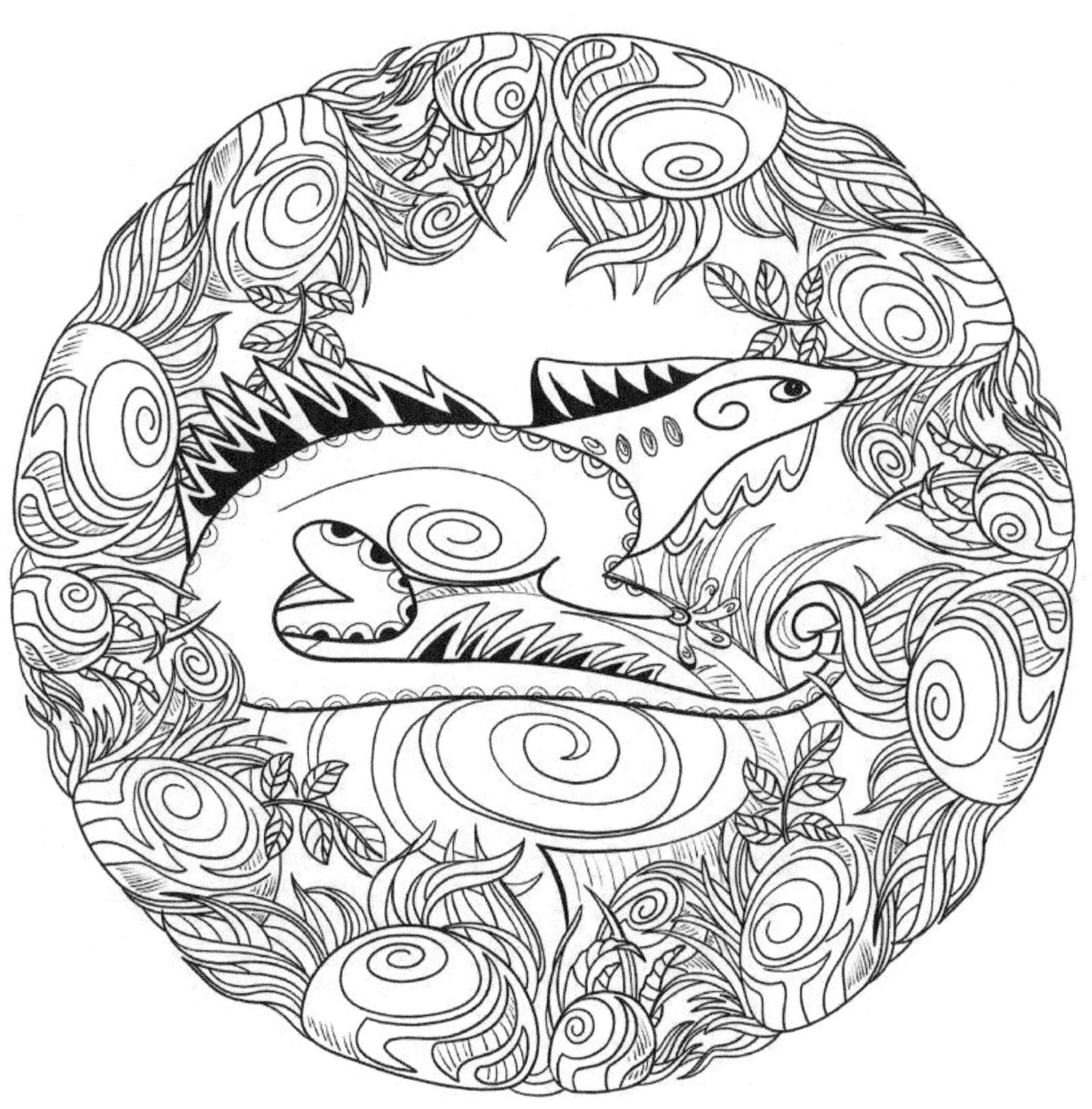

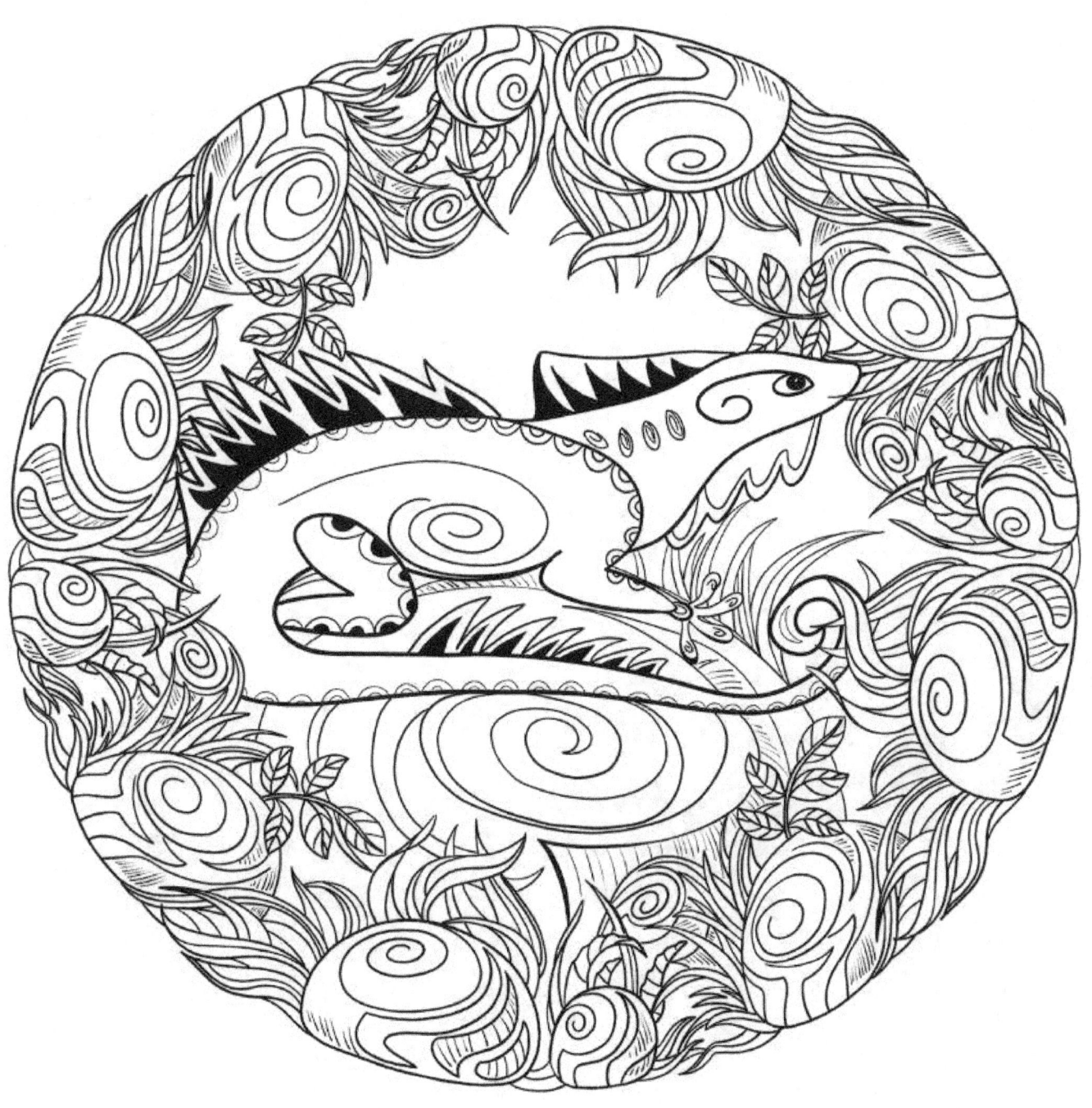

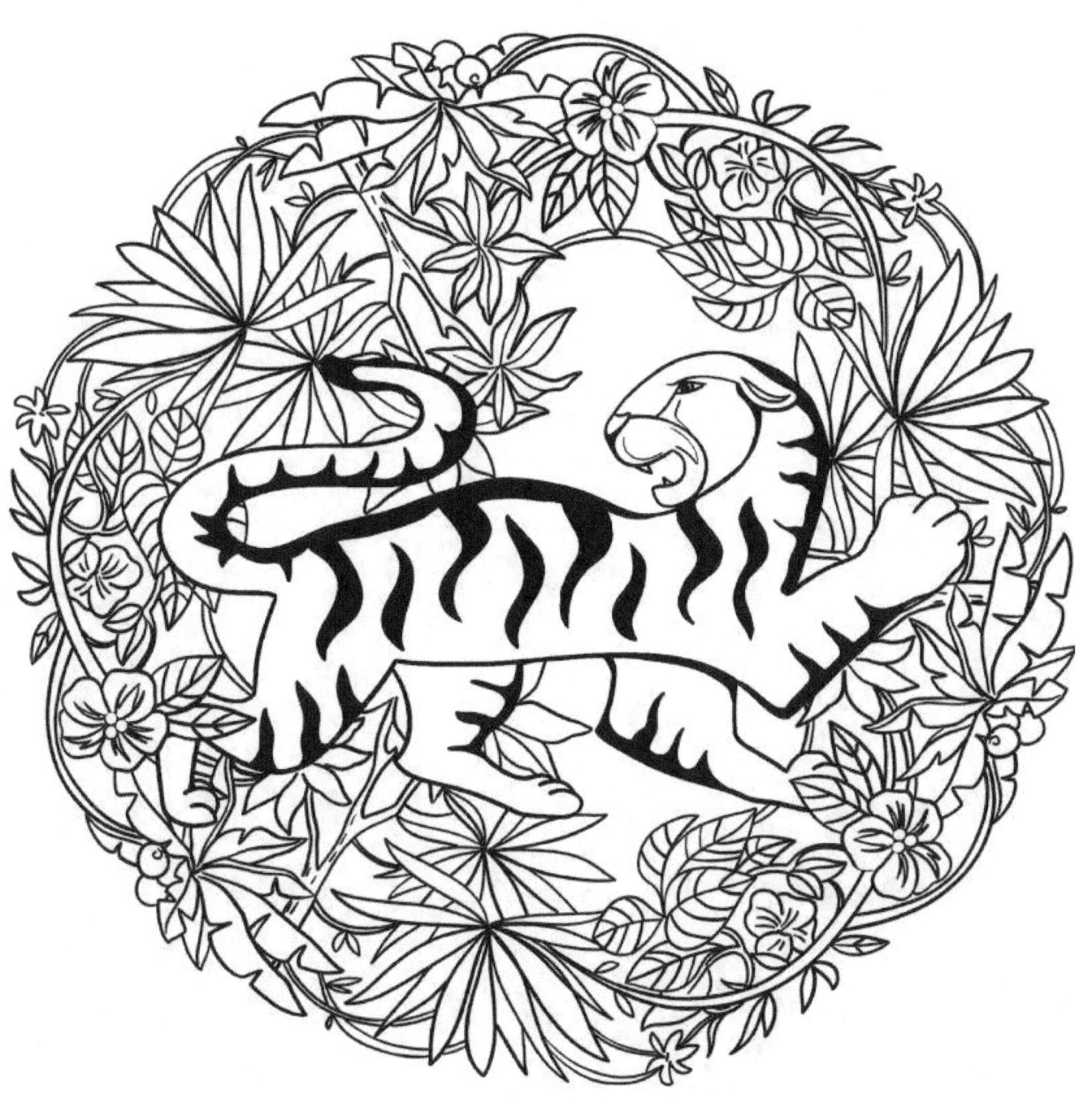

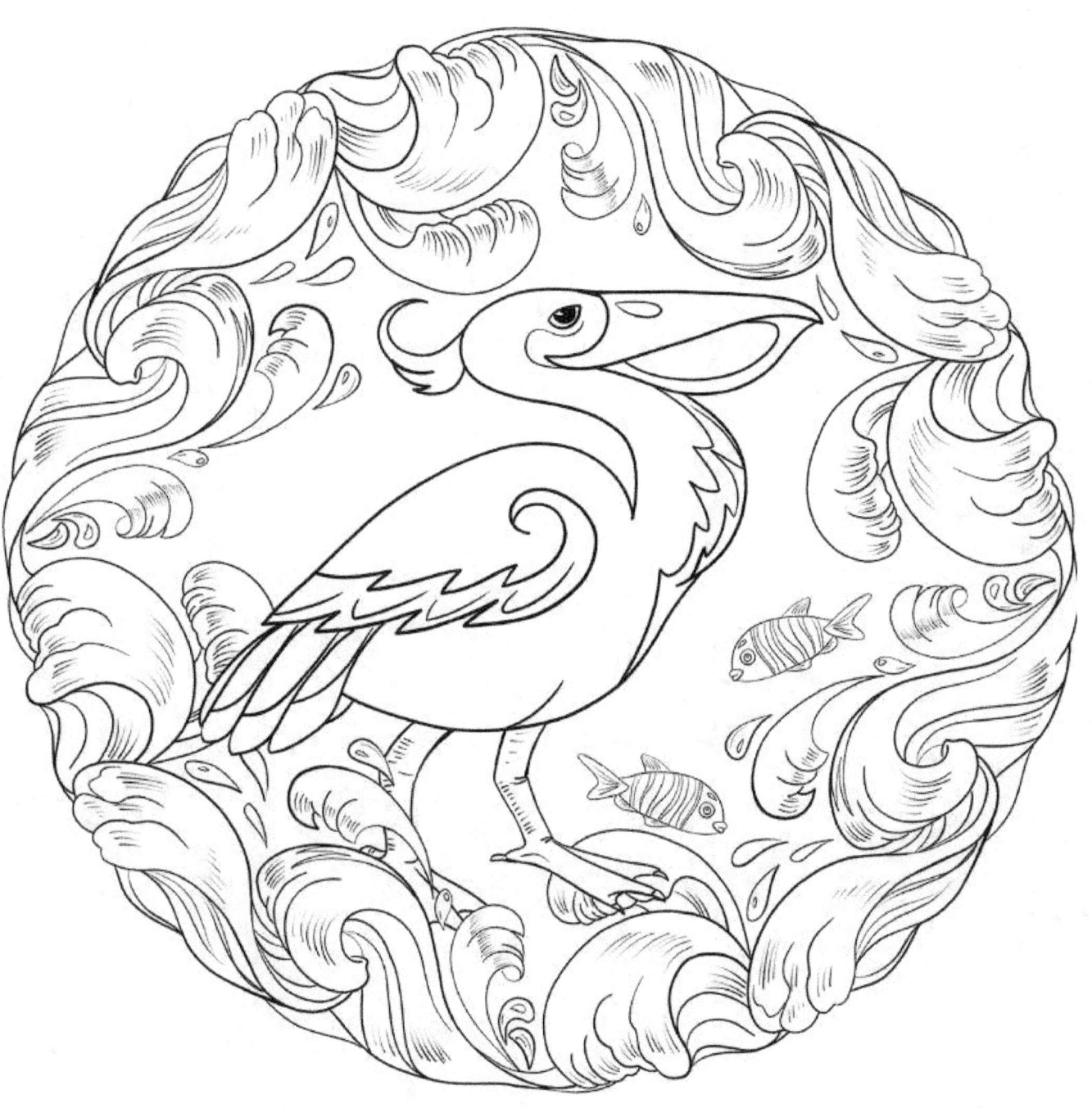

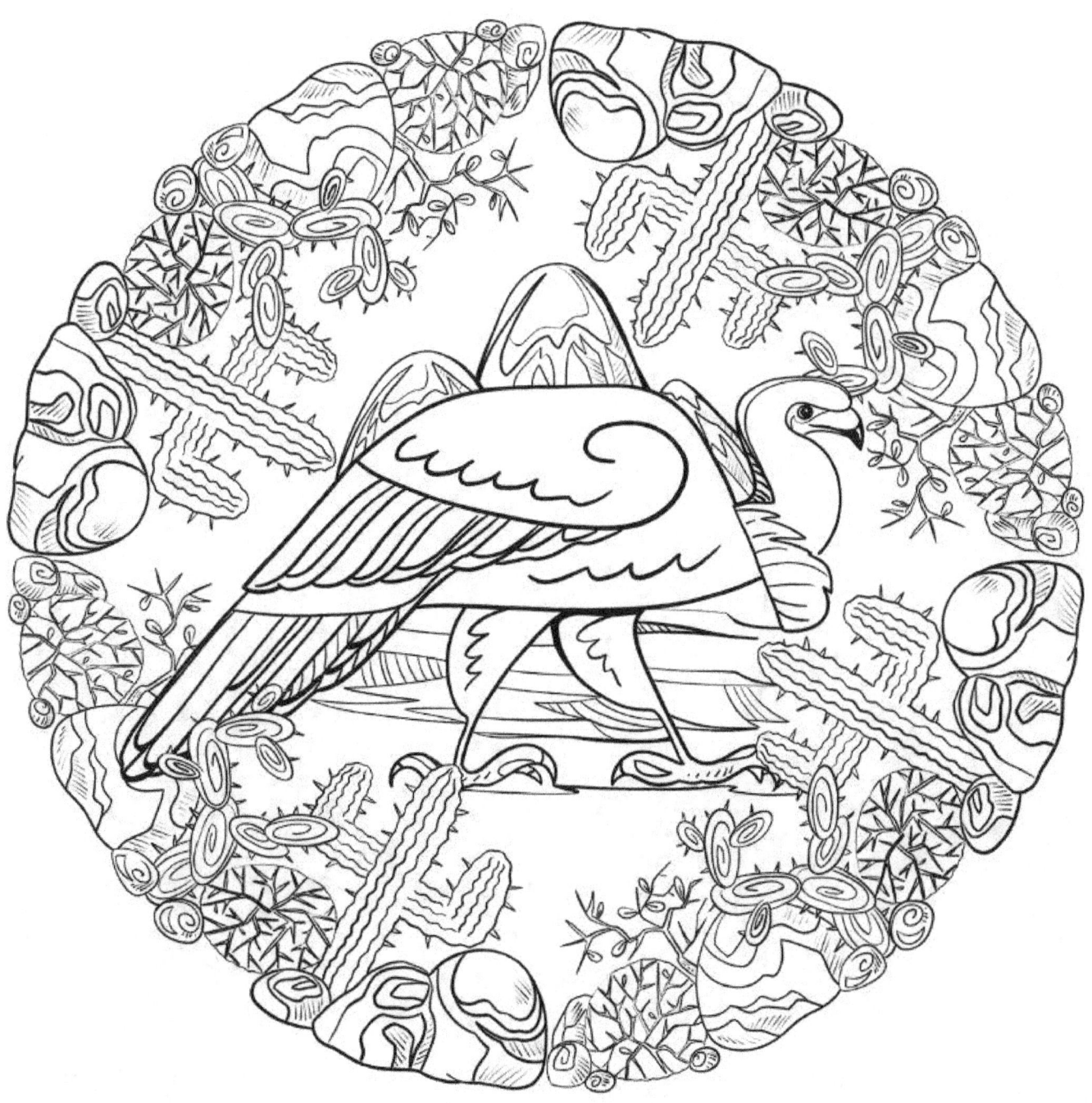

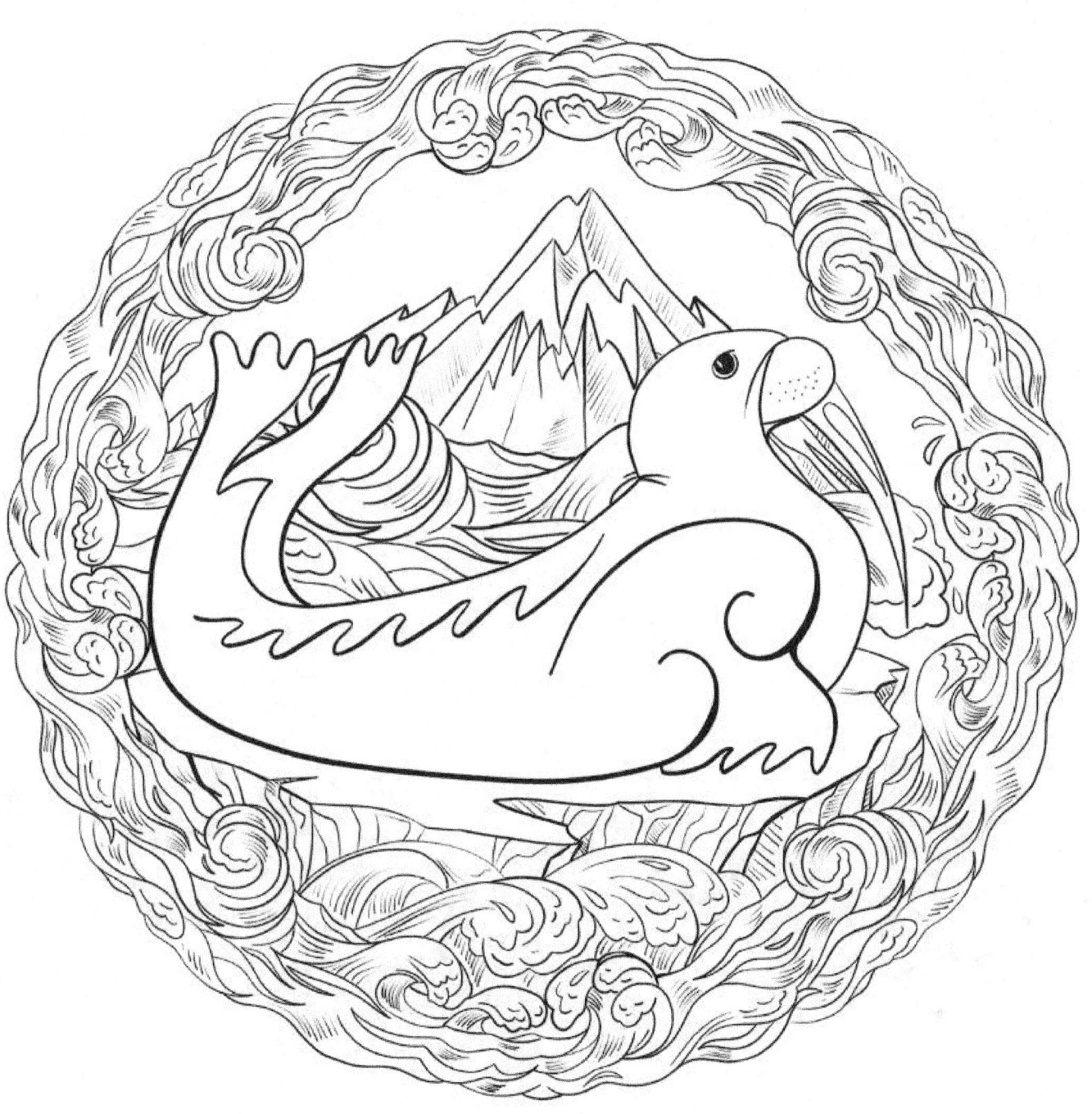

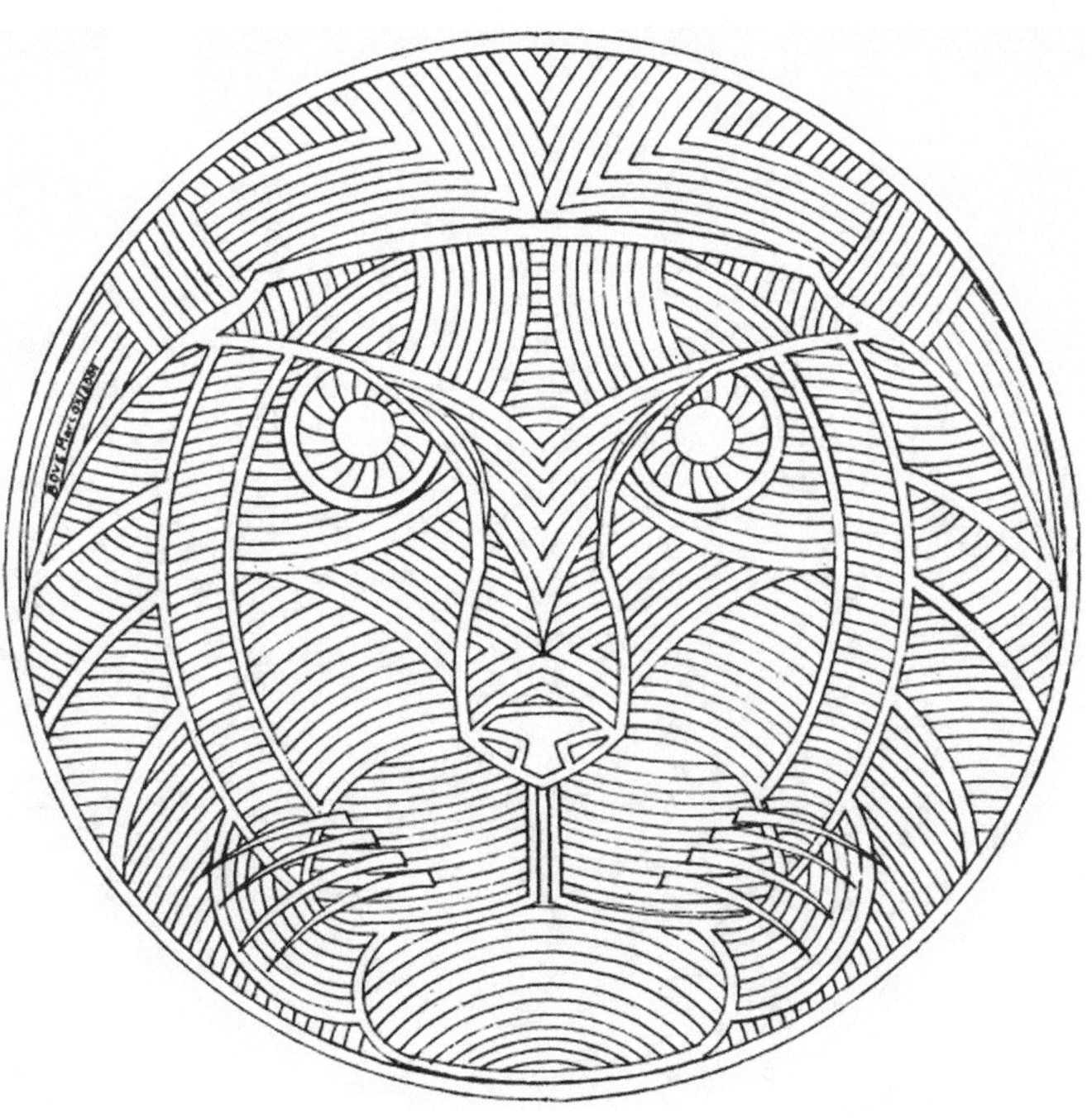

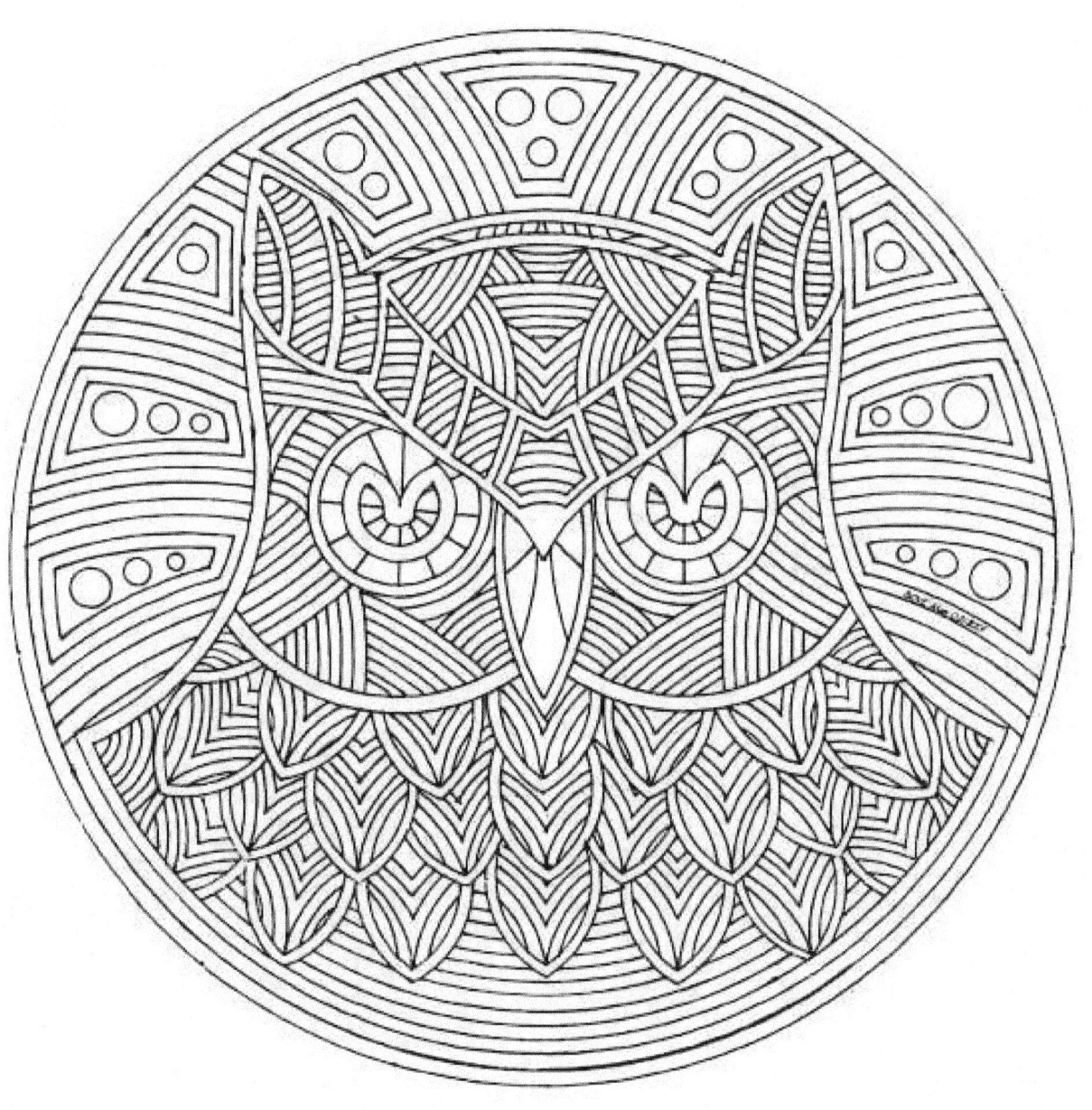

Book No. 3

Mandalas andSugsrt Skull

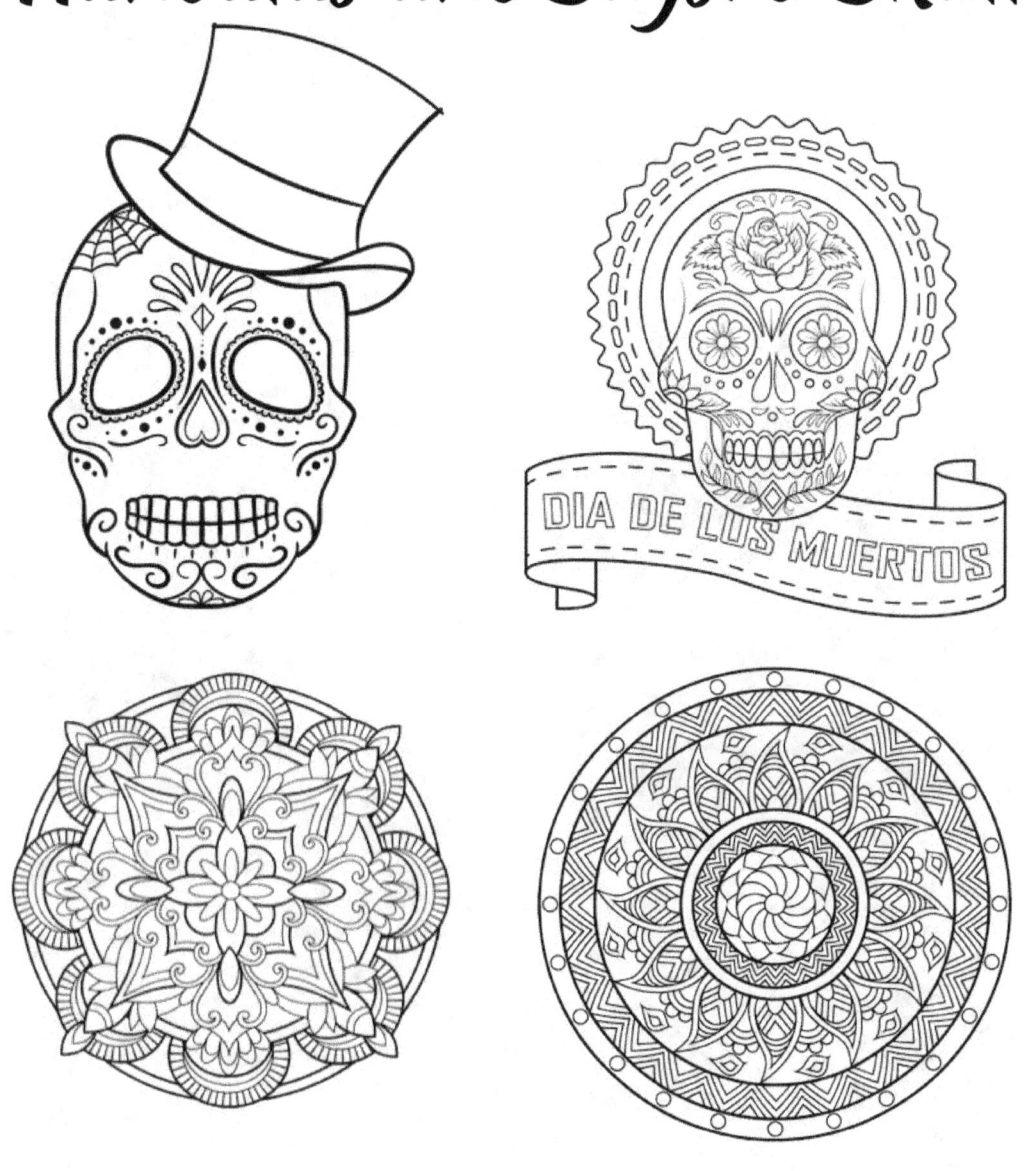

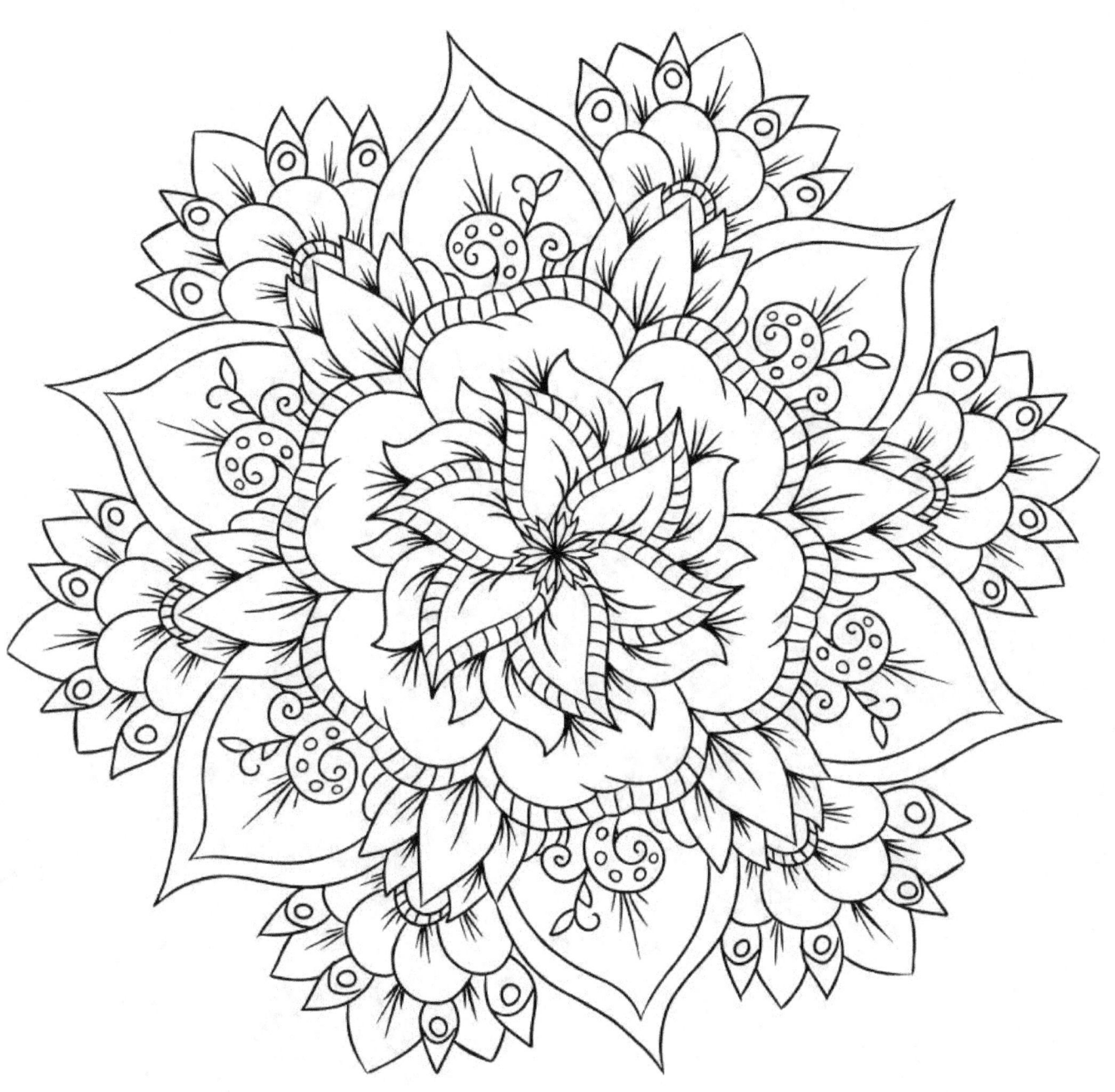

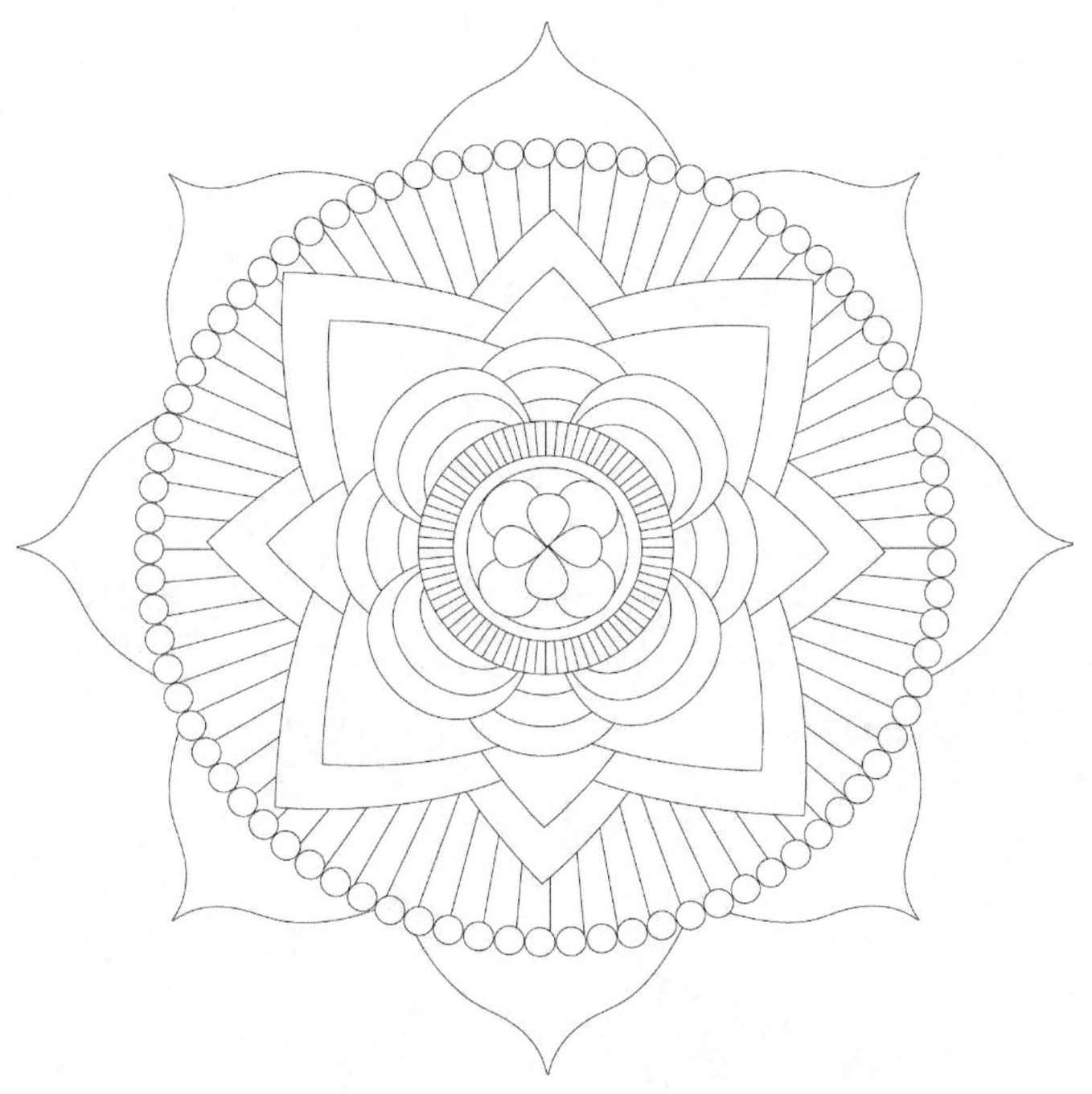

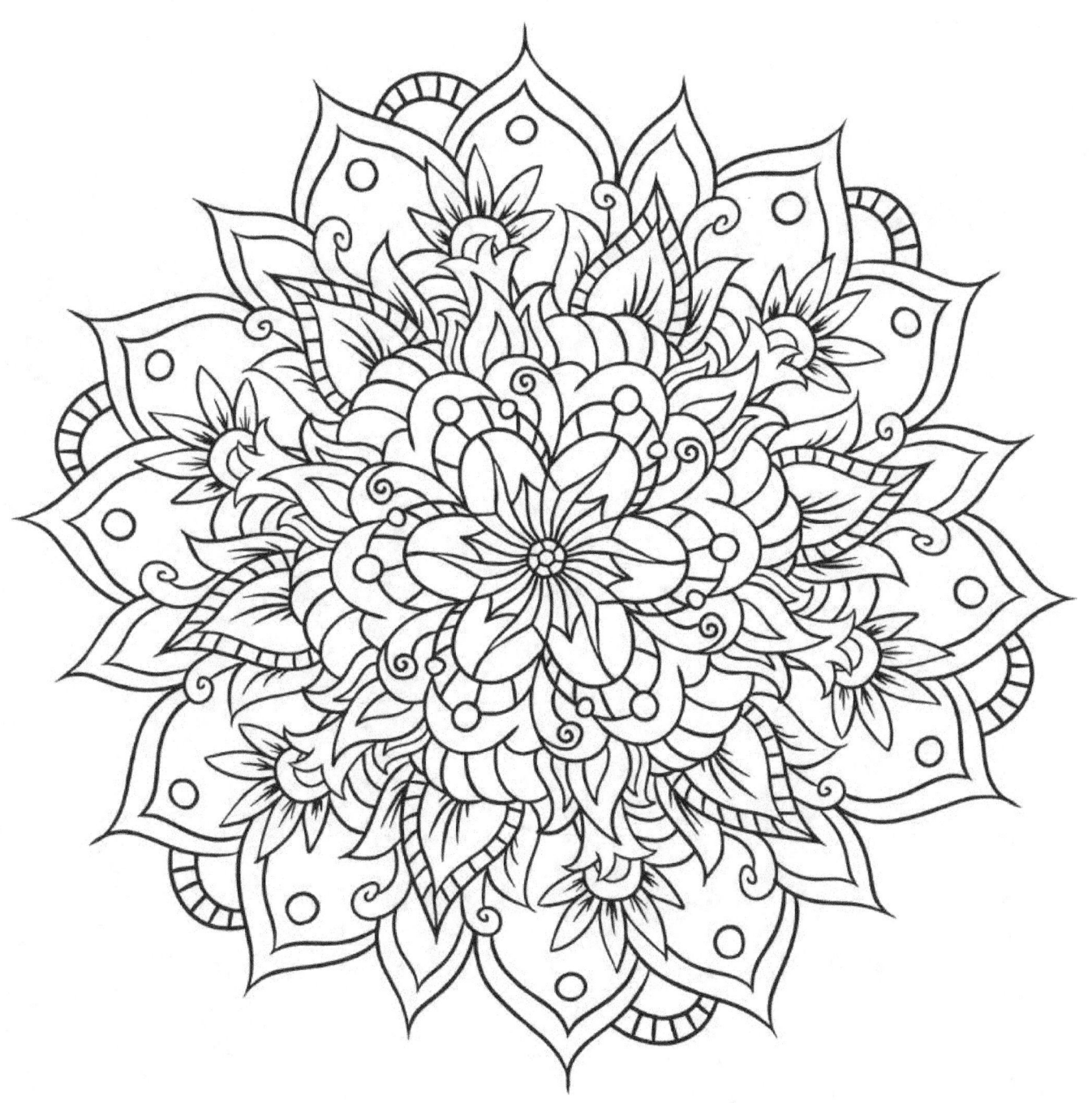

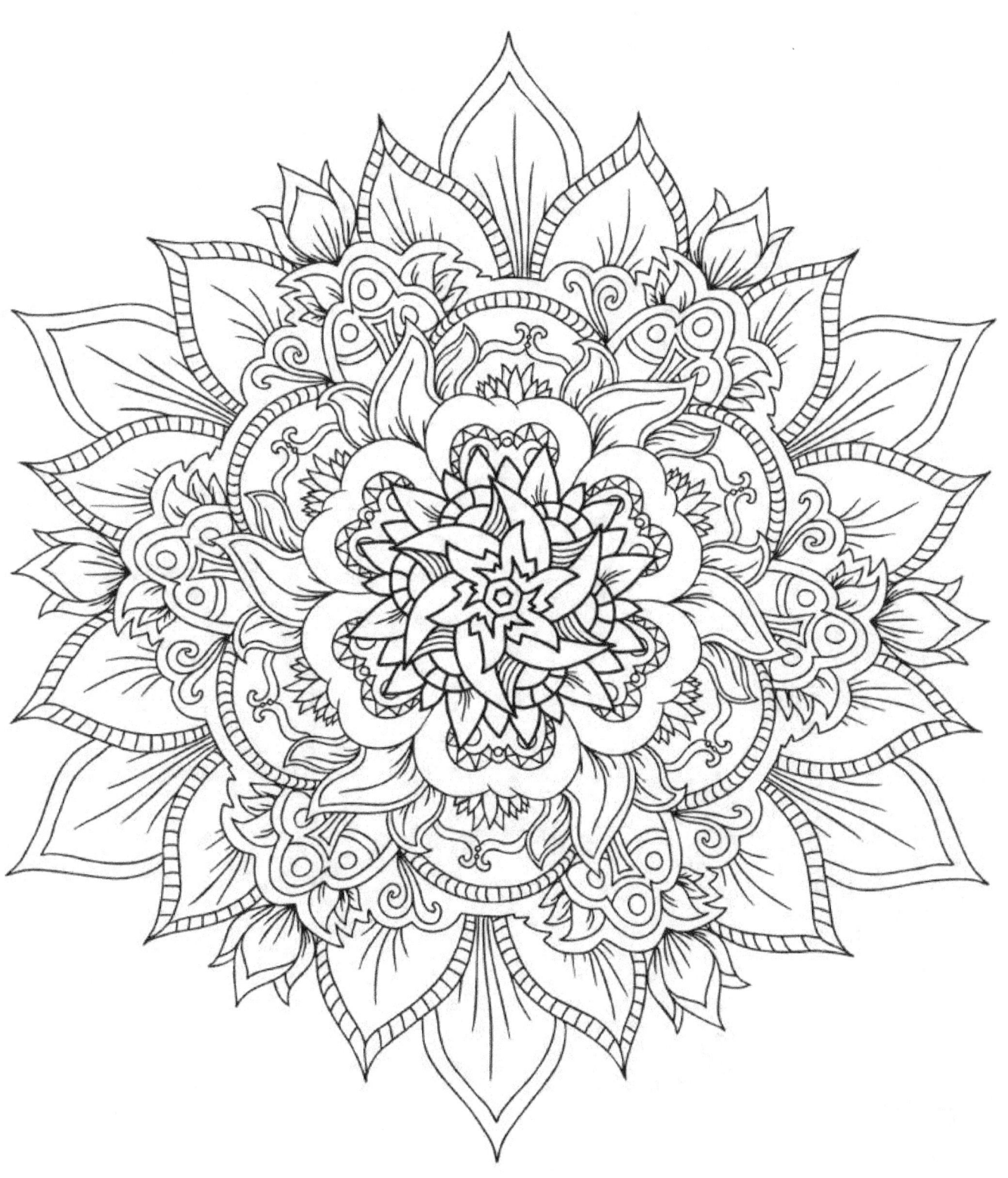

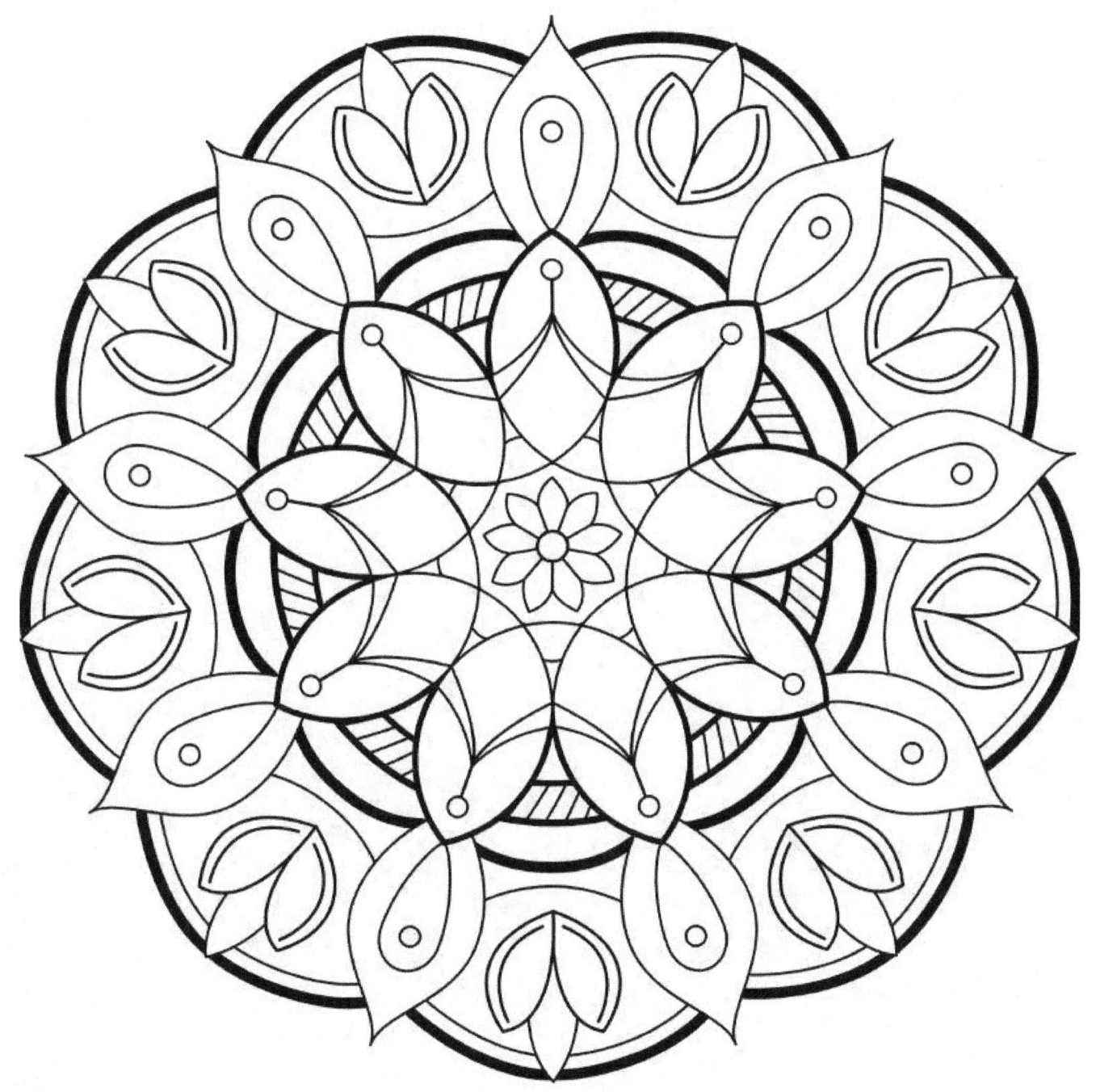

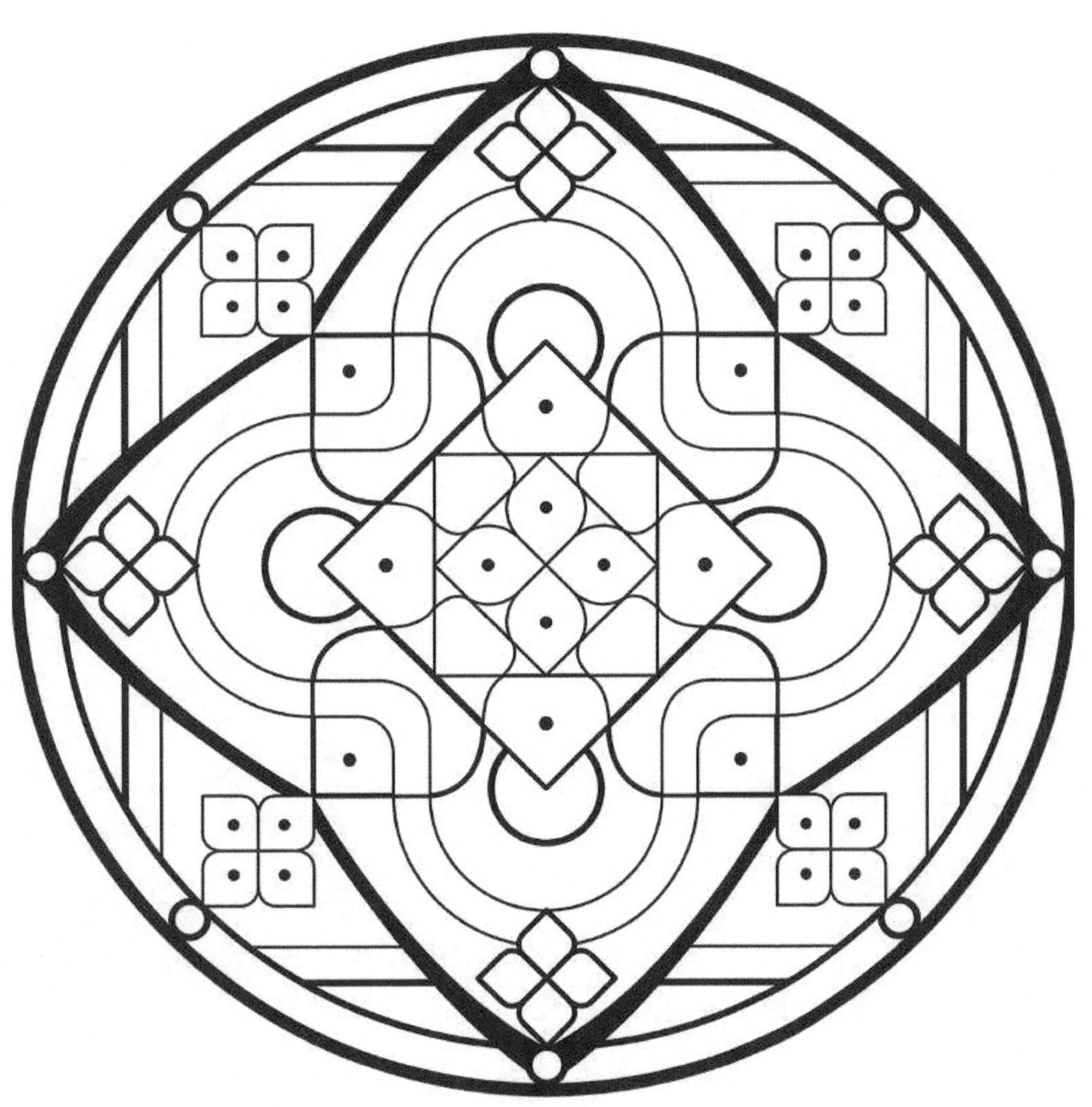

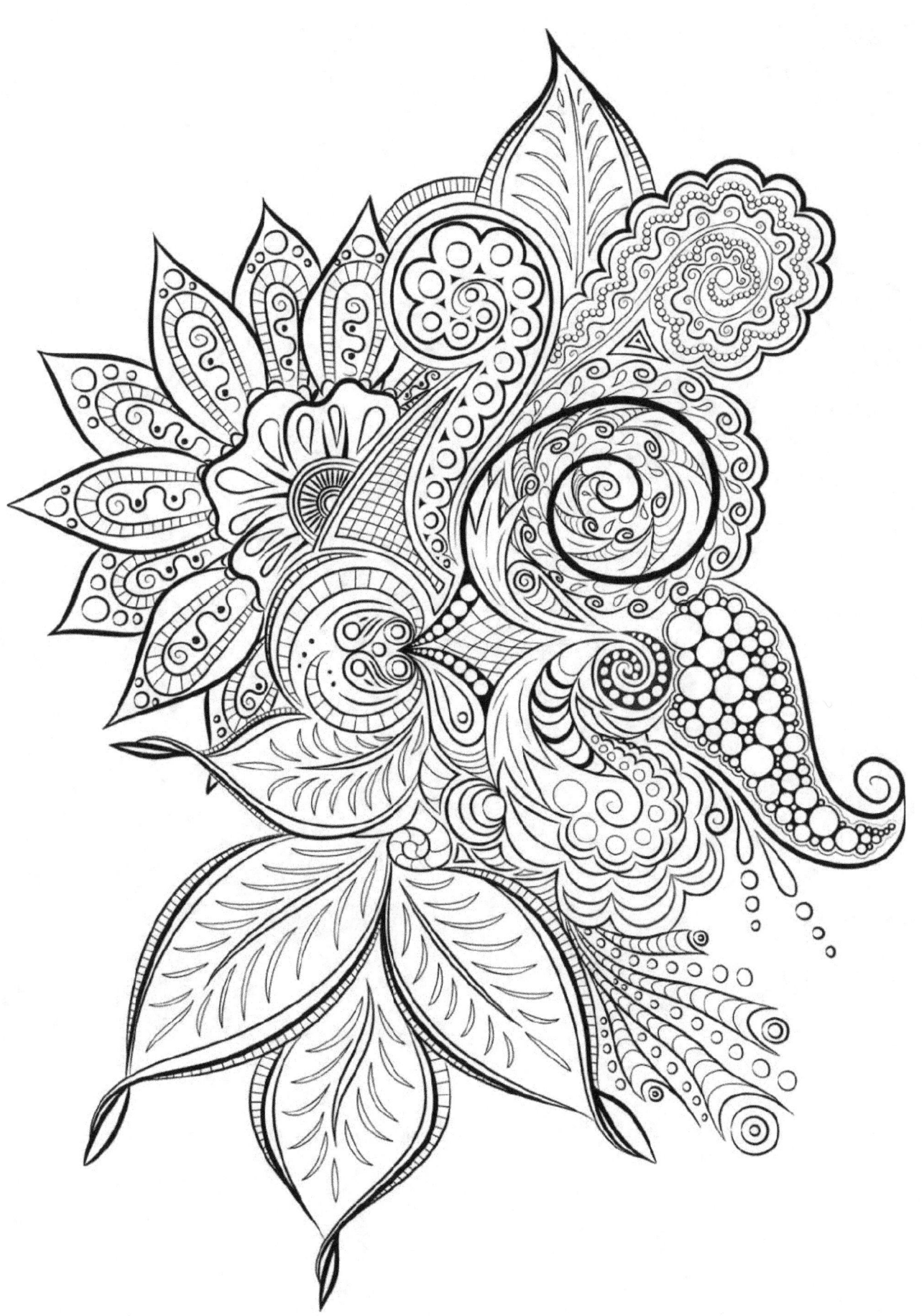

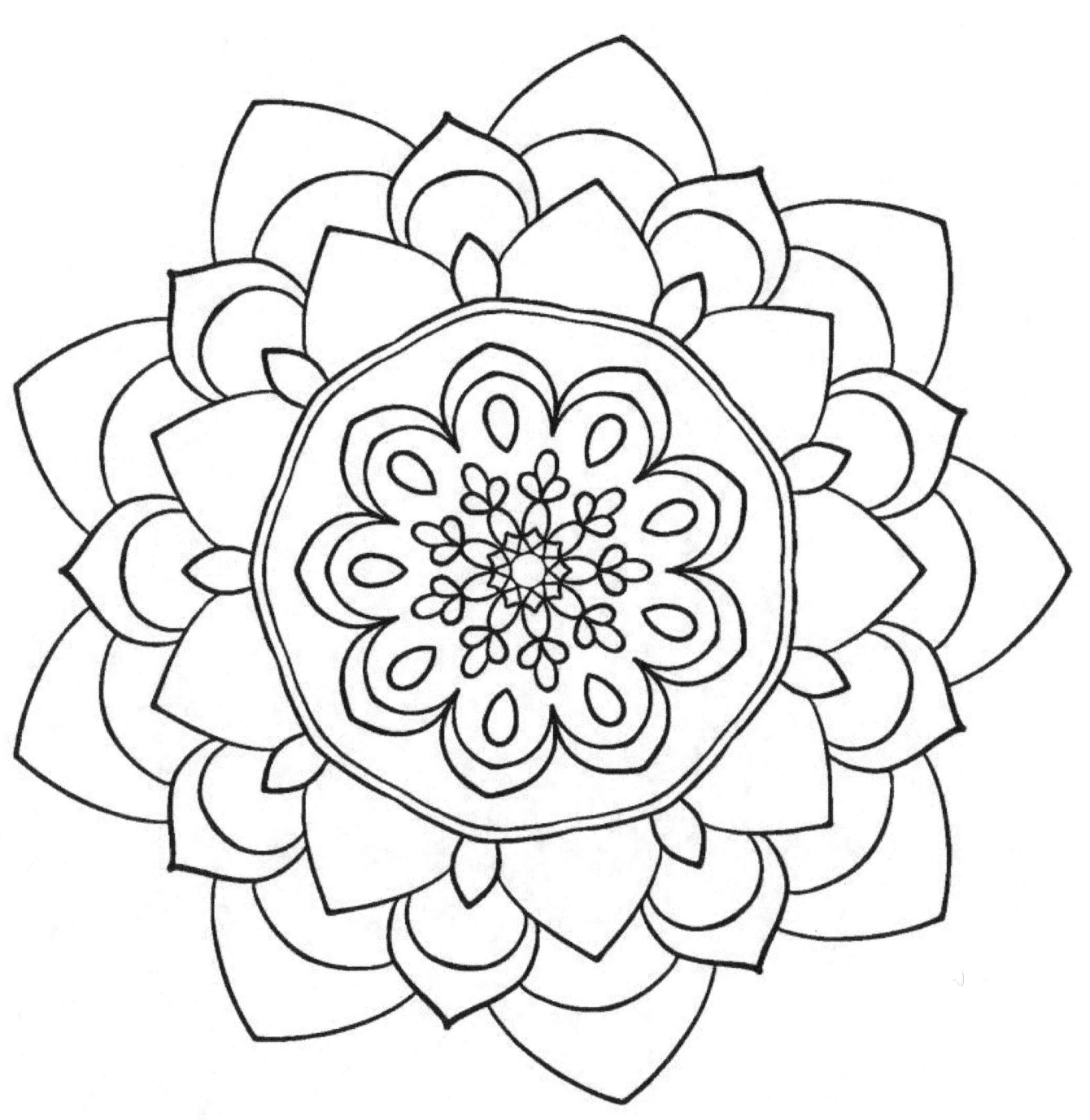

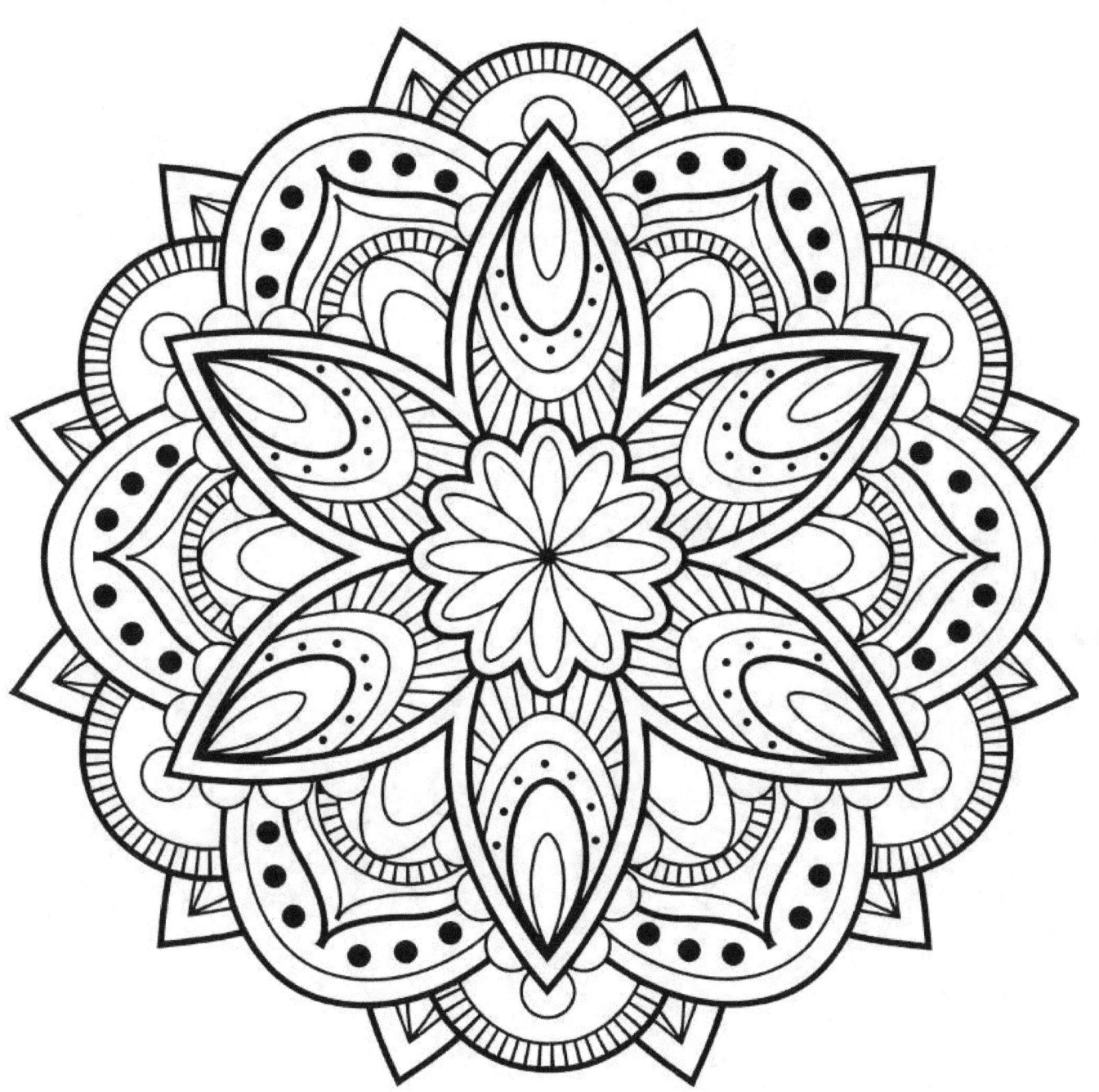

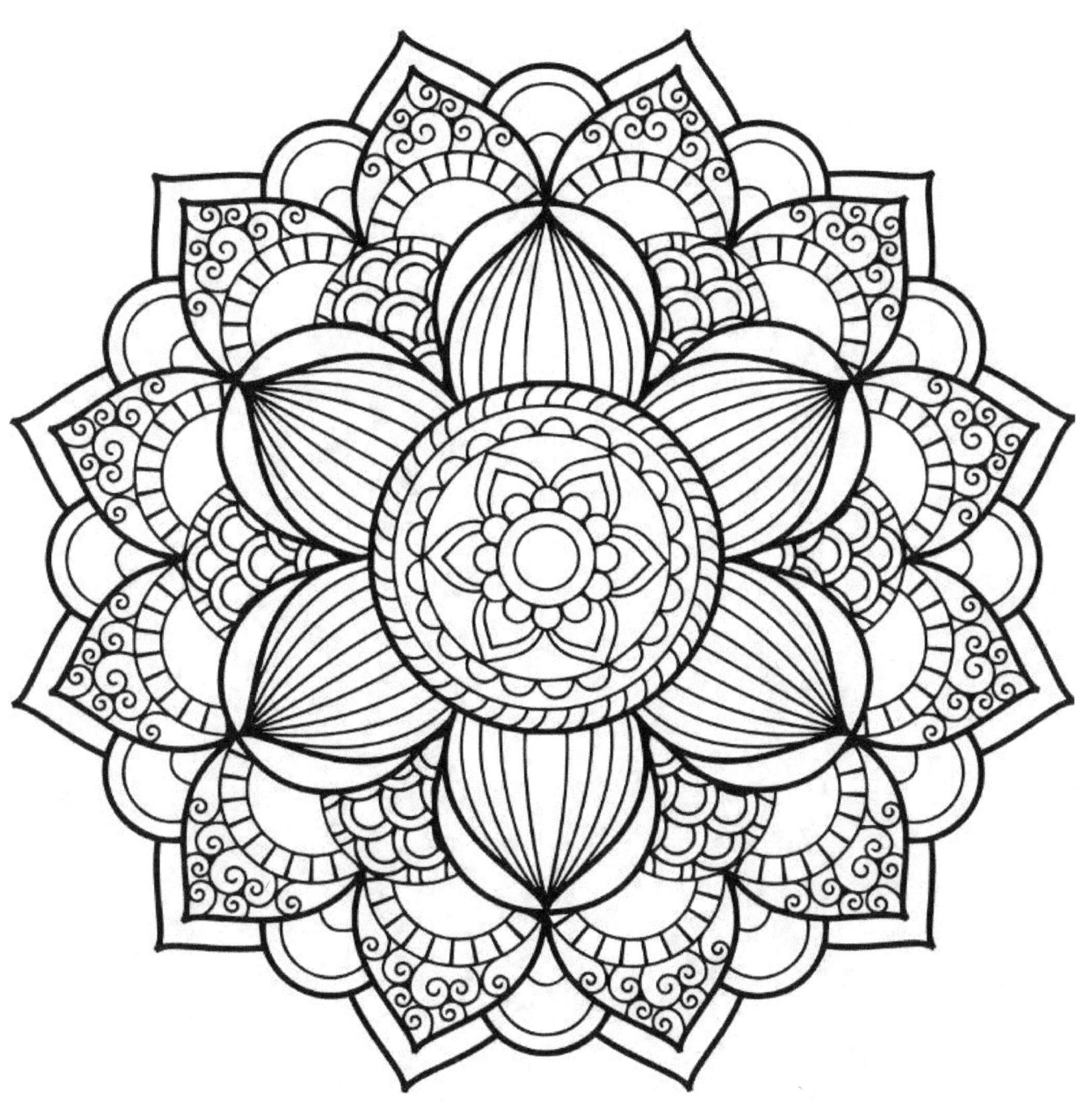

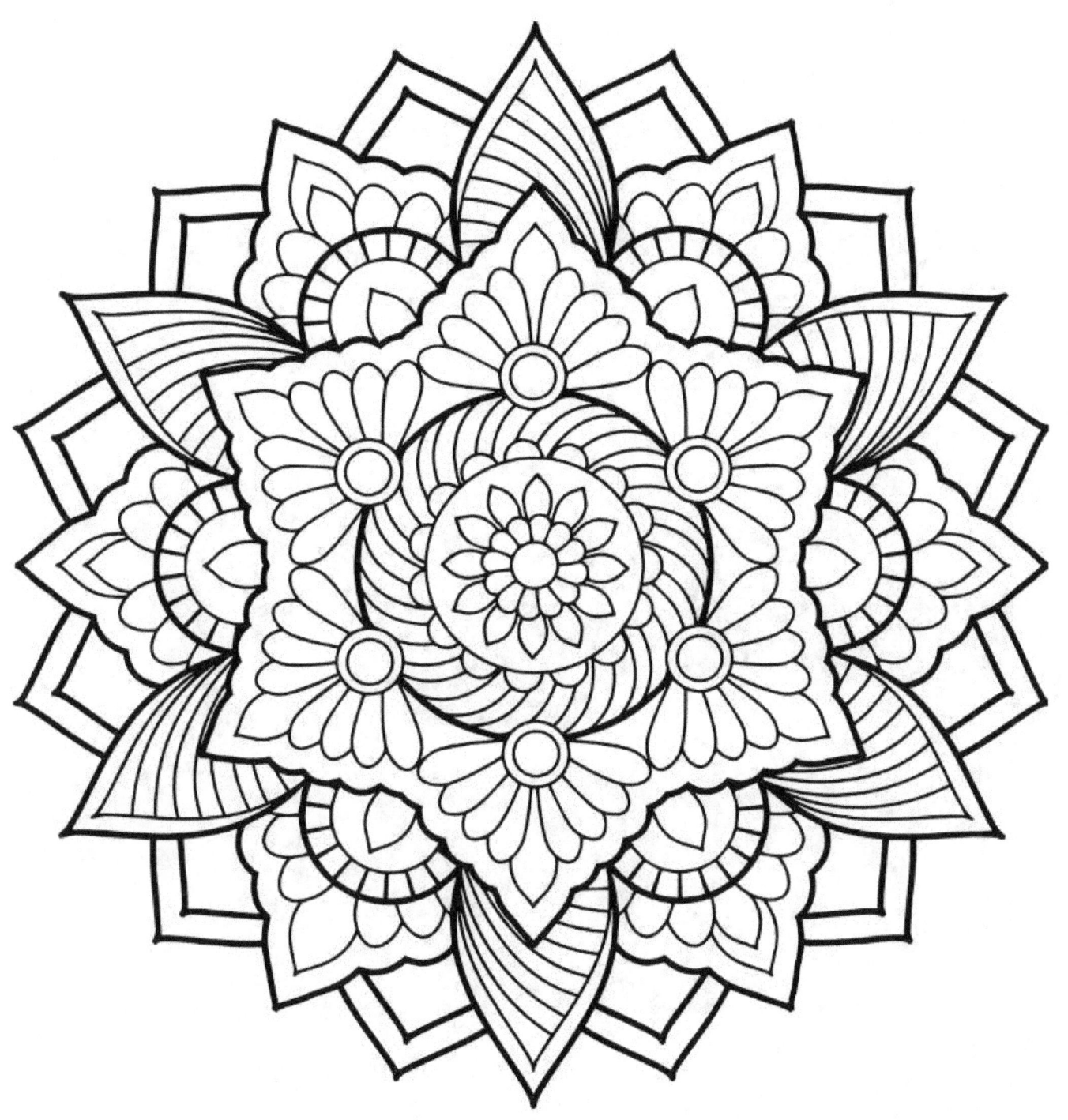

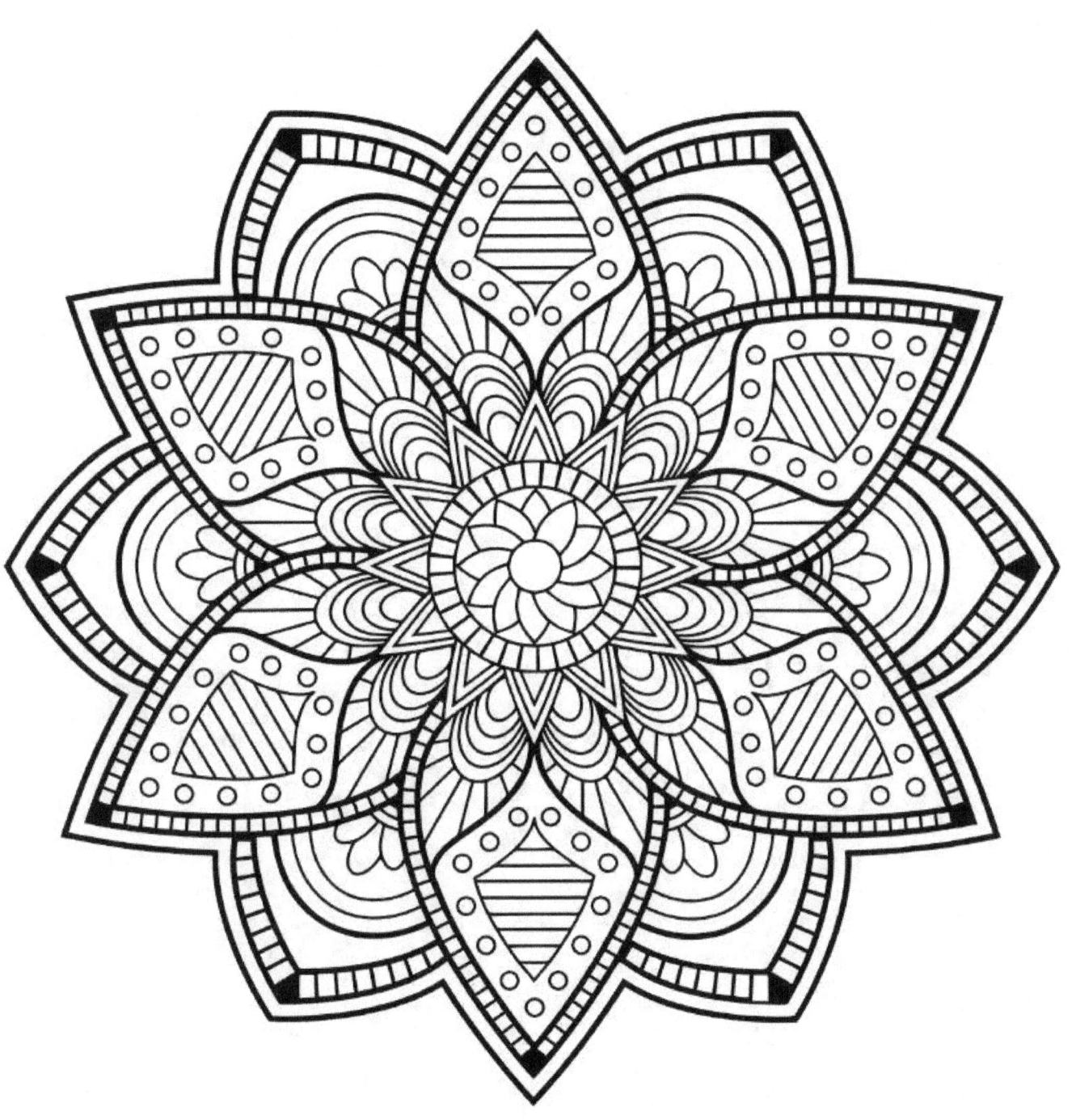

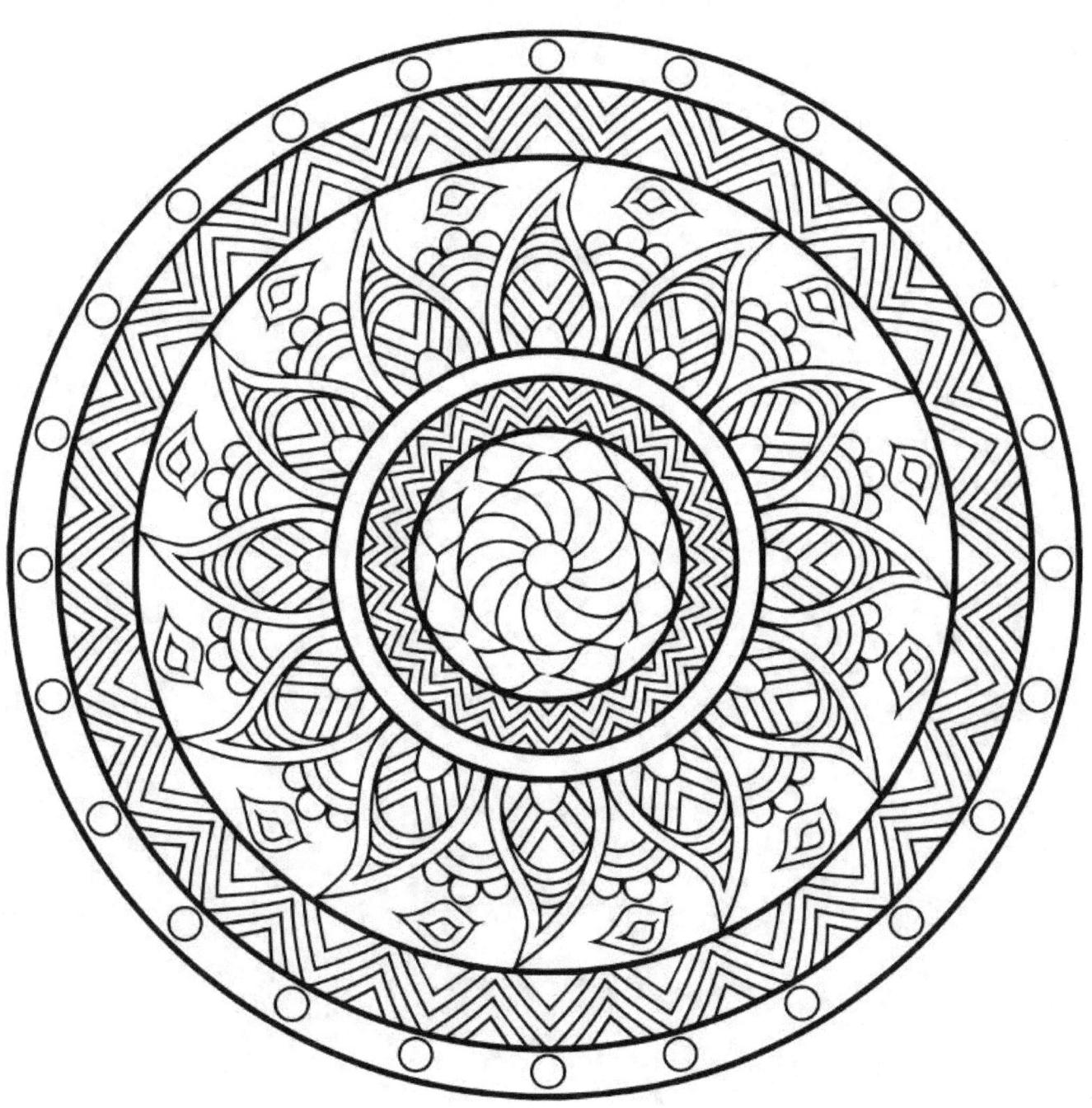

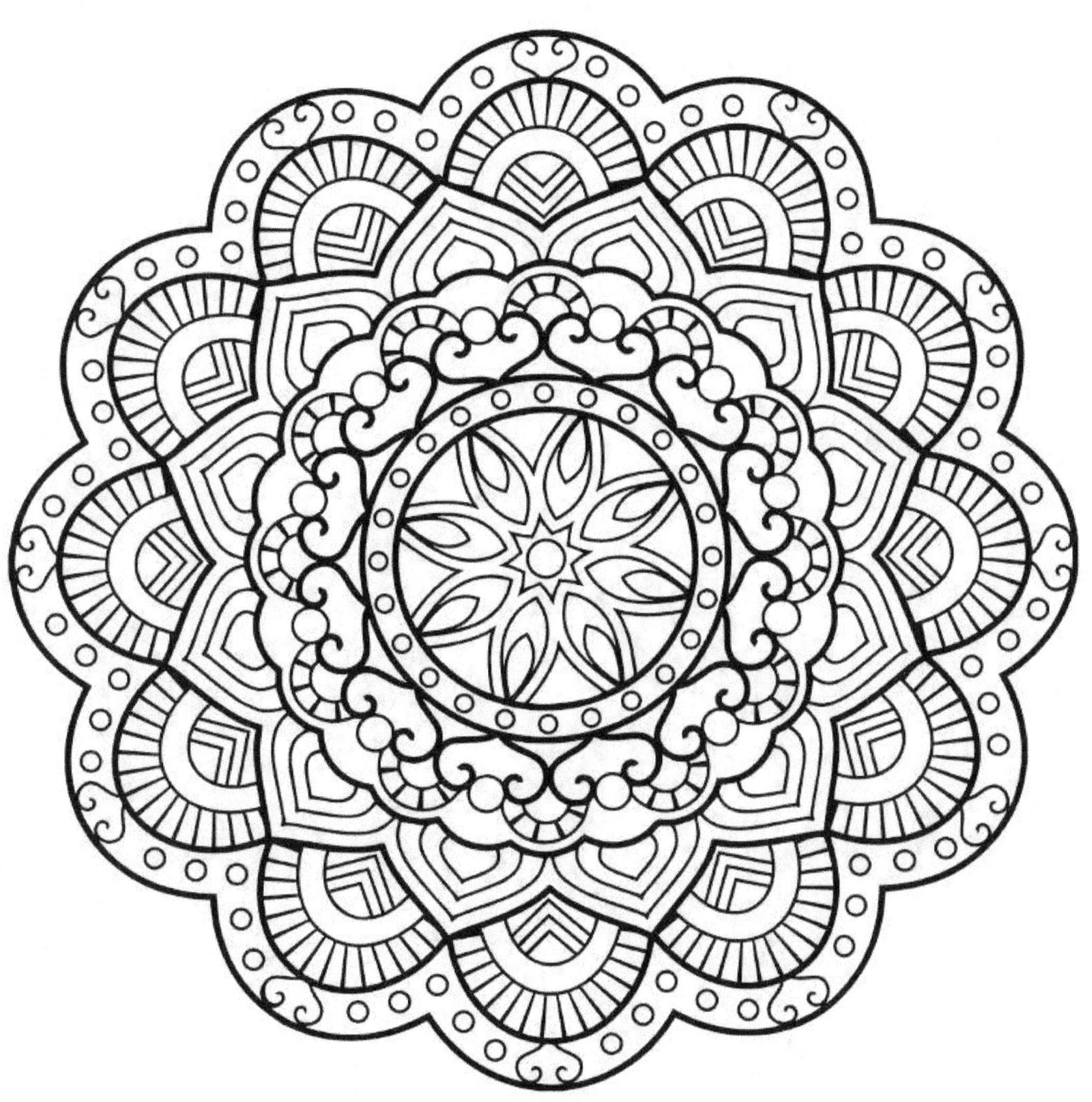

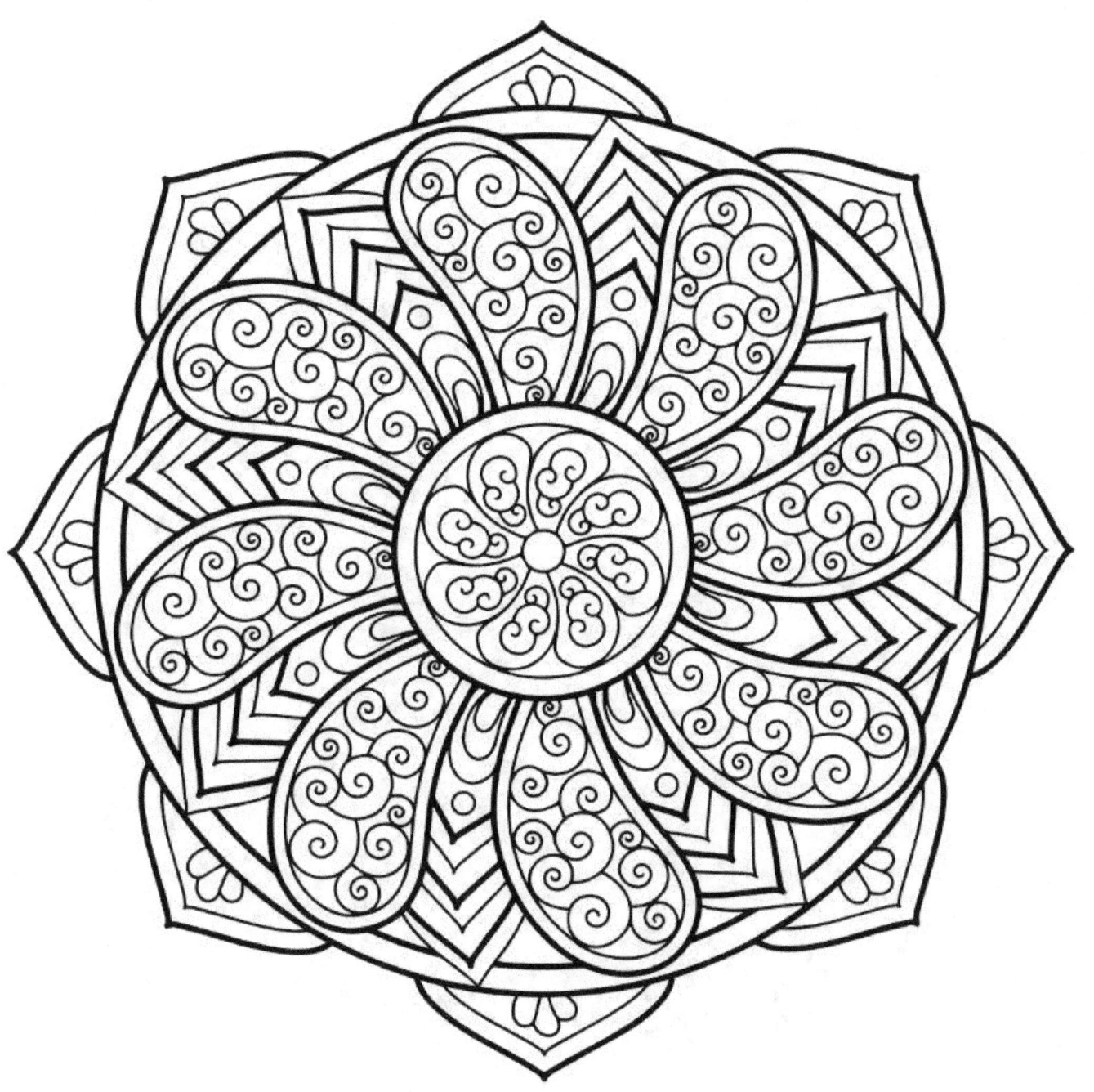

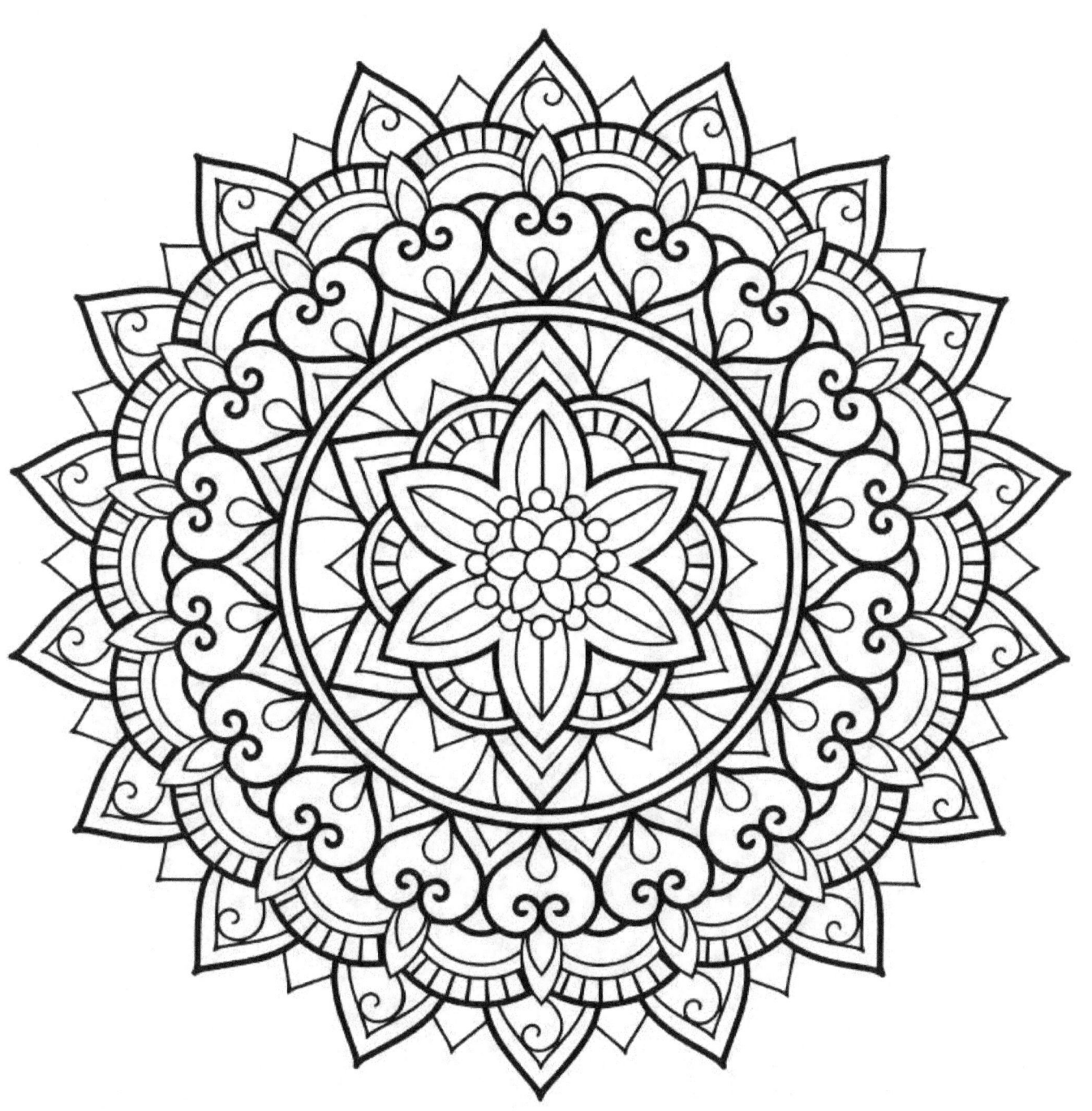

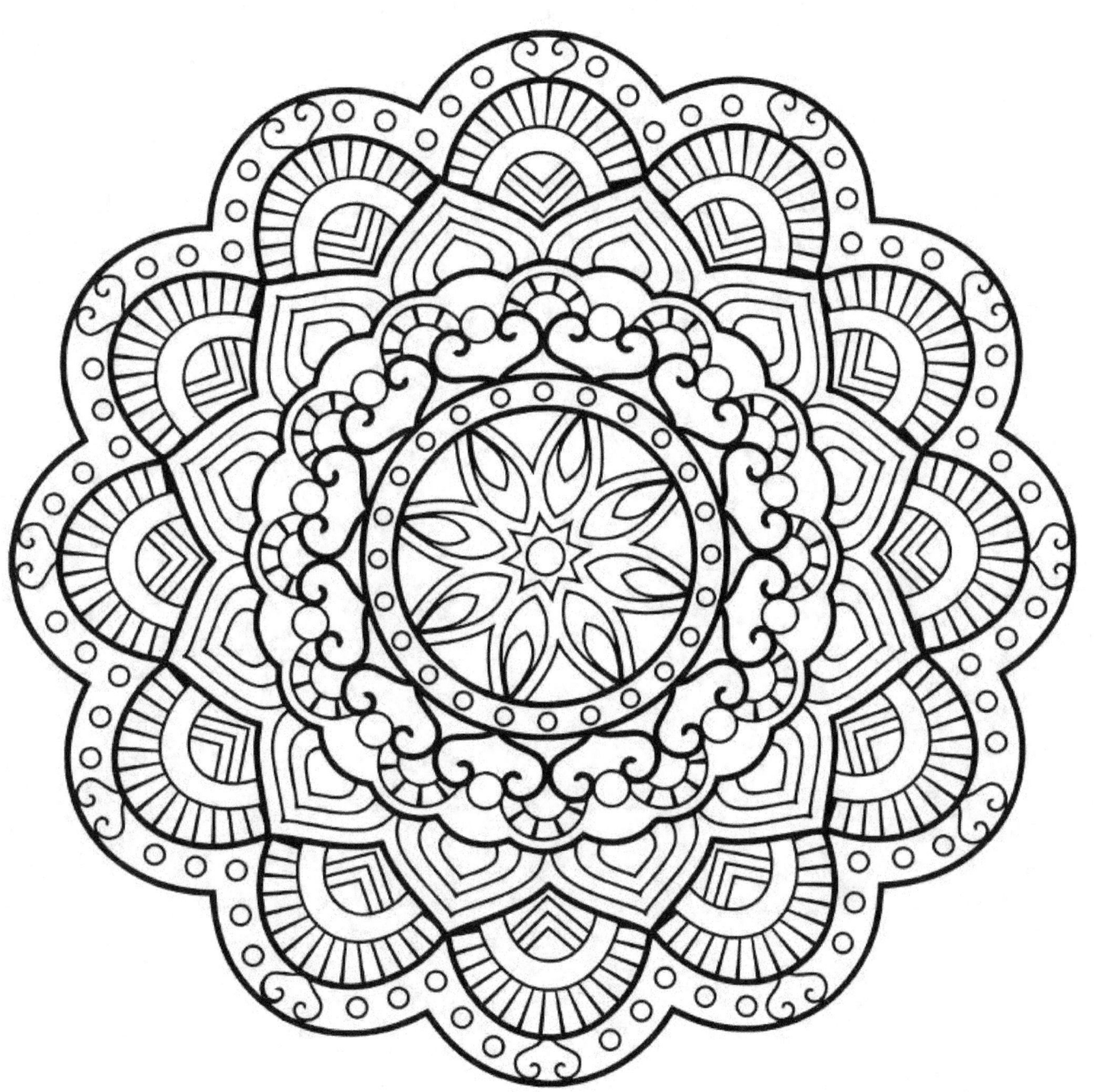

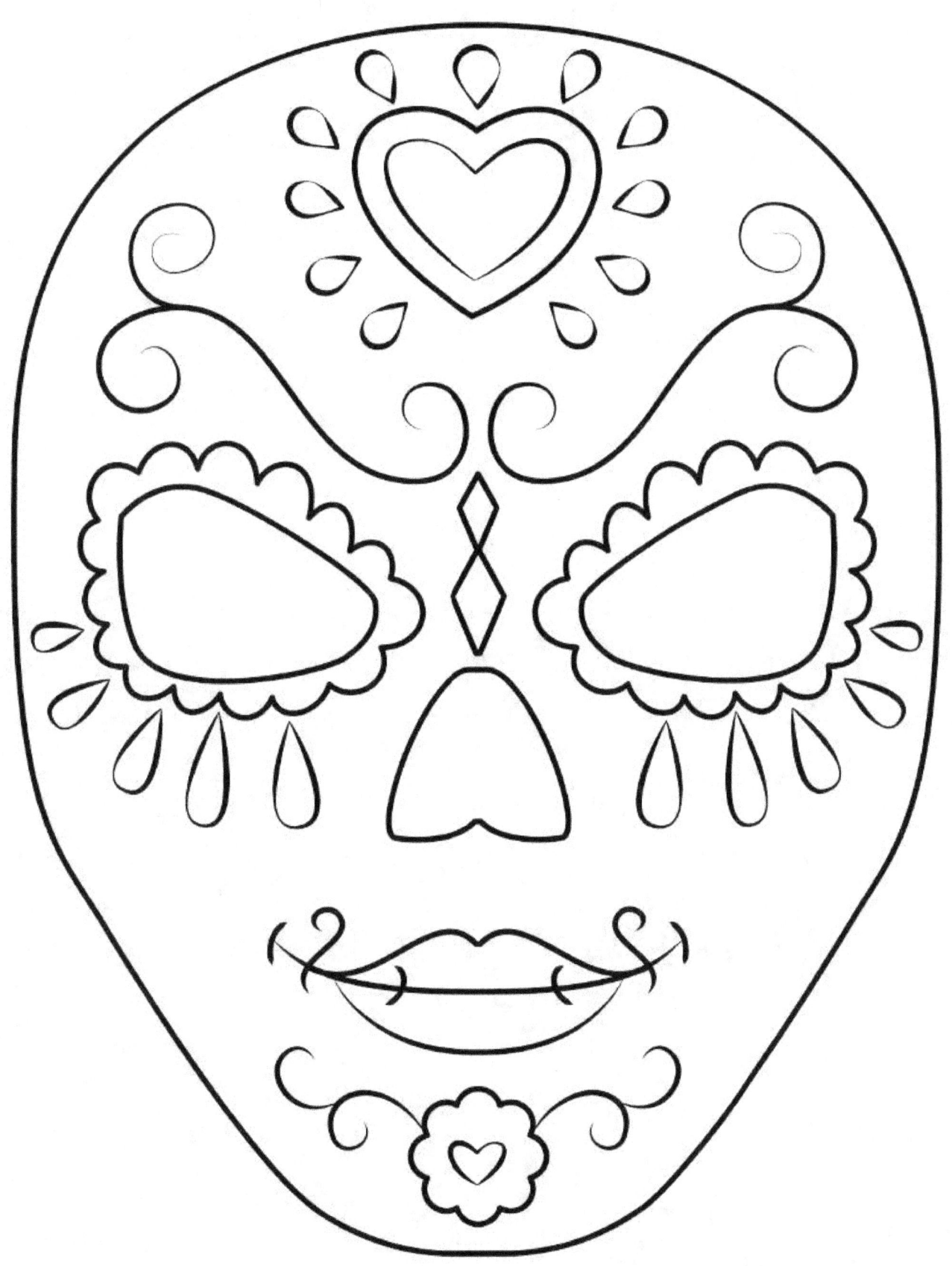

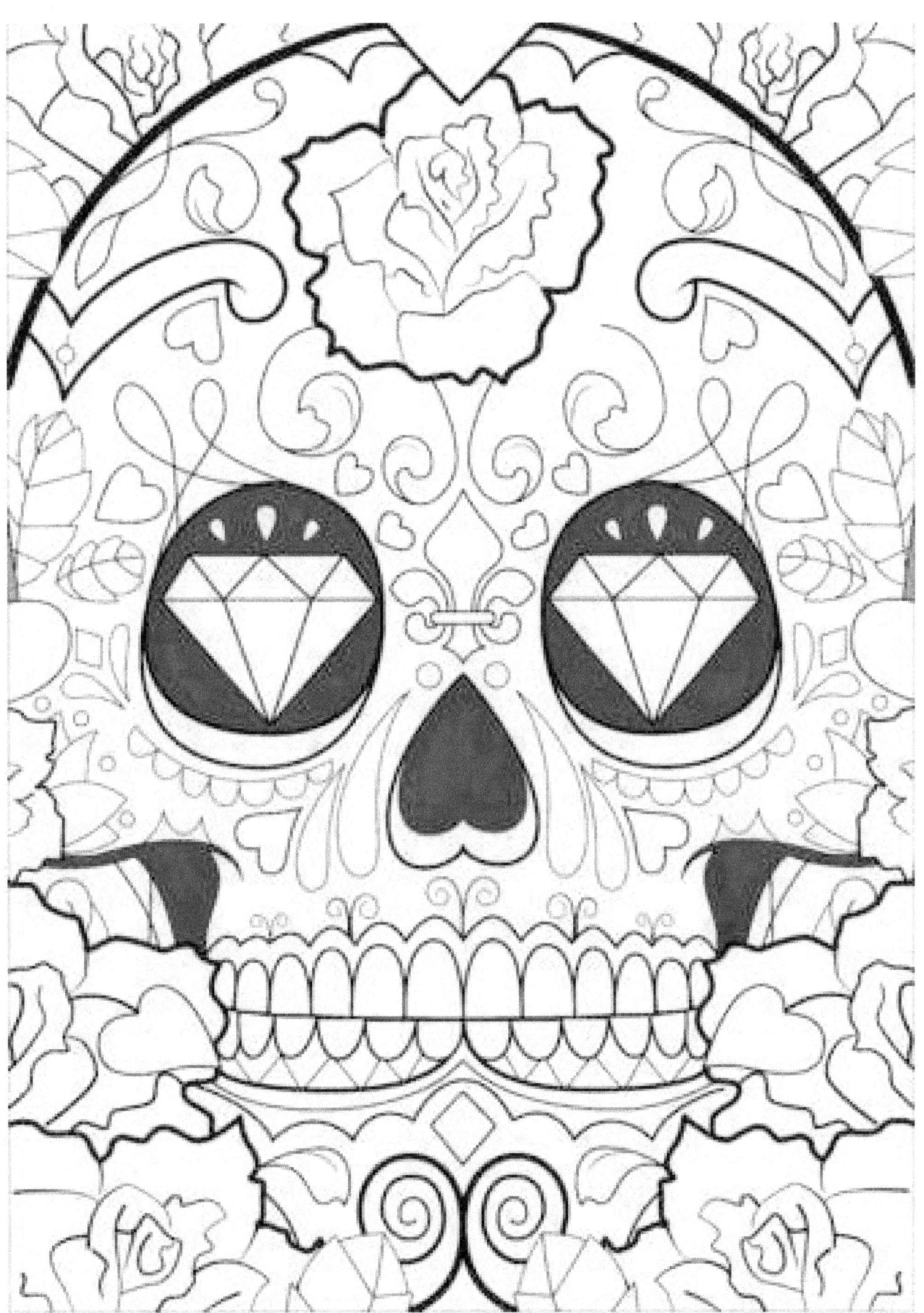

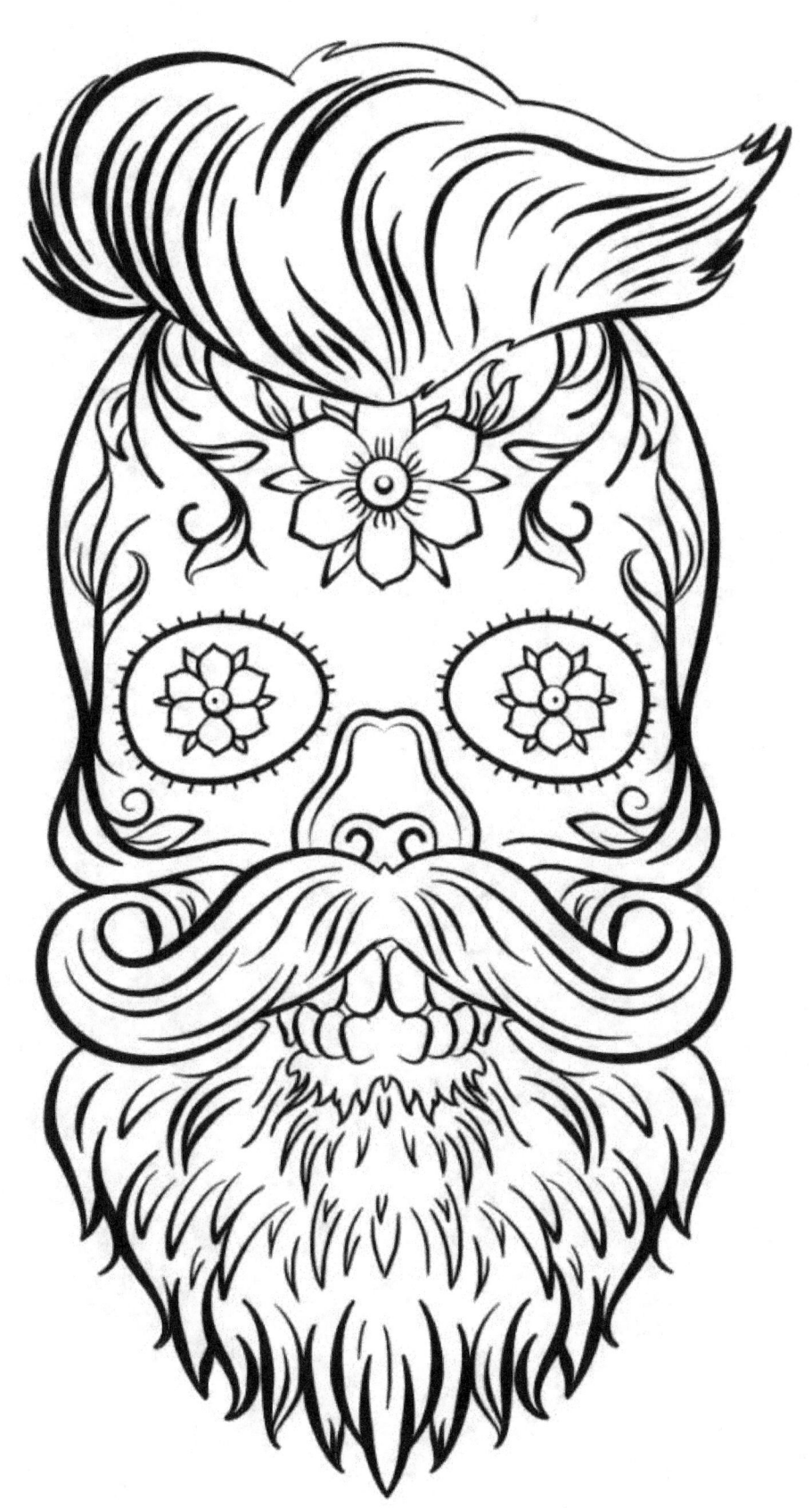

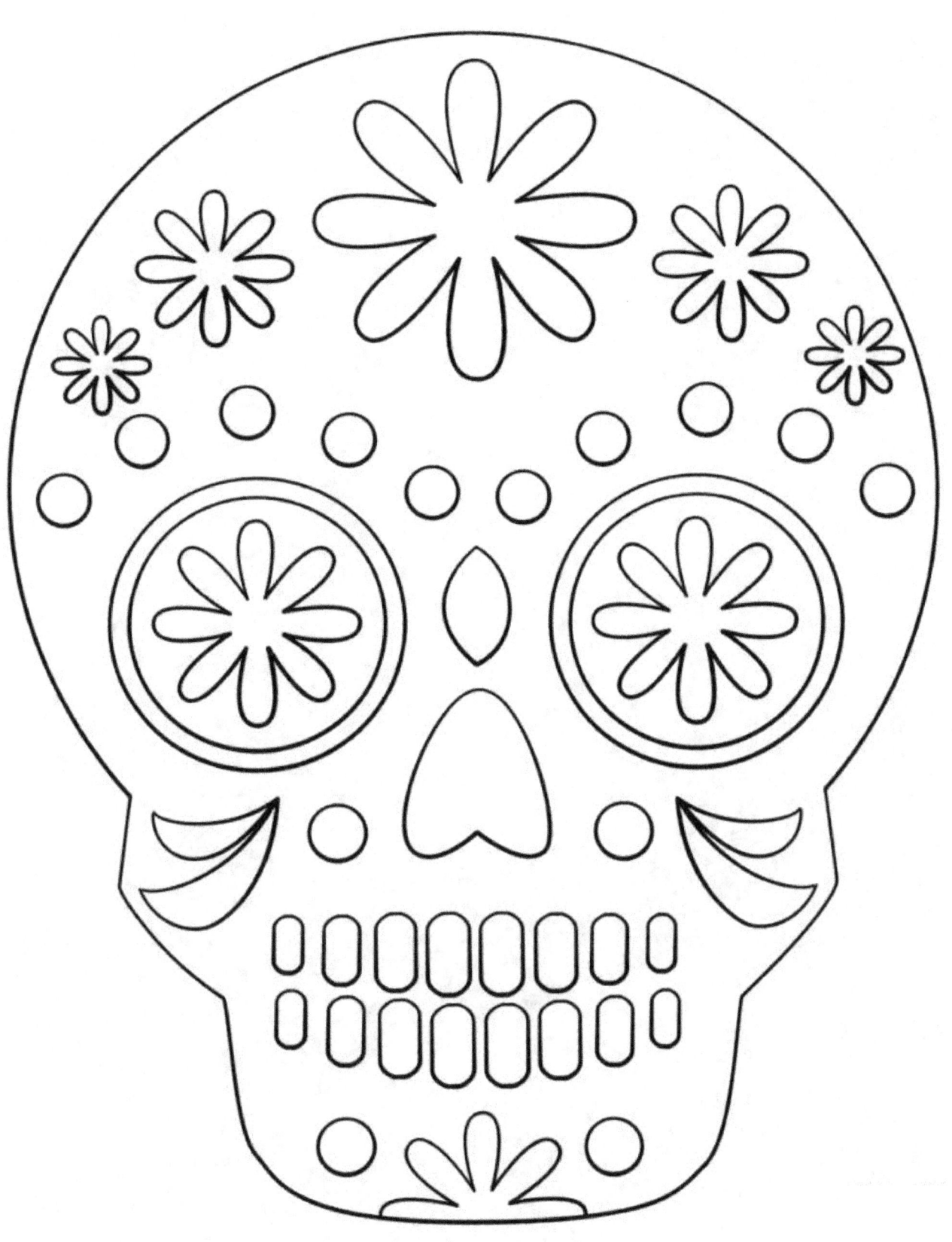

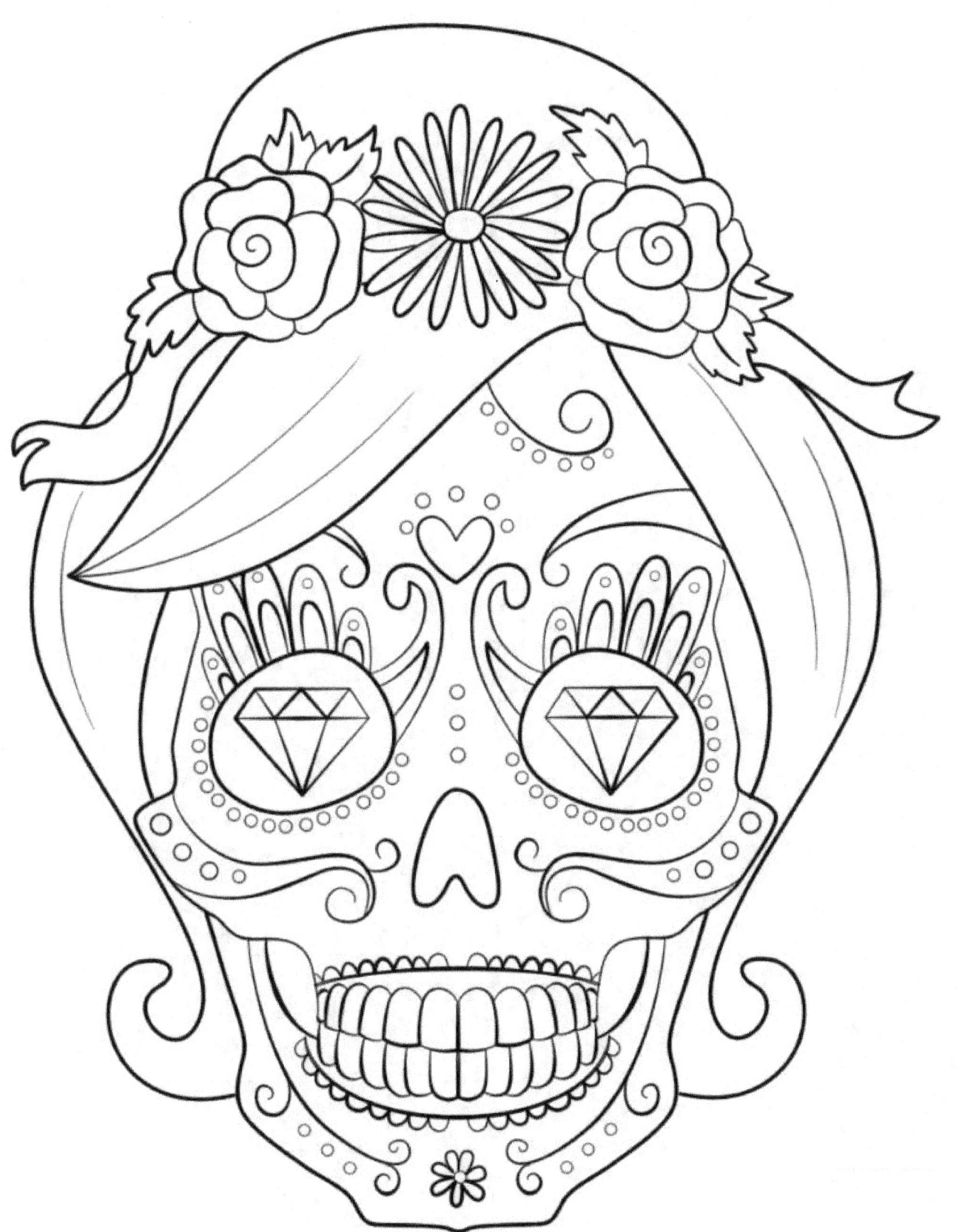

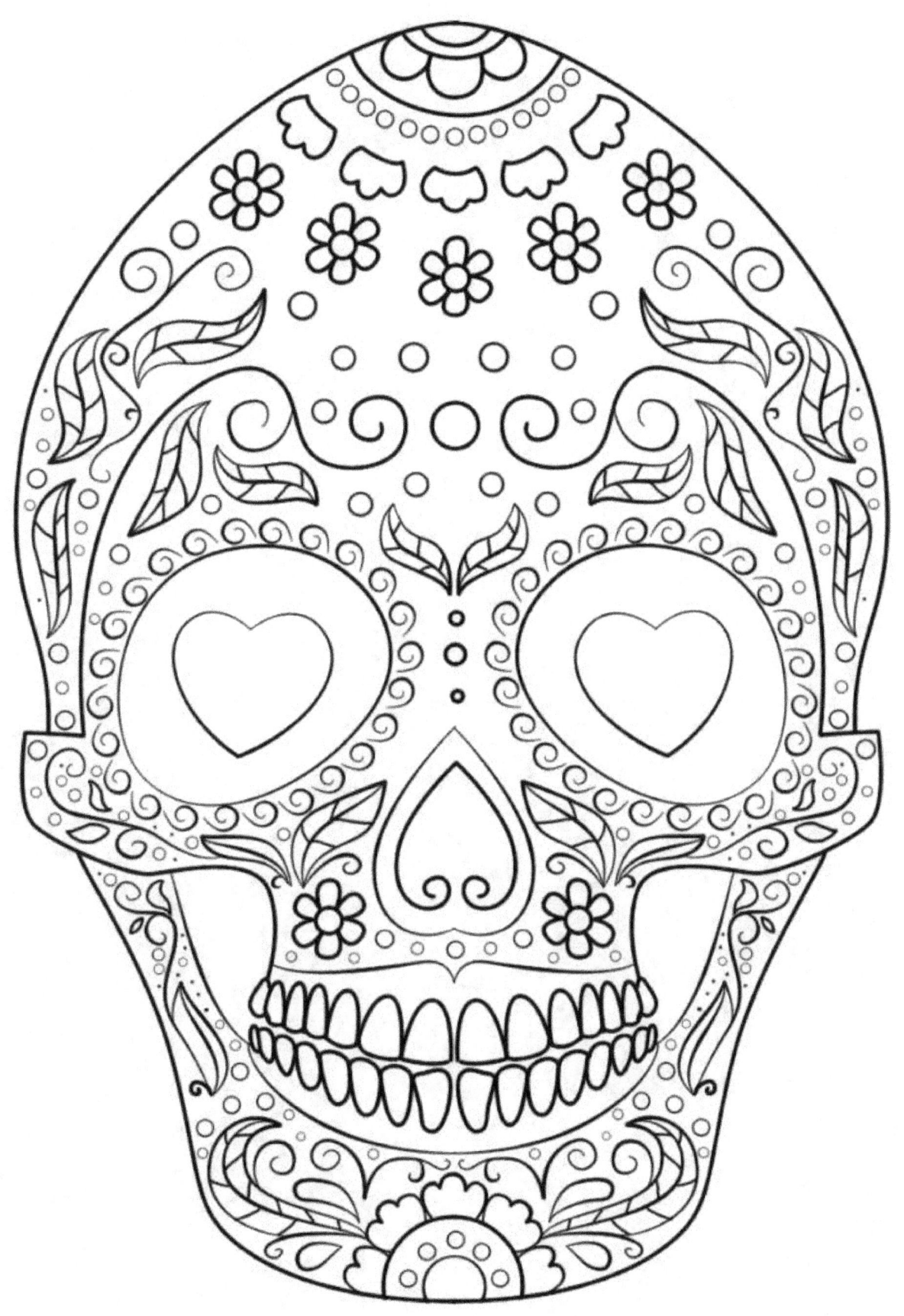

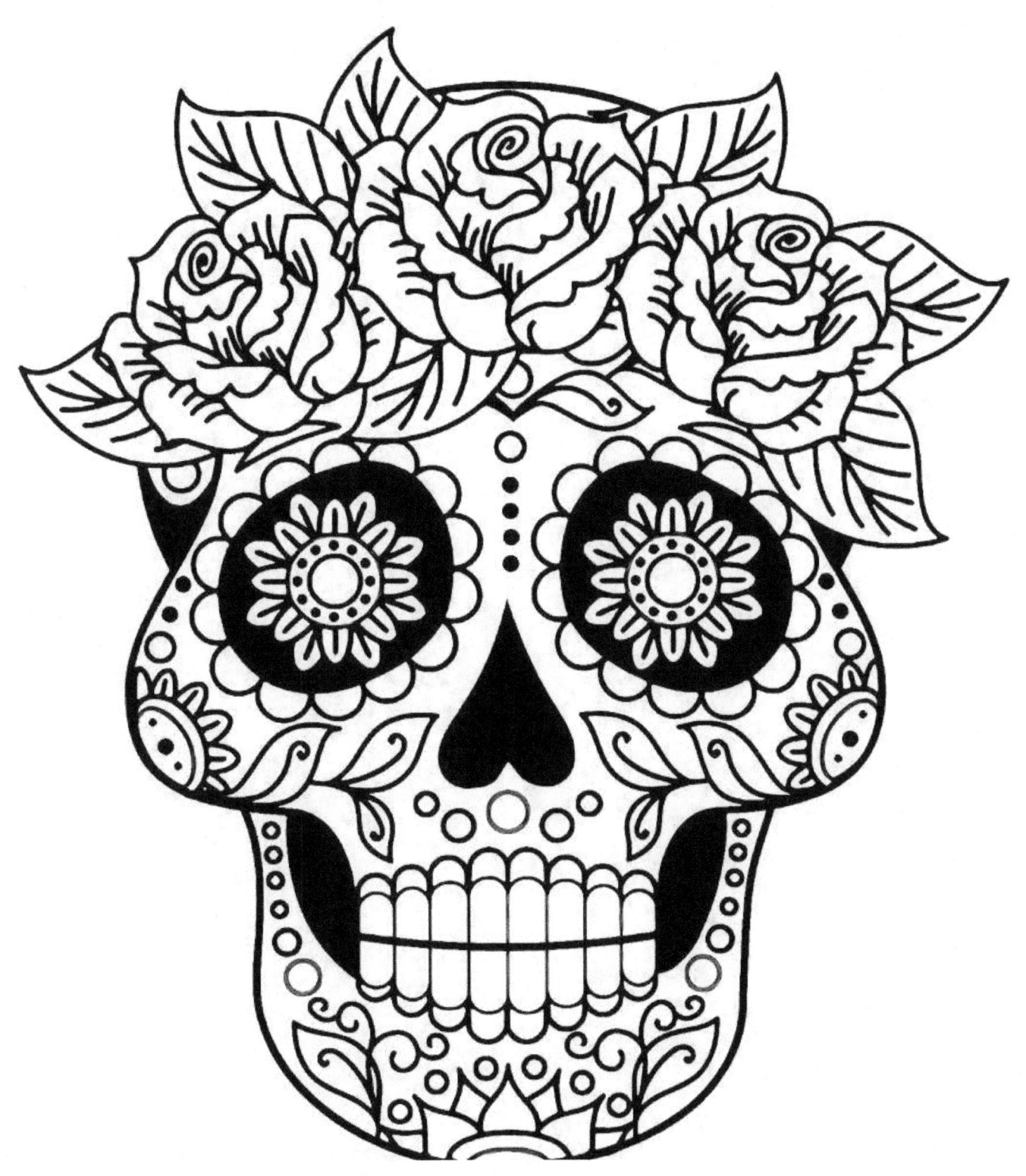

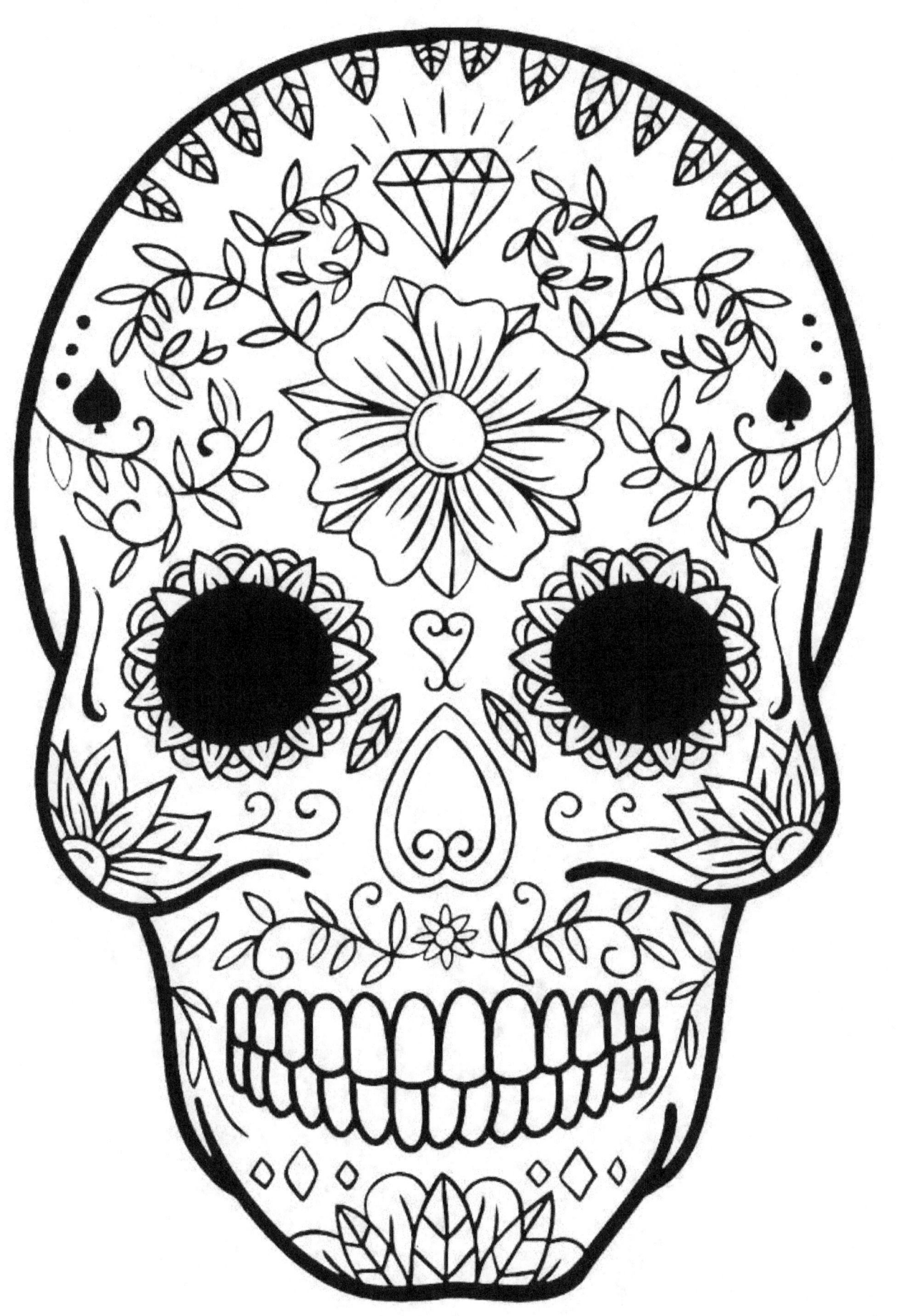

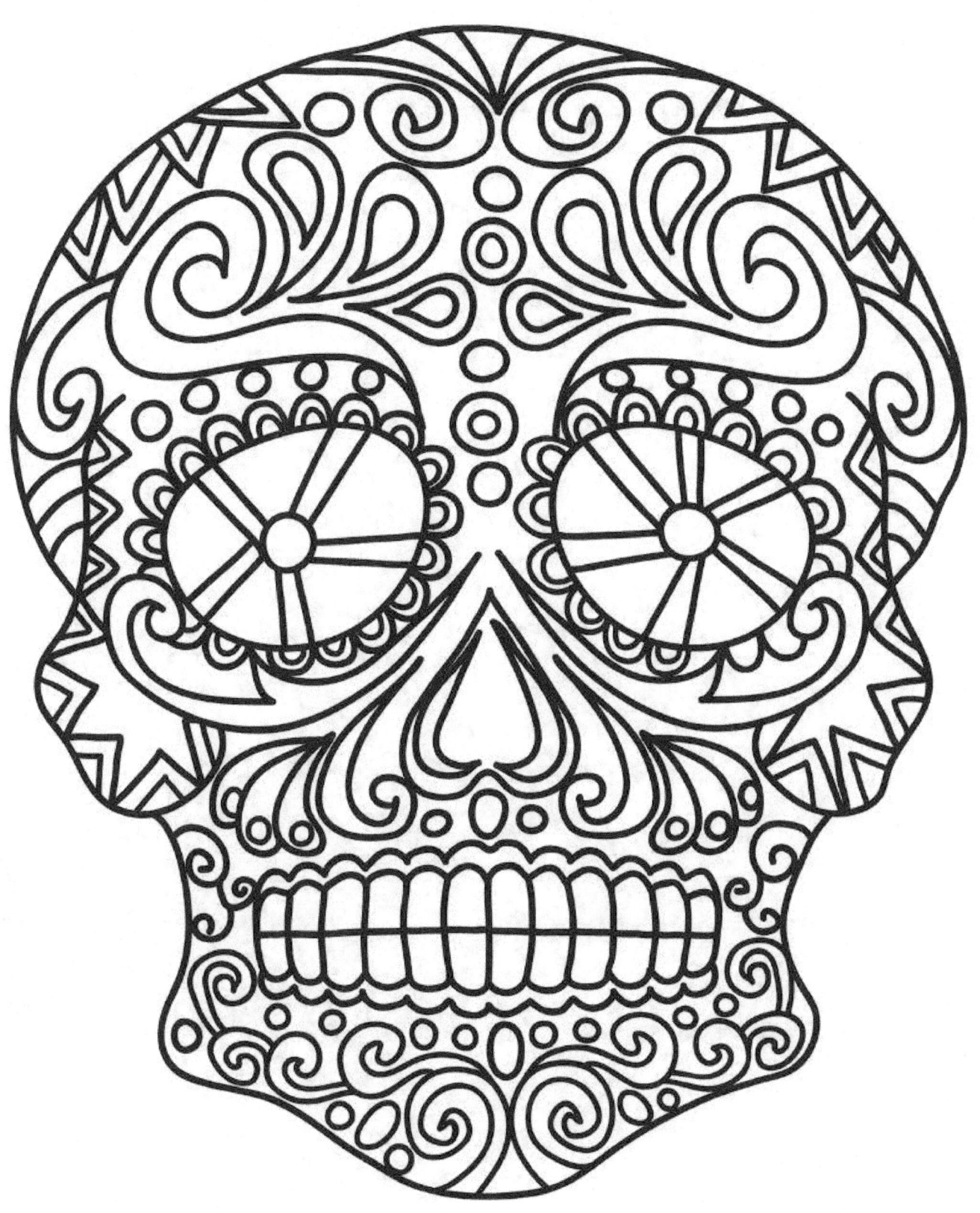

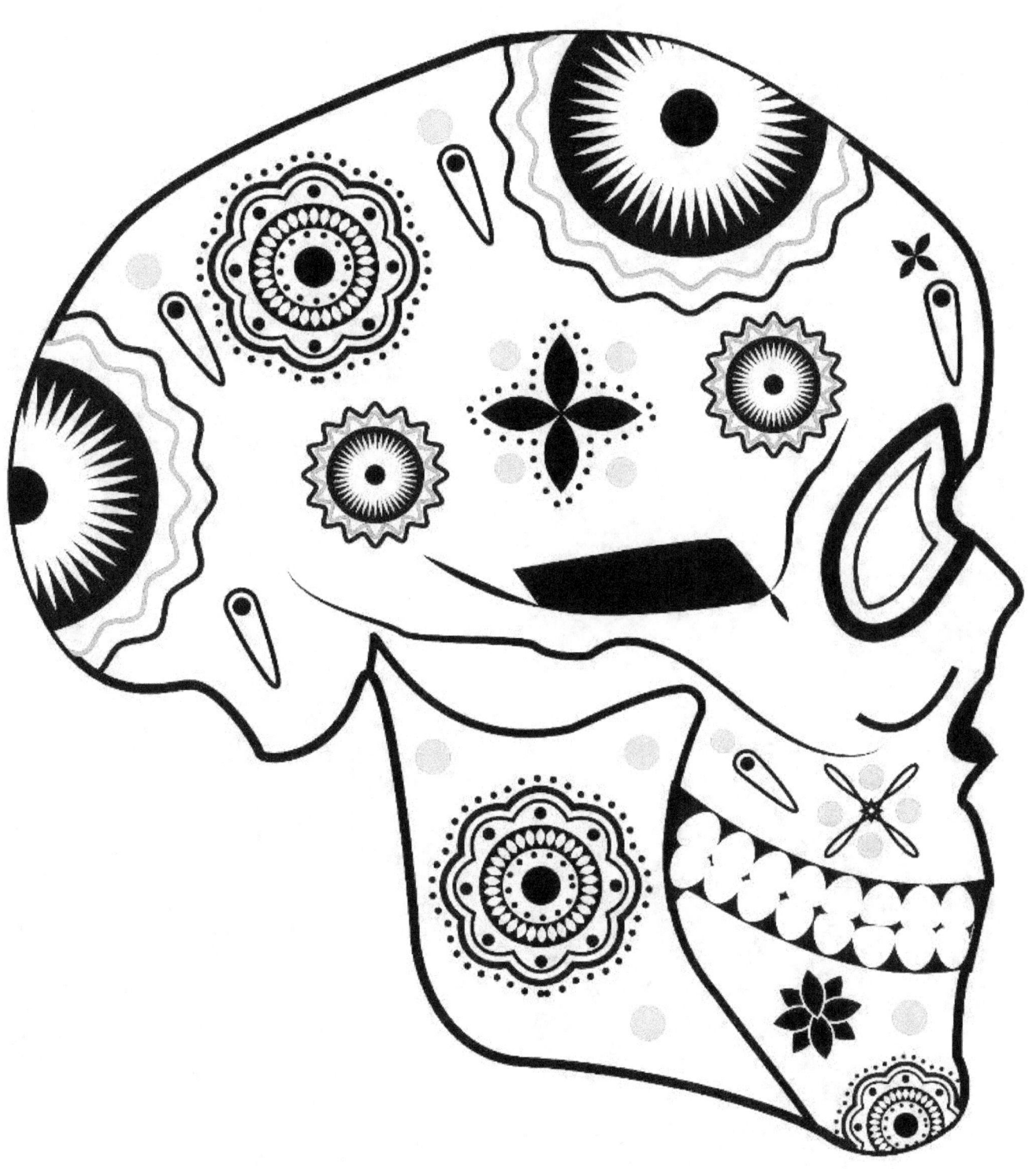

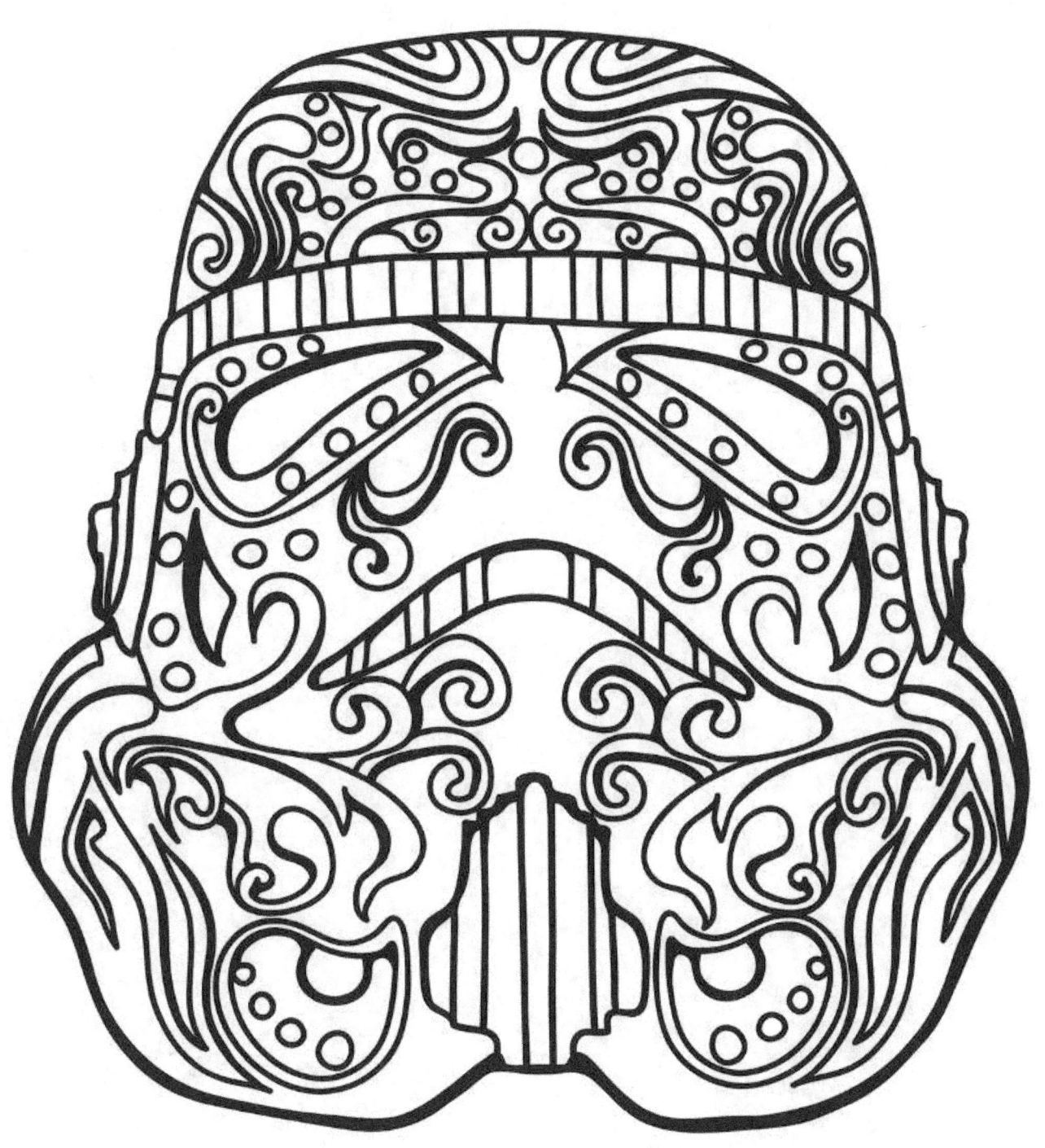

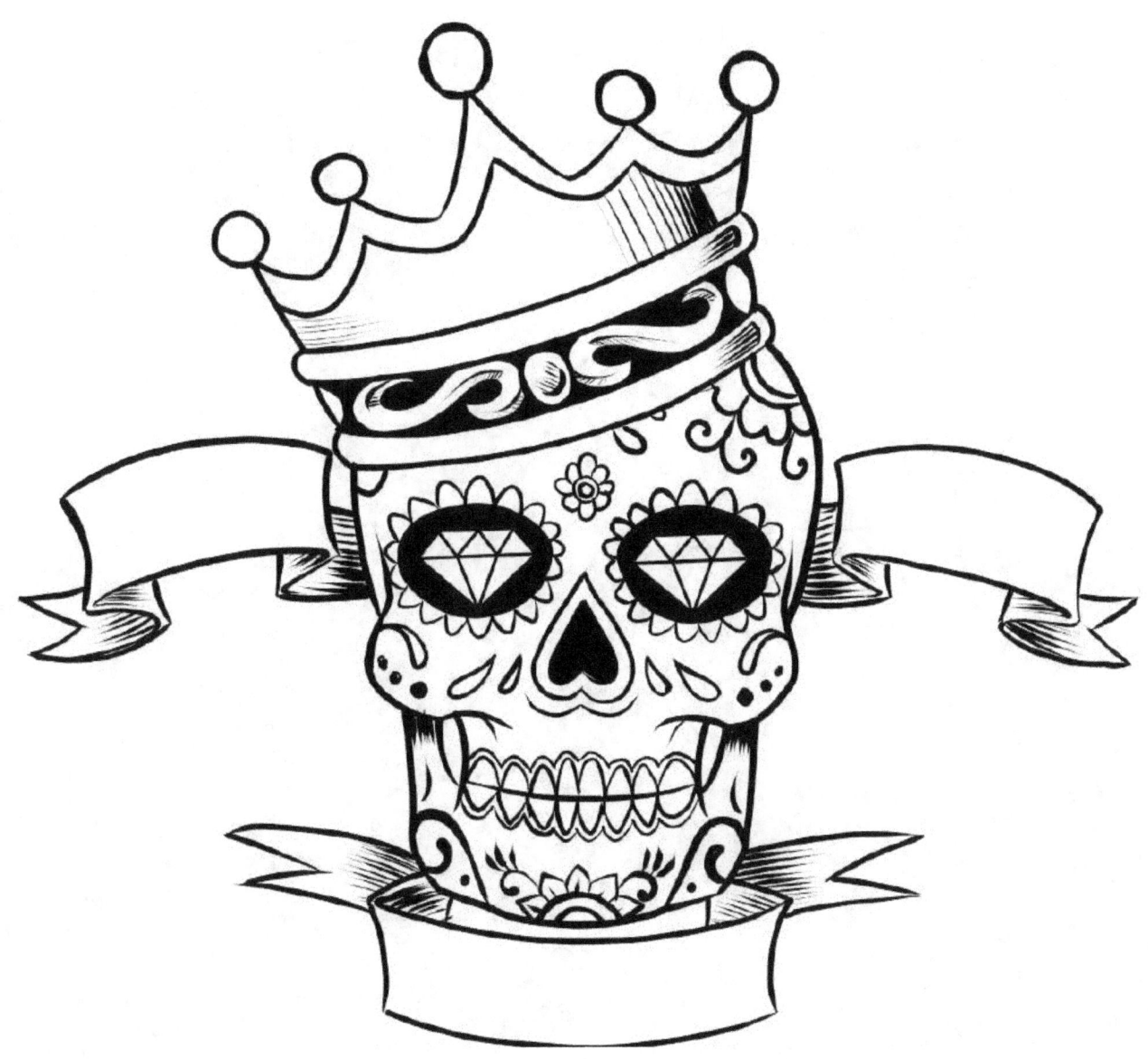

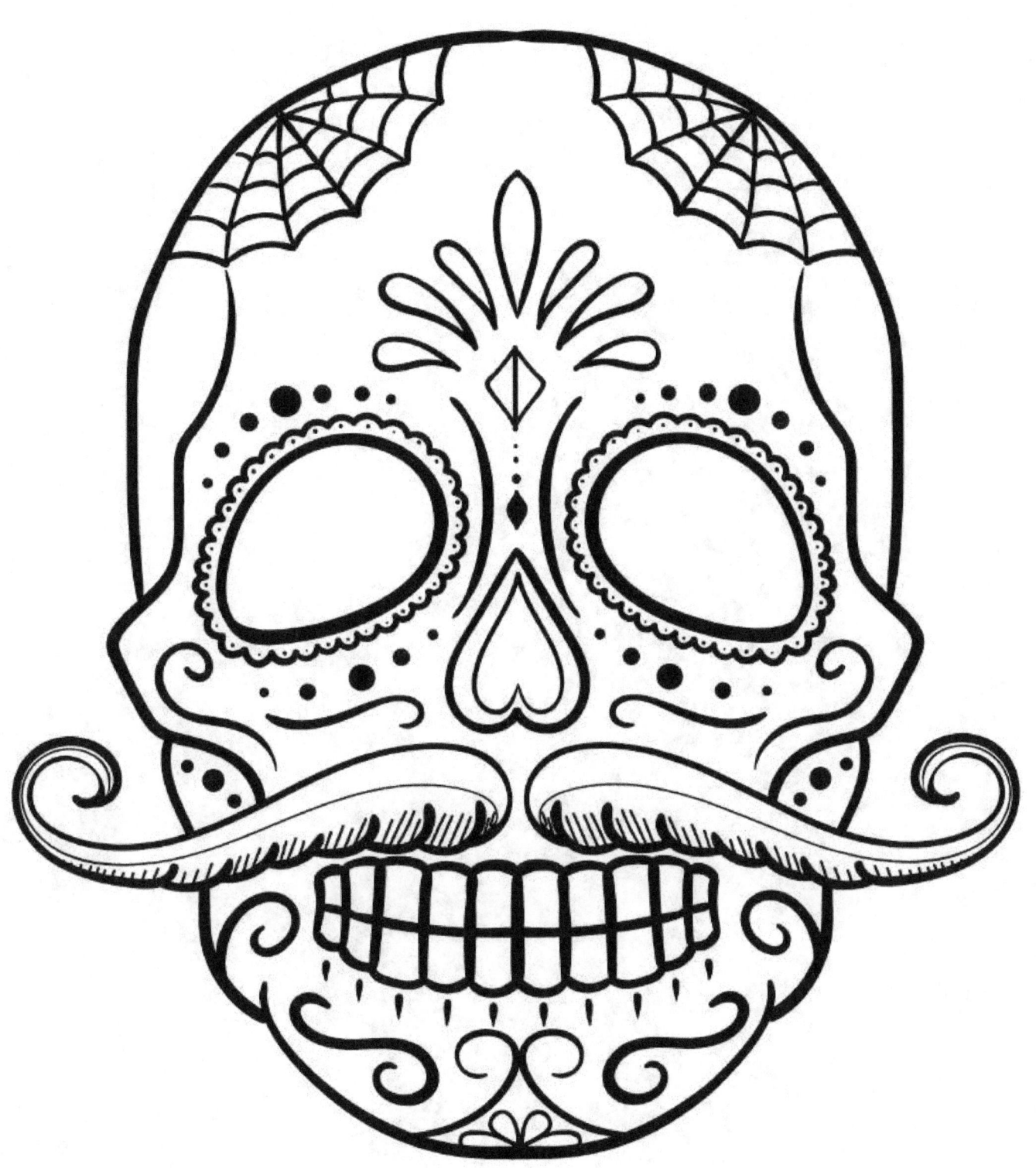

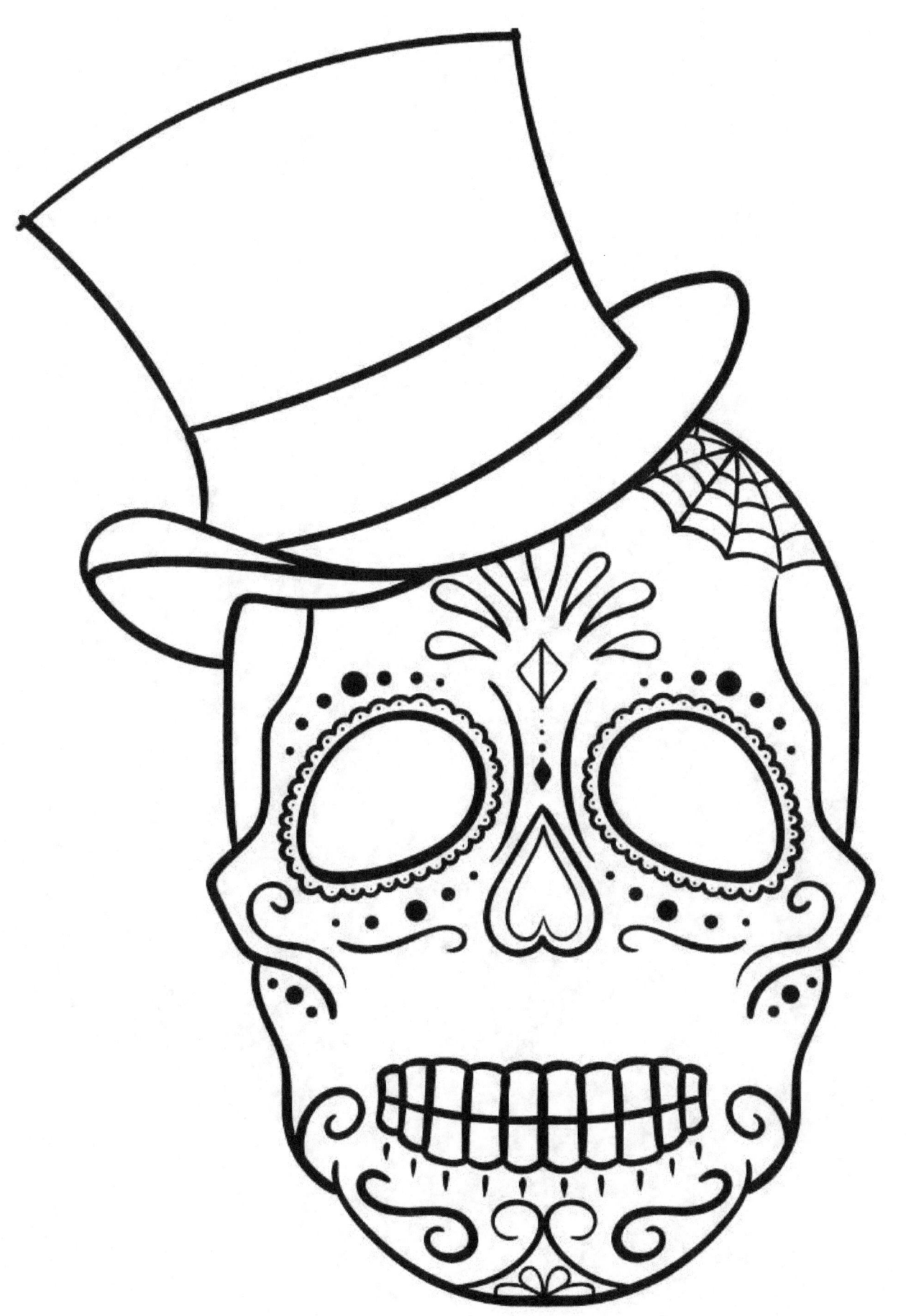

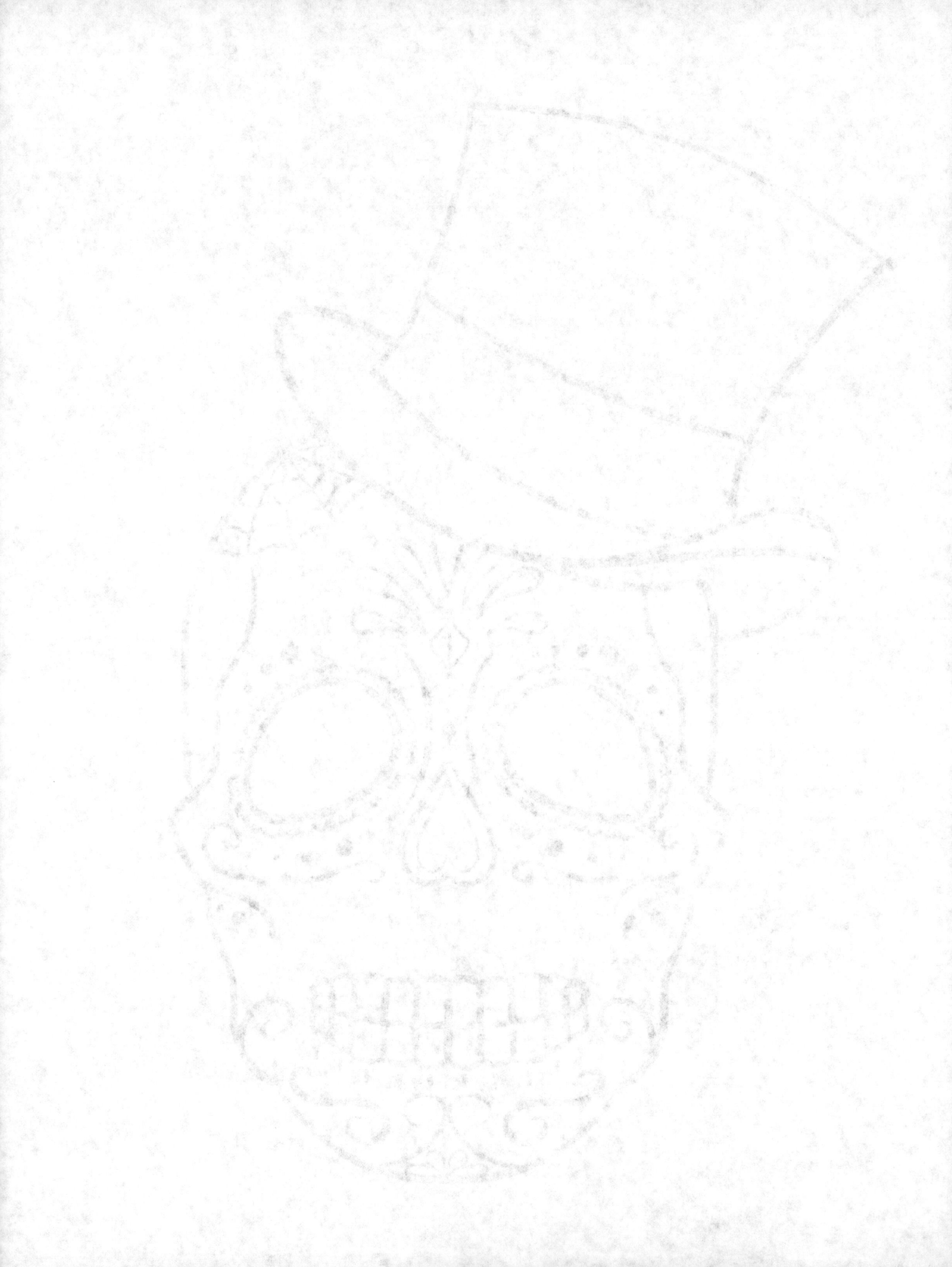

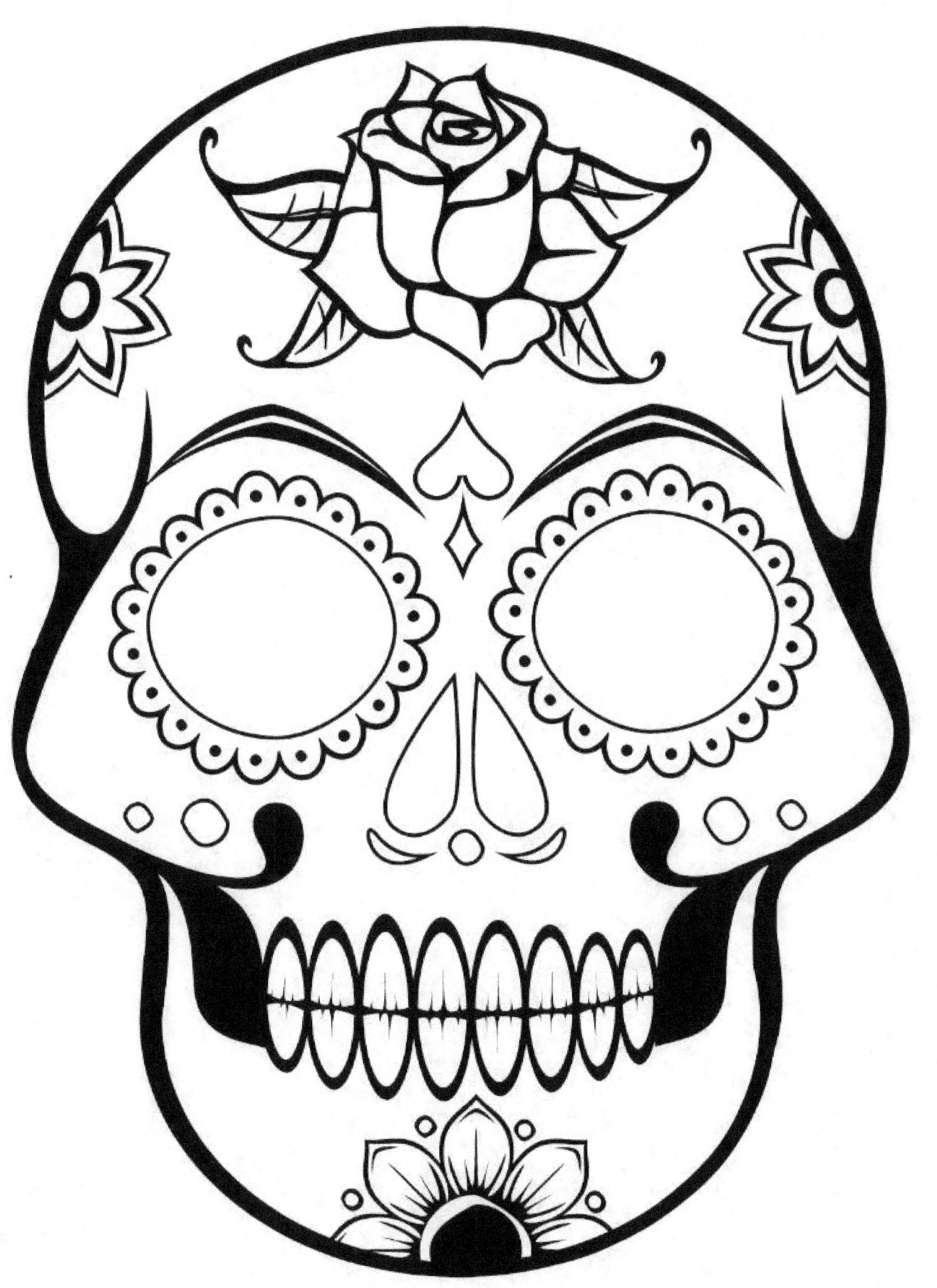

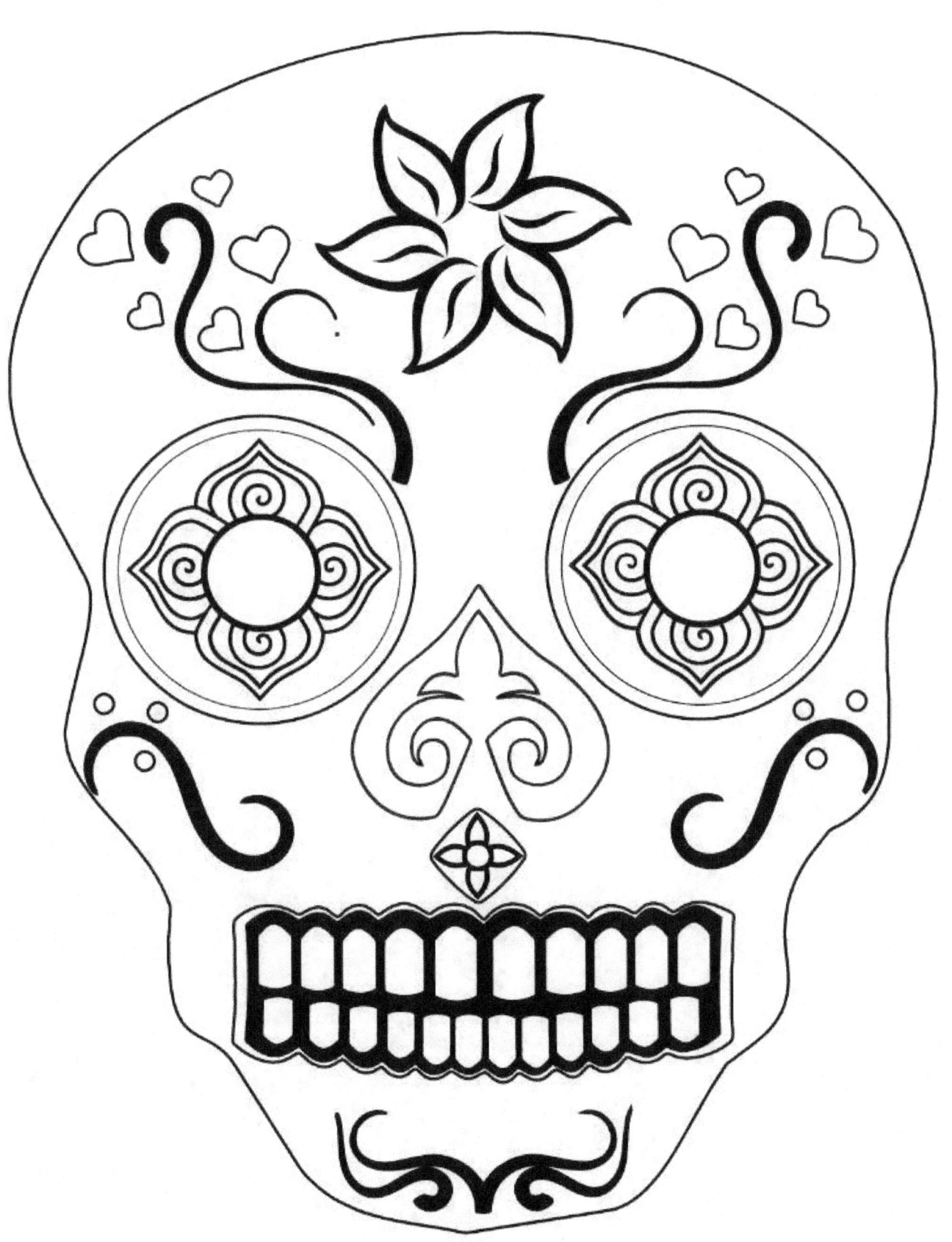

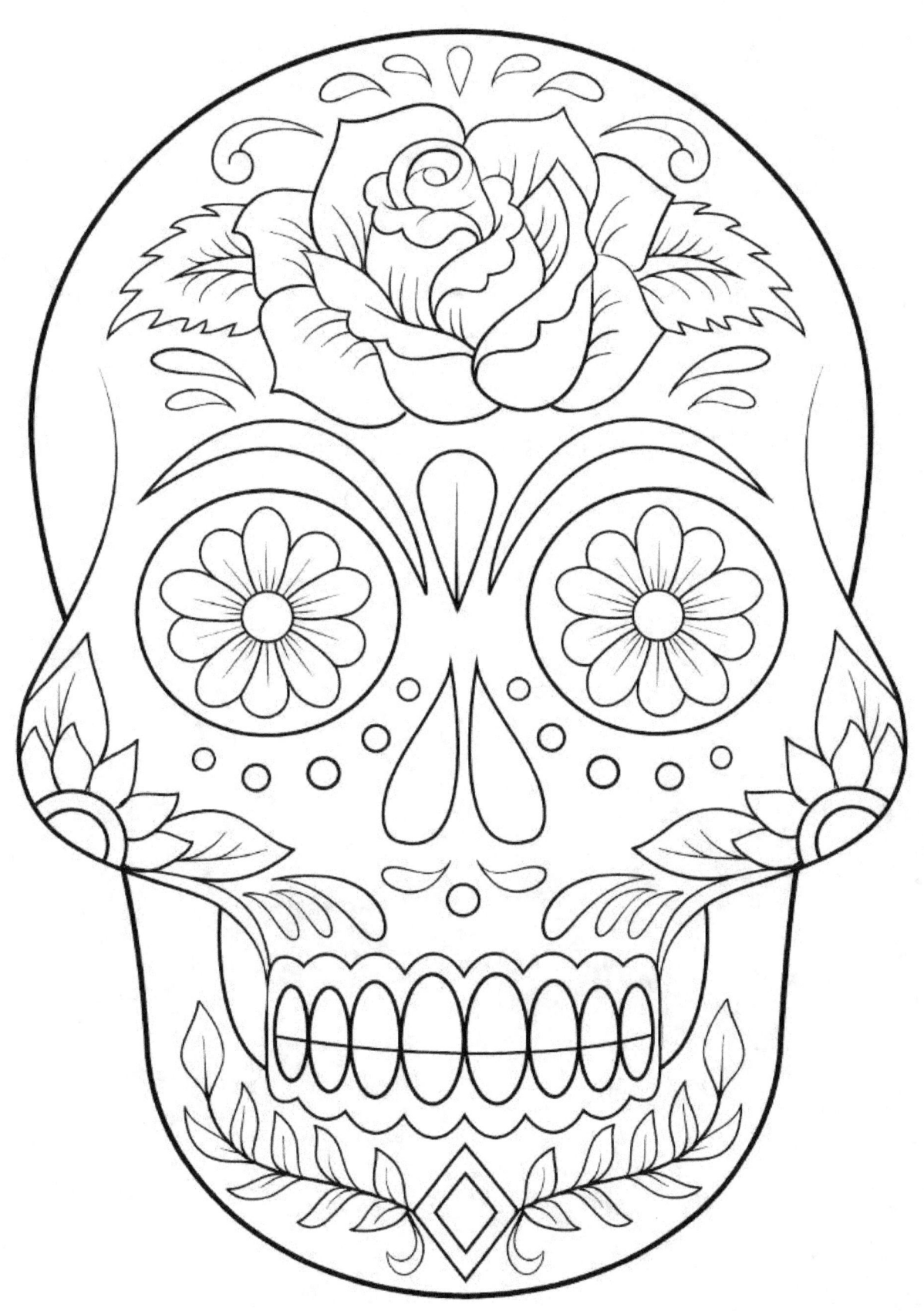

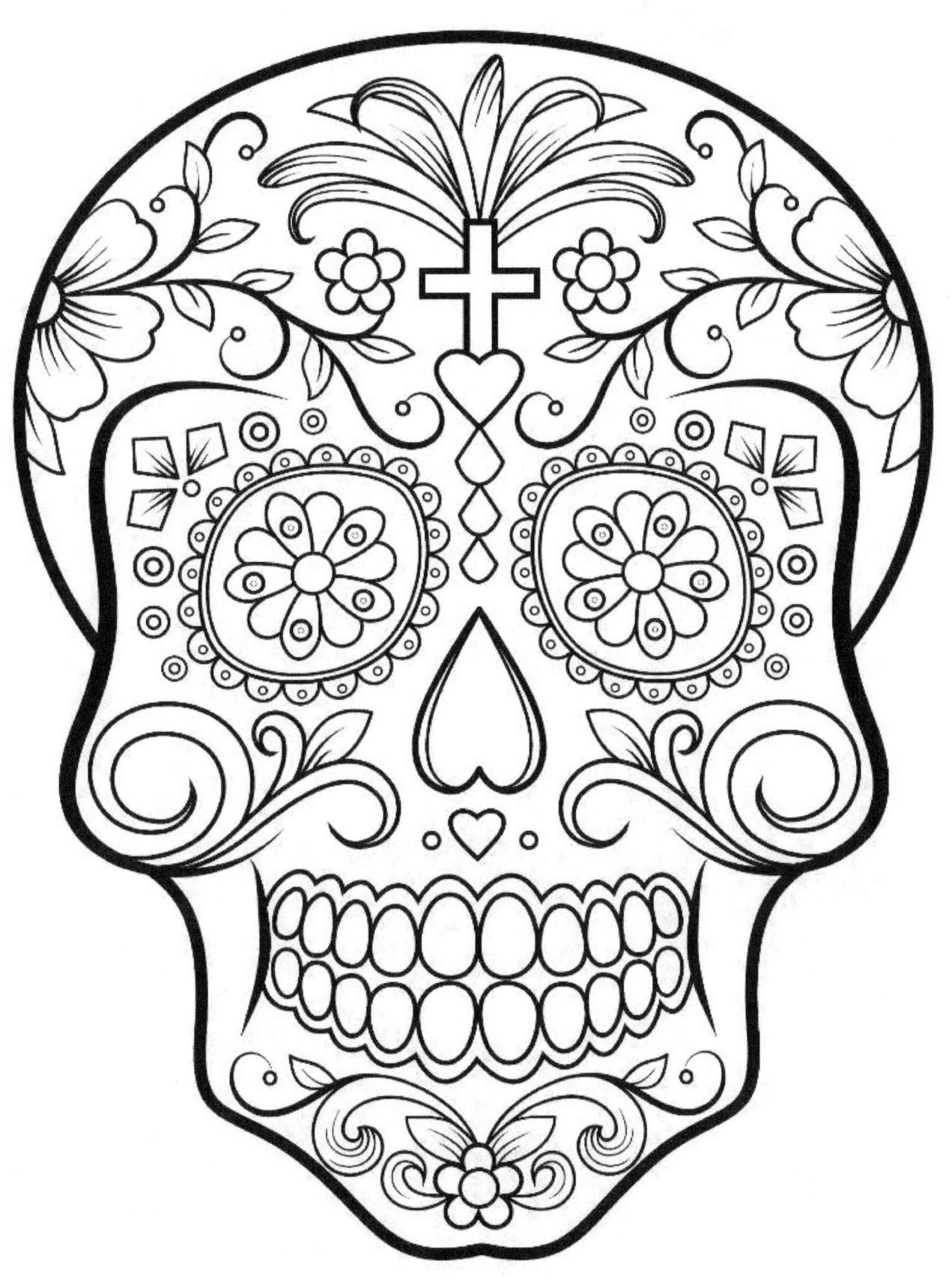

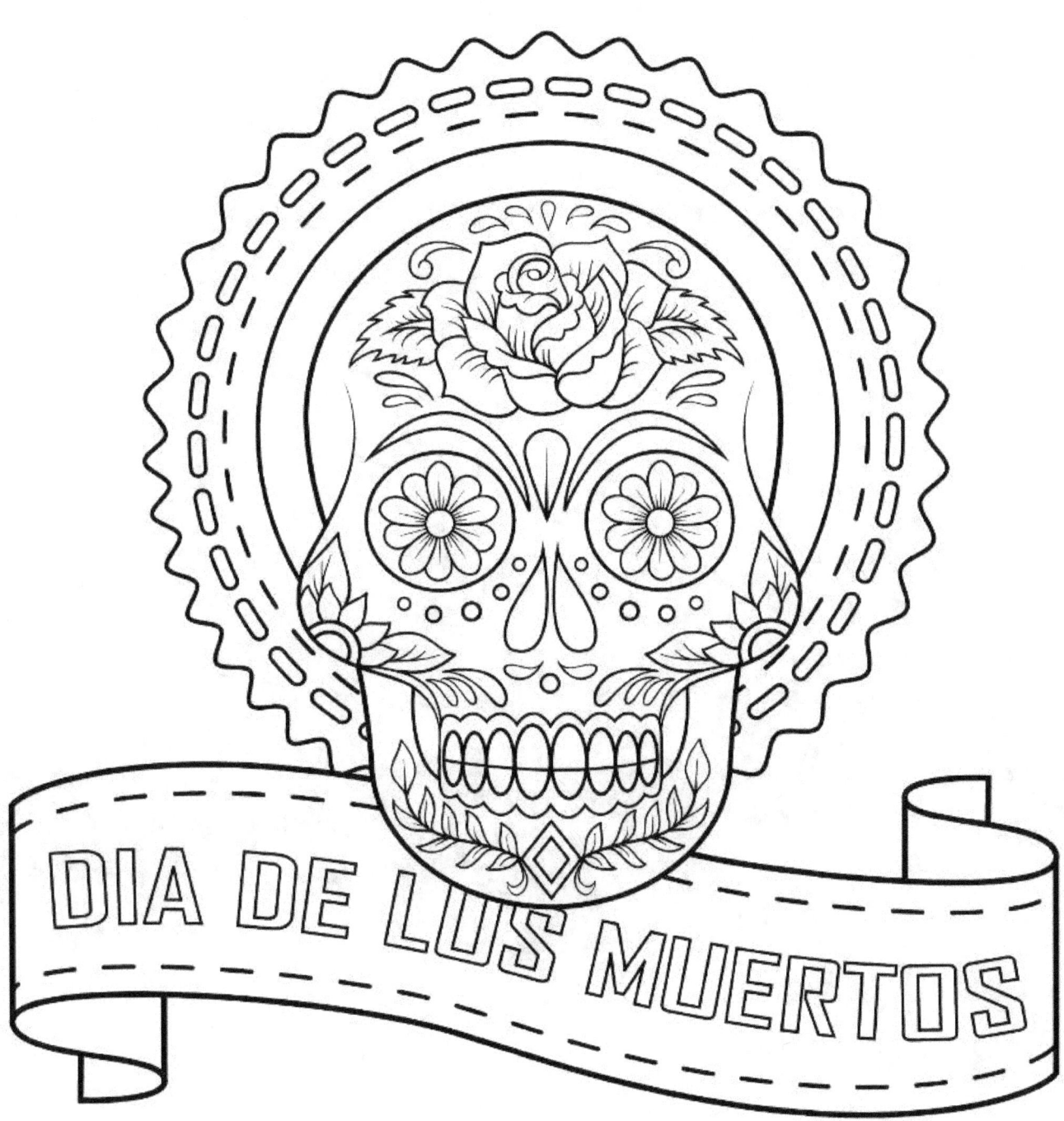

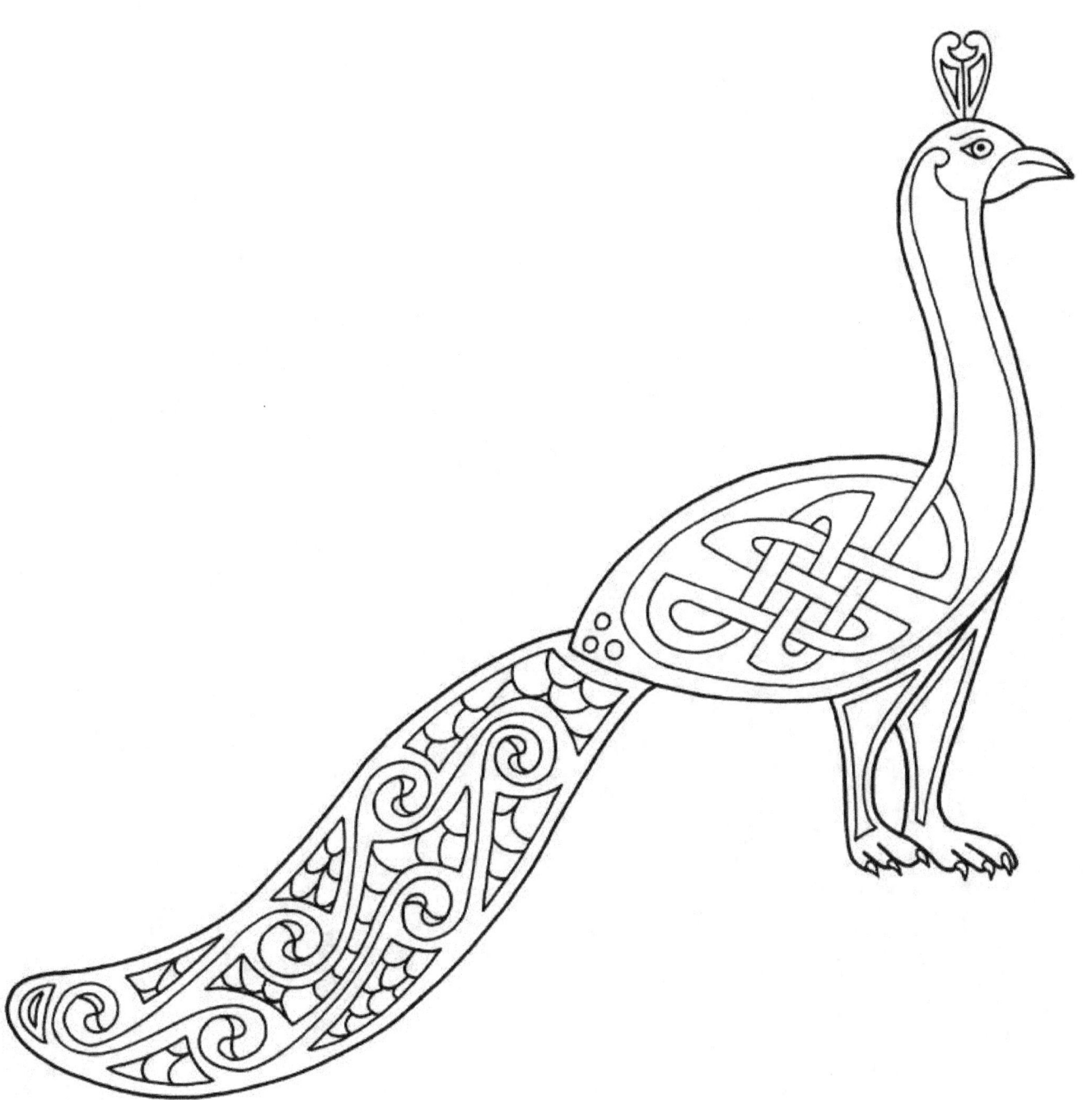

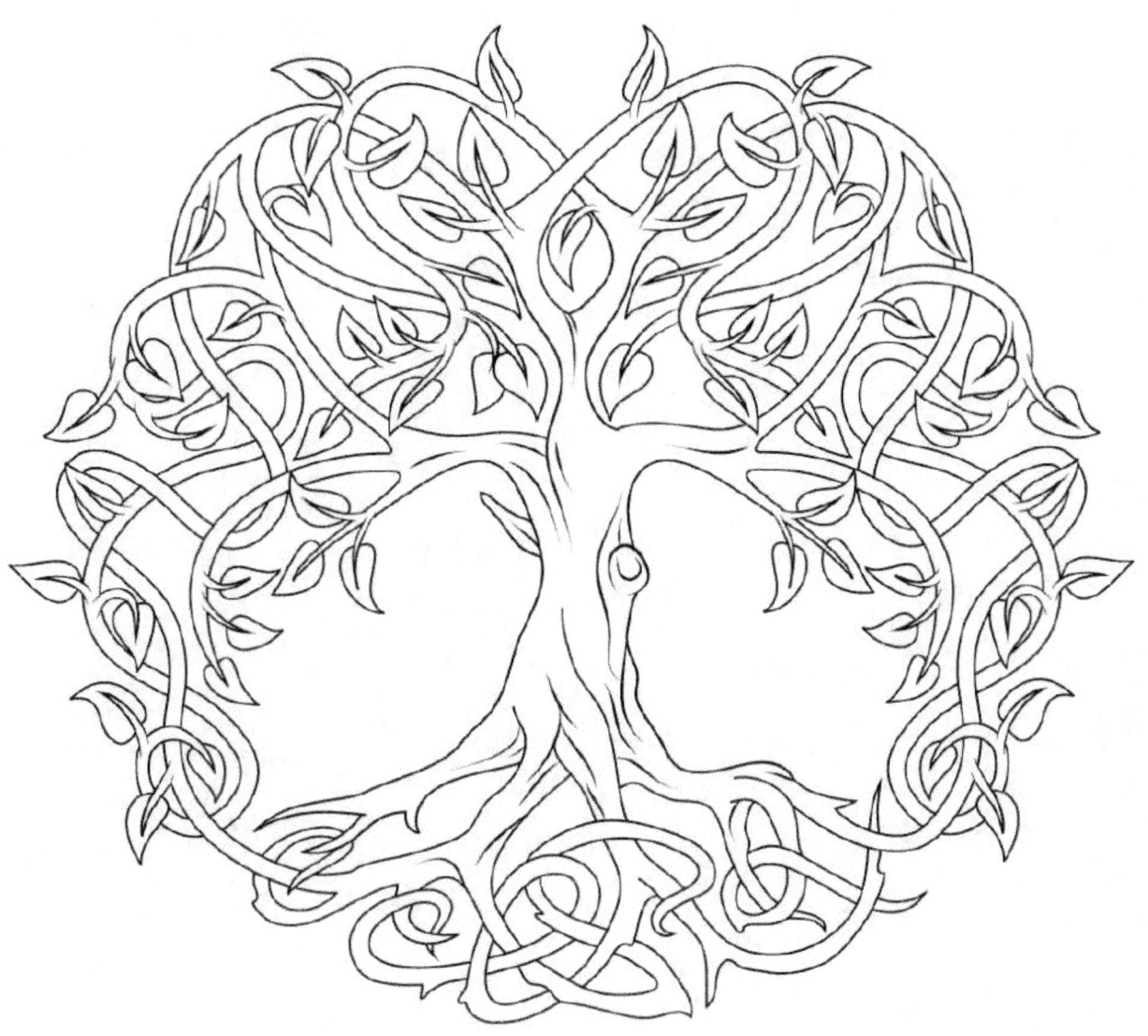

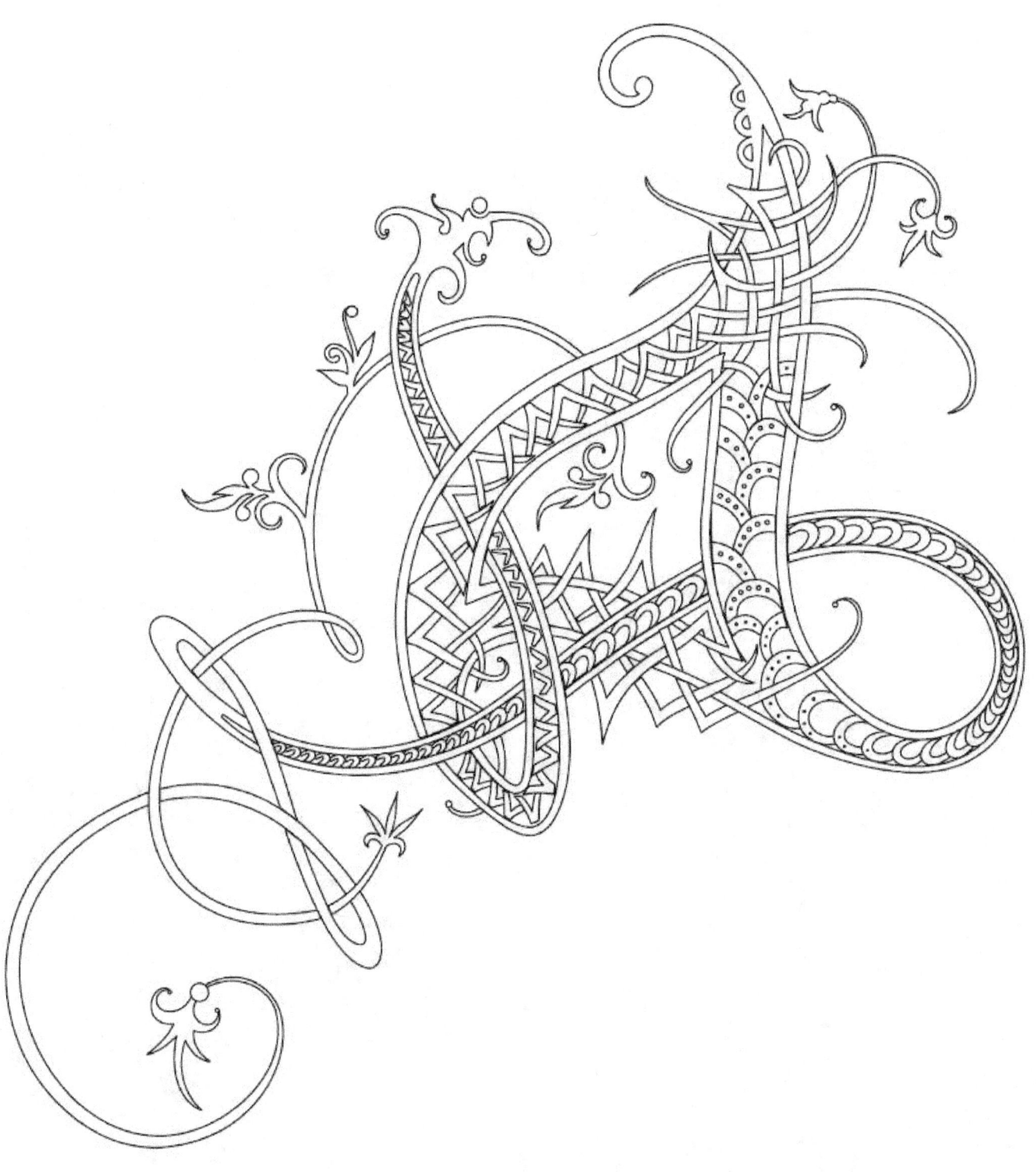

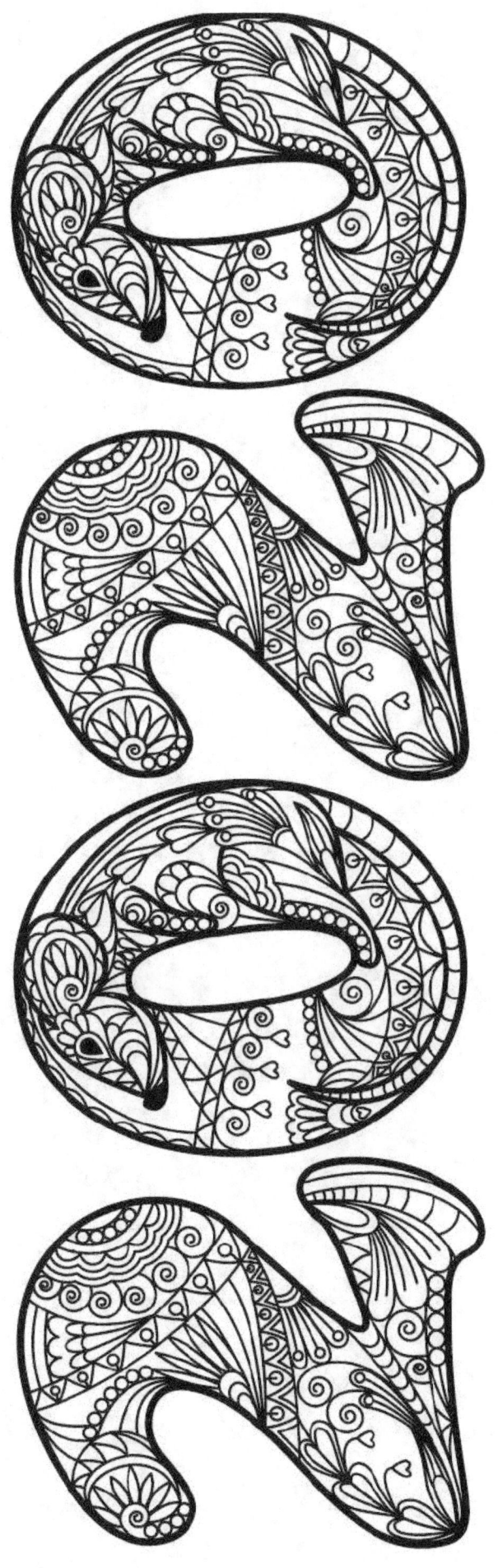

FROM THE AUTHOR

One last thing...
Thanks for coloring our book! I hope it was relaxing and I hope you had a lot of fun with it.
I would like to ask you for a *smallt favor.
We love to hear your feedback about this book!
If you enjoyed this book or found it useful, we would be very grateful if you posted a short review on Amazon. Your support does make a difference and we read every review personally.
If you would like to leave a review,
It will help the buyers to make a decision and your feedback will be priceless to our illustrators
Thank you for your support!

www.ingramcontent.com/pod-product-compliance
Lightning Source LLC
Chambersburg PA
CBHW080541220526
45466CB00010B/2994